NOMADS
of the
WIND

NOMADS of the WIND

A Natural History of Polynesia

PETER CRAWFORD

BBC BOOKS

CONTENTS

Published by BBC Books, a division of BBC Enterprises Limited,
Woodlands, 80 Wood Lane, London W12 0TT

First published 1993
© Peter Crawford 1993
ISBN 0 563 36707 5

Endpapers and maps by Line and Line

Set in Galliard by Ace Filmsetting Ltd, Frome
Printed and bound in Great Britain by
Butler & Tanner Ltd, Frome and London
Colour separations by Technik Ltd, Berkhamsted
Jacket printed by Lawrence Allen Ltd, Weston-super-Mare

PICTURE CREDITS

BBC Books would like to thank the following for providing photographs and for permission
to reproduce copyright material. While every effort has been made to trace and acknowledge
all copyright holders, we would like to apologize should there have been any errors or
omissions.

Ardea pages 51, 117 (J-P. Ferrero), 123 *left* (J. Mason) and 181 (J-P. Ferrero); **Auscape**
pages 96 (J-P. Ferrero), 138 (J-P. Ferrero) and 142 (B. Saunders); **British Library** pages 56–
7; **British Museum** page 113; **Michael Brooke** page 154; **Phil Chapman** pages 86, 91, 151,
152, 153, 178, 195 and 196–7; **Claude Coirault** pages 32 and 43; **Bruce Coleman** pages
24–5 (N. de Vore), 35 (J. Burton), 79 (Frithfoto), 89 (Frithfoto), 166 *bottom* (C. Roessler),
187 *top* (C. Zuber), 209 (S. Krasemann), 230 (G. Cubitt), 238 (G. Cubitt) and 244
(F. Furlong); **ET Archive** pages 42–3 and 148–9; **Frank Lane Picture Agency** pages 140
(Silvestris) and 245 (G. Moon); **Frithfoto** pages 69 and 123 *right*; **Jennifer Fry** page 228;
Genesis Space Photo Library/NASA page 180; **Roger Green, University of Auckland**
page 82; **David Hamilton** page 254 *bottom*; **Robert Harding** pages 17 (P. Plisson), 23
(P. Plisson), 159 (S. Grandadam), 163 (S. Grandadam), 198 and 208 (K. Krafft);
Michael Holford page 149; **Island Image** pages 136–7 (E. Smith); **Mark Jacobs** pages 50,
59, 132 and 217; **Jack Jeffrey** page 213; **Susan Kennedy** page 20; **Georgia Lee** page 187
bottom; **Rod Morris** pages 98 *both*, 126, 131, 145, 164, 192, 204, 229 *right* and 241;
National Maritime Museum, London pages 53, 56, 193, 223 and 250 (on loan from the
Admiralty); **Natural Science Photos** pages 211 (*both* D. Fleetham) and 216 (D. Yendall);
NHPA pages 55 (A.N.T.), 67 (A.N.T./K. Uhlenhut), 99 (A.N.T.) and 233
(*top* J. Carmichael, *bottom* B. Jones and M. Shimlock); **New Zealand Tourist Board** page
260; **Joël Orempuller** page 166 *top*; **Pierre Ottino** page 172 *left*; **Oxford Scientific Films**
pages 10 and back cover (*inset* frigate bird, M. Birkhead) and 232 (F. Huber); **Pacific Stock**
pages 128 (E. Robinson), 200 (E. Aeder), 215 (R. Mains) and 219 (K. Rothenborg);
Michael Pitts pages 146 and 155; **Neil Rettig** pages 71 and 114–15; **Dieter Rinke,
Brehm-Fonds Südsee Expedition** page 91 *left*; **Paddy Ryan** pages 66, 111, 124, 125, 229
and back cover (*bottom, inset*); **Syndication International** pages 48, 247, 252 and 254 *top*.

All other photographs were taken by **Peter Crawford**.

PREFACE

I am never happier than when by the ocean. Since my boyhood, I have been fascinated by the story of Captain Cook and his voyages to the South Seas. In more recent years, my own travels as a writer and producer of television programmes have given me the opportunity to meet and make friends with people in many distant parts of the world. Until this project, my ambition to follow in the wake of Captain Cook had only been a dream.

This book, and the television series which it accompanies, sets out to tell the story of Polynesia, that vast triangle of islands scattered across the Pacific, our greatest ocean. Ever since my first exploratory visit to Tahiti and New Zealand in 1990, I have been captivated by the people of Polynesia and by the natural history of their island world. Almost four years and many thousands of miles later, I feel I know them well. This is their story, and I am indebted to all the Polynesian friends who made us so welcome.

This book also explores the natural landscapes and native wildlife of the Polynesian islands and the vast ocean that links them together. It is an extraordinary world, fashioned by its remoteness. Even today, I find it difficult to imagine just how far away from our own it really is; only when clambering through the Samoan rainforest or reaching the summit of Easter Island's tallest crater, does the isolation become real. But for the native people and wildlife of Polynesia, this was, and still is, their essential home, their *fenua*.

Ask any Polynesian where they came from, and they will tell you a different story; they are even less certain about the origins and natural history of the plants and animals that share their islands. For guidance about the islands' geology and biology, their archaeology and anthropology and for linguistic and other cultural insight into the origins and pre-history of the Polynesian people, I have drawn on the wealth of research which has been conducted by dedicated experts throughout the Pacific during the last few decades. Without their help, this book and the television series, would not have been possible. I am particularly indebted to those who kindly read my chapters and made suggestions for their improvement. In Tahiti: Bengt and Marie-Thérèse Danielsson; on the Marquesas Islands: Pierre and Marie-Noëlle Ottino; in Fiji: Dr Paul Geraghty of the Institute of Fijian Language and Culture, Dr Andrew Crosby at the Fiji Museum, Dr Patrick Nunn at the University of the South Pacific; in Hawaii: Dr Yoshihiko Sinoto of the Department of Anthropology, Bishop Museum, and the writer and artist Herb Kawainui Kane; on Easter Island: Dr Georgia Lee, Editor of the Rapa Nui Journal; in New Zealand: Dr Atholl Anderson of the Anthropology Department at Otago University, Dr David Mackay at the History Department of Victoria University, Wellington, and Fergus Clunie, formerly Director of the Fiji Museum. Their generous advice has inspired many of the ideas in this book, but any mistakes or misconceptions are probably mine.

Many other experts have given up their time to discuss ideas with me while I was exploring the vast subject of Polynesia. Notable amongst them have been Thor Heyerdahl of the *Kon-Tiki* museum in Oslo; Roger Green and Geoff Irwin at the Unviversity of Auckland; Maeva Navarro and Mark Eddowes at the Department of Archaeology, Tahiti; Leon Grice and his colleagues at the Department of Conservation, Wellington; and Geoff Hicks and his colleagues of the Natural History Unit at the National Museum of New Zealand. I hope when they read this book and view the television series, they will consider their efforts worthwhile.

Television reaches a wide audience. This series will bring the epic story of Polynesia into the homes of families across the world. In this endeavour, I have been suported by an enthusiastic and talented team of film-makers, notably cameramen: Mike Lemmon and Niel Rettig and production team: Phil Chapman, Sally Cryer, Thea Gazidis, Mark Jacobs, Julia McDade, Alisa Robbins and Anna Thomas. They have all played valuable roles in this television voyage of discovery. I am particularly grateful to Phil Chapman for his special help and encouragement when I was writing the book. Above the call of duty, he and my wife, Pat, have had more influence than anyone on its style and content.

At BBC Books, I have enjoyed working with another creative team: Sheila Ableman, Linda Blakemore, Jennifer Fry, Charlotte Lochhead, Anna Ottewill and Anne Wilson have diligently and sensitively edited my manuscript and the pictures to produce this handsome companion to the series.

Writing this book has given me a special perspective on the Polynesian story and an opportunity to explore and expand on themes that I find particularly revealing. I hope that readers will enjoy sharing in this exploration of the Pacific, whether or not they also see the television films. Book and series are each designed to have their independent appeal, but they tell the same story, that of the Polynesian people and their ocean world. My hope is that both accounts respect and celebrate their voyaging heritage.

Peter Crawford, Bristol, November 1993.

for Betty

PROLOGUE

The Polynesian Triangle
is like an ancient spearhead
thrust across the great Pacific Ocean.

Long ago
a voyaging people
made this their home.

The story of the Polynesians
is an epic natural history
Man and Nature
each shaping the destiny of the other.

1000 miles

1000 kms

CHINA

PACIFIC

South
China
Sea

PHILIPPINES

HAWAIIAN
ISLANDS

POL

MICRONESIA

INDONESIA

BISMARCK
ARCH.

NEW
GUINEA

SOLOMON
ISLANDS

MELANESIA

VANUATU

NORTHERN
COOK IS.
Manahiki

WESTERN
SAMOA

AMERICAN
SAMOA

Vitilevu

FIJI

SOUTHERN
COOK IS.
Rarotonga

NEW
CALEDONIA

TONGA

AUSTRALIA

20°S

North
Island

NEW ZEALAND

South
Island

40°S

120°E   140°E   160°E   180°

NORTH
AMERICA

O C E A N

40°N

20°N

Hawaii

Y N E S I A

Christmas
Island

equator

LINE
ISLANDS

SOUTH
AMERICA

MARQUESAS
ISLANDS

SOCIETY
ISLANDS

Rangiroa

TUAMOTU
ISLANDS

Tahiti

Henderson

AUSTRAL
ISLANDS

PITCAIRN
ISLANDS

EASTER
ISLAND

°W

140°W

120°W

100°W

CHAPTER ONE

The FARAWAY HEAVEN

Everyone has their own idea of paradise. We all dream of faraway places beyond the horizon.

On Tahiti, jewel of the South Seas, the international airport is busiest at night. Most of the passenger jets that call at this remote tropical island set off from Los Angeles in time to reach the other side of the Pacific just after dawn the next day. Flights from Auckland, Sydney and other cities on the western rim set off in the evening and arrive in America in the middle of the same day. Whichever direction they fly, these transpacific jumbos start their descent into Papeete, the capital of Tahiti, when most Tahitians are asleep.

From 5000 feet, the distinctive figure-of-eight shape of the island is faintly outlined by a necklace of flickering lights along the coastal road. Tahiti was formed from the tips of two volcanoes which are now joined by a narrow neck and embraced by a coral reef that roars to the constant beat of the Pacific. On a moonlit night, you can see the surf from the air. Like a white chalk mark, it separates this speck of land from the unending blackness of the sea. If you have flown from the west coast of North America, it has been nine hours since land. For the passengers left on board, it will be another ten hours before they reach the other side of this seemingly endless ocean.

Some 25 000 islands are scattered across the Pacific, which, at its greatest depth, is six miles deep. That is deep enough to swallow Mount Everest with a mile to spare. Many of the volcanic Pacific islands, such as Tahiti, have risen several thousand feet into the sky. They are the weathered tops of extinct volcanoes which under their own weight are slowly sinking back into the depths

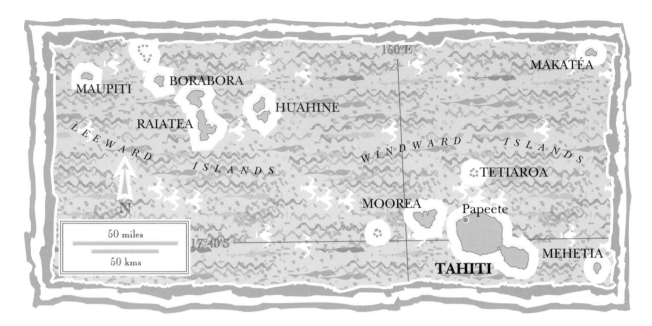

of the ocean. Tahiti burst to the surface perhaps two million years ago. That is young by island time. Some islands of Hawaii, for example, date back almost forty million years. New Zealand is very much older. It was once part of an ancient continent and has been an island group for at least 135 million years.

As the jumbo turns into the prevailing easterly wind to make its final approach to the two-mile runway built on the reef near Papeete, passengers on the right-hand side catch a glimpse of Tahiti's profile and her violent volcanic past. The cone-shape is still very evident. It rises symmetrically at a slope of almost forty-five degrees from the reef. Often shrouded in clouds, the 7000-feet-high summit is a jagged range of peaks, sculpted by the wind and rain that have beaten against this young island ever since it thrust its head above the sea.

Tahiti is at the very heart of the Polynesian Triangle. Geographically, the three corners marked by Hawaii to the north, New Zealand to the south-west and Easter Island to the south-east are almost the same distance away. Culturally, Tahiti is also central to the human story of Polynesia. Many of the epic voyages of the Polynesian people started or finished here. Together with a handful of other islands that make up the group now called the Society Islands, Tahiti is at the centre of the Polynesian world.

As the plane touches down on the tarmac, it is easy to forget just how remote these islands are. Before the French administration built the airport in the late 1950s, the only way to discover the charms of Tahiti was by a long and often arduous voyage. For almost two centuries, only the most adventurous tourist came in search of the South Seas idyll made famous by Captain Cook and those other European explorers. Tahiti is no longer a dream beyond our reach; now we can jet into paradise.

As visitors and transit passengers make their bleary-eyed way to the terminal, the hot moist air of the tropics mingles with the sound of today's South Pacific music. To the unrelenting accompaniment of Hawaiian guitar and ukulele, smiling young Tahitian women with flowers in their hair welcome the new and returning immigrants to the capital of the South Seas. Necks draped with sweet-smelling garlands, the new arrivals make their dazed way through French immigration towards a fleet of mini-buses to be transported to their long-awaited beds.

Papeete is much like any other French provincial town. Bars and bistros, banks and boutiques spill onto the pavement; the sounds and smells of traffic pervade the daytime air. At night, you could be back in any Mediterranean port. Along the quayside, mobile food-stalls light up to the aromas of kebabs, brochettes and fresh pizza. Papeete is bustling and cosmopolitan; very little is conspicuously Polynesian. As the food-stalls pack up and drive away, the night-people of Papeete withdraw to the bars and clubs which pulse to the latest transpacific culture. It is only occasionally in the faces of the people of Papeete that you can glimpse something of their long and distinctive heritage, one that links them with the other Pacific islands, across two millennia and almost a third of the globe.

Papeete did not exist when Captain Cook came to Tahiti; it is now a cosmopolitan city of 100 000 inhabitants, and the capital of French Polynesia.

Tahiti has only one main road; it circles the island. Along its two sides live today's Tahitians. A few tracks lead inland along steep-sided valleys carved by rivers that for a million years have tumbled from the island's peaks. A track, close by the airport, leads almost to the summit of Mount Marau. Rising 5000 feet above the ocean, this peak dominates the town of Papeete, but few locals ever go there. Here, high above the town, is the island's television relay station. The French, in their colonial wisdom, have provided their Pacific island outpost with one of the most up-to-date telecommunication systems in the world. There are few mountain tops in French Polynesia which do not bristle with antennae and parabolic dishes. One unexpected bonus of the track to Mount Marau is that, in under an hour, it can transport you back in time to the birth of Tahiti.

As you leave the island's circular road and head inland, the route takes you through orchards and market gardens. Plantations of Caribbean pines replace the traditional groves of coconut palms. Along the river, pandanus and ironwood trees give way to stands of the Tahitian chestnut with its magnificent buttresses. African tulip trees, once confined to gardens, bring splashes of imported colour to the native forest where often the only relief from lush green are the deep red plumes of the puarata tree (*Metrosideros collina*). Another less welcome botanical escapee is miconia, a devastatingly successful shrub which on Tahiti and several other islands is threatening to overwhelm the native bush. The impact of recent introductions has so changed the face of Tahiti that it is difficult to imagine how the island might once have looked.

For the final thousand feet, the tortuous route to Mount Marau has few lookout points; the eventual view from the top is breathtaking. You stand on the rim of a great cauldron which plunges 2000 feet to the river valley. On the distant flank, giant cascades are dwarfed by the overall grandeur of the panorama. From this high point, dawn and sunset evoke a sense of the primordial nature of this land. At first light, the distant Diadème peaks stand out as if adorned with haloes. It is not difficult to visualize how rain and wind fashioned these peaks from the silent volcano.

Up here there are few birds and insects. The only sounds are the distant roar of waterfalls and the dripping of the rainforest. The early morning atmosphere is cool and very damp. These high peaks lie in the path of the south-east trade winds which for most of the year bring moisture-laden air from the open Pacific and saturate the windward slopes with rain. The combination of minerals leached from the volcanic rocks and this abundance of fresh-water endows all

To climb Mount Marau, just inland from Tahiti's international airport,
is to step back in time.

such high tropical islands with extraordinary natural fertility. Up here, despite the cold, each square inch of soil and rock is covered with vegetation. Lichens and mosses cling to every crevice and ferns festoon the bark of trees stunted by the wind. On the slopes below, giant tree ferns add to the primordial scene. Other than the television relay tower, there is no evidence of man. Bustling Papeete on the coast, although out of sight, is only a short drive away.

As the sun climbs above the eastern peaks and the shadows retreat, the cauldron below seems to turn to steam. Water vapour billows upwards from the lower altitudes, obliterating the view and embracing the spectator in a sudden rush of tropical warmth. As if at the beckon of the gods, the water-laden gusts of hot air roll up the precipitous sides of the mountain to join the other clouds that assemble each day on the majestic summits of Tahiti. Here they play their part in the natural cycle that sustains life in the middle of the world's largest ocean.

The problem for Tahiti is that it *is* so far away. Isolated from the continents that flank the Pacific, it has been cut off from the mainstream of nature. Like so many oceanic islands, it is simply out of the natural reach of many plants and animals that would otherwise thrive in its benevolent climate and rich soils. There are no native land mammals here, not even bats. There are no amphibians and only four species of land reptile. Few species of land-bird have ever made the long ocean flight which separates Tahiti from the continents where their ancestors evolved. The list of birds that have successfully made land-fall is small and very select. In contrast, insects and spiders, because they can be borne by the wind over great distances, are better represented; so are several families of plants which by virtue of their wind-blown seeds are notable oceanic voyagers. Compared with islands closer to Asia or Australia, this speck of land is not blessed with natural diversity. Its full potential was not realized until the arrival of the Polynesians. The first people to set foot on Tahiti and her neighbouring islands arrived 1300 years ago.

Tahiti is the largest of the Society Islands, but the group includes seven other volcanic islands with the same kind of terrain and vegetation. Some are within sight of each other, such as the beautiful island of Moorea which is only seven miles to the west of Papeete. Volcanic peaks rise steeply from its many sheltered bays and a fringing coral reef surrounds the island, protecting it from the full force of the ocean. Today the slopes of Moorea are covered with pineapple plantations, a sure sign of the natural fertility of the soil. A little further away to the north of Tahiti, but visible on a clear day, is the atoll called Tetiaroa,

From every jagged peak of Tahiti cool fresh-water cascades back towards
the ocean from which it came.

Tahitian for 'far in the ocean'. Geologically much older than Tahiti and the other 'high' volcanic islands, Tetiaroa consists of twelve small islets grouped in a circle. This configuration is all that remains of an ancient volcano which, after millions of years, finally sank beneath the sea. The islets are the surviving fragments of the coral reef which originally circled the island and which grew upwards as fast as the core of the island sank towards the ocean floor, to be replaced by a lagoon.

Some atolls are huge. The lagoon of Rangiroa in the Tuamotu Archipelago, an hour's flying to the north of Tahiti, is so extensive that the entire island of Tahiti could fit within its perimeter. Unlike high volcanic islands, such atolls are usually less attractive to life, whether human or otherwise. The absence of a mountainous interior means that rainfall is far less frequent; the lagoon is deep blue because of the lack of dark, water-laden clouds overhead. The soil is not only dry but, being formed essentially from the coral which created the atoll, also lacks many of the vital minerals that are needed for plant nourishment. Atolls look very attractive to the twentieth-century Western eye; they are the classic postcard image of a South Seas paradise. Their sheltered lagoons and extensive reefs are rich in fish, but as permanent homes for people, they have less to offer than the diverse landscapes of younger 'high' volcanic islands.

Above Moorea erupted more recently than its close neighbour, Tahiti; but violent
erosion by sea and rain has sculpted its extinct volcano into a castle-like island
set in a fairytale lagoon.
Left The idyllic atoll of Tetiaroa lies twenty-five miles north of Tahiti. Seen from
the air, the twelve small islets clearly show the shape of the reef that once fringed a high
volcanic island, now completely eroded by time.
Overleaf The spectacular volcanic plug and huge lagoon of Borabora.

A hundred miles or so to the north-west of Tahiti lie the Leeward Islands,
so named because of their position in relation to the prevailing wind. The most
spectacular is the island now called Borabora, infamous for the exploits of
American GIs based there during World War Two. Borabora's natural beauty
comes from its age. The volcano erupted three or four million years ago, since
when its central core has split and eroded. What remains today are dramatic high
peaks created by the volcanic chimneys, surrounded by a vast lagoon quite out
of proportion to the size of the surviving core of the island.

Twenty-five miles to the west of Borabora lies the tiny island of Maupiti. It is here that archaeologists have unearthed one of the oldest settlements found so far in this part of Polynesia. Two other islands in the Leeward group have a long history of occupation. One of these is Huahine, which looks like two islands joined by a common fringing reef. Legend claims that the Polynesian god Hiro split the island with his canoe. Geologists tell us that the caldera of the original volcano did indeed do just that. A man-made bridge now reconnects the two halves. Archaeological excavations on Huahine have revealed traces of settlements as old as those on Maupiti. Stone tools, bone or mother-of-pearl fish-hooks and wooden objects such as house timbers, canoe planks, tools and weapons have been remarkably preserved in the swampy soil. They give an insight into the way of life on Huahine more than 1200 years ago.

The other main island of the Leeward group is Raiatea, which in Tahitian means 'the faraway heaven'. For generations it has been regarded a sacred isle. Its coastline is jagged with deep bays; inland its vegetation is particularly lush. Native and introduced species of fruits and vegetables grow in luxuriant harmony. As you drive around the island road, which twists and turns following the indented coast, you pass little fields of pawpaw and banana, terraces filled with taro and vast plantations of pineapple; as far as the eye can see, there are coconut palms of all shapes and sizes. Beneath the shade of all this tropical greenery are archaeological remains of a very ancient civilization that was born on Raiatea many centuries before Captain Cook encountered this 'faraway heaven'. He recorded in his journal that the island had once been called 'Havaii', a name which is met in various forms throughout Polynesia. Maybe it was here that the first Polynesians navigated through the reef and decided to set up home.

We can visualize that first encounter. An ocean-going double-hulled canoe, perhaps fifty feet long, powered by the wind, makes its way towards a gap in the fringing reef. The navigator carefully observes the effects of the prevailing wind and current, and selects a sheltered approach. On board, a weary but elated group of seafarers search the shoreline for clues to the island's nature. They carry a precious cargo of seeds and cuttings of favourite vegetables and cultivated plants. Transported in basketwork cages is a selection of their domestic stock, including pigs, chickens and dogs. On the long voyage to this new homeland, the travellers had nurtured their stock with care. It was from these plants and animals that a new landscape would be created on the island that they had

Each voyage of settlement transported cultivated plants and domestic stock
with which the Polynesian pioneers would re-create familiar landscapes to support
their island way of life.

come so far to find. As they steer the craft into the shelter of the lagoon, they praise their gods for their safe arrival on the shores of a new world.

They had survived the rigours of a long ocean crossing, but ahead lay challenges of a different kind. They had come equipped with lines and hooks to catch fish in the lagoon, they were knowledgeable about the other edible inhabitants of the reef, but on land there would be new problems of survival and their future was uncertain. Generations of voyaging had taught the Polynesians that the smaller the island and the more remote its location, the less able it would be to support their needs.

For the first few months or even years, they may have been able to survive simply as hunters and gatherers. The reef was there to be gleaned and the forests harboured a few edible plants and creatures. Of the wild plants that were already inhabitants of these remote islands, only purslane, seaweeds and the nuts of pandanus and the coconut palm provided any real sustenance for people.

Whilst the original wild coconut (*Cocos nucifera*) is certainly capable of spreading itself from island to island, no experienced Polynesian voyager would have left home without this indispensable and versatile plant. The other plants carried on board their ocean-going canoes included bread-fruit, bananas, taro, yams, arrowroot, sugar-cane and a woody-stemmed lily called *ti* (*Cordyline fruticosa*). Very rich in sugar, the tuber of the *ti* was used by ancient Tahitians to make a candy, and its large leaves served as clothing and to wrap food for cooking. The Polynesian canoe was a veritable botanical Noah's Ark.

Like settlers the world over, the Polynesians strove to change the landscape to suit their needs. As ocean voyagers they were unsurpassed, but once back on land their survival depended on the management of their new surroundings and on the establishment of a cultural system that would sustain their way of life. With the arrival of people on the islands of Polynesia, many plants and animals began to decline and some were eaten to extinction. Large strong-flying pigeons (*Ducula* spp.) had reached almost every island in the Pacific long before the Polynesians. They bred prolifically and, once established on a group of islands, developed into local species. In the Society Islands and the Tuamotu Archipelago just to the east, there is an endemic pigeon (*Ducula aurorae*) and further north, the Marquesas group has its own distinct pigeon (*Ducula galeata*). There were once other species across eastern Polynesia as far as Easter Island, but they are now extinct. They fell victim to the Polynesians or to the Polynesian rats which came with them.

The most widespread species of land-bird in Polynesia is the sooty rail (*Porzana tabuensis*). It is found from Fiji in the west to the island of Ducie in the Pitcairn group almost 4000 miles to the east. From the bones found by biologists, it is known that there were related species of this rail on Easter Island and other remote islands but that they ended their existence baking in the Polynesian oven. Other birds have fared better despite the coming of people to the islands. Kingfishers (*Halcyon* spp.), widespread and very beautiful, are often revered by local people. Despite their name, they ignore the plentiful fish in the rivers and reefs, and instead hunt for insects and lizards in the forest. Warblers and flycatchers followed the insects to many Pacific islands, and the Pacific swallow (*Hirundo tahitica*) is found everywhere from Fiji to Tahiti. Some islands have their own colourful lorikeets. The grey-green fruit dove (*Ptilinopus purpuratus*) has also evolved into numerous different subspecies throughout eastern and western Polynesia, and in Tahiti and the other Society Islands it is still a handsome member of the native fauna. Wherever there are fruiting trees, flocks of these plump little birds gorge themselves until disturbed; then, with a noisy whirring of wings, they take off into the forest.

Many centuries passed between the time that the first Polynesians set foot on these islands and their 'discovery' by European explorers who sailed to the South Seas in the eighteenth century. The strange foreigners were recounted tales about Tahiti, told of myths and legends through which the Tahitians traced their long ancestry and celebrated their rich culture. During the last 200 years, experts from all over the world have attempted to unearth and unravel the story of the Polynesians. Much of that work has centred on Tahiti and her neighbouring islands, particularly Huahine and Raiatea. Archaeologists have scratched in the soil to reveal the physical world of the Tahitians. Linguists have analysed the Tahitian language and compared it with other Pacific tongues. Biologists have studied the bones and other remains of plants and animals that had a place in the lives of ancient Tahitians. Anthropologists have helped piece together a picture of the prehistoric Polynesian world.

The chronicles and drawings made by the early European explorers and scientists were remarkable. Without them today's historians would have very little first-hand evidence about this civilization that, unknown to the rest of the world, flourished in the middle of the Pacific. Once discovered, its fame spread far. The impact of Tahiti on Europe was as sensational as the impact of Europe on Tahiti. Descriptions of the place conveyed by returning scientists and sailors came close to rhapsody. Samuel Wallis, the English naval captain of the first European vessel to encounter Tahiti in 1767, reported that bread grew on trees and that palm trees supplied milk. The following year, the Frenchman, Louis de Bougainville, arrived with his crew and declared that he had been transported into the Garden of Eden. The naturalist Joseph Banks, who accompanied Captain Cook to Tahiti a year later, claimed that the Tahitian women were the most elegant in the world.

It is clear that, at the time of those first European encounters, Tahiti was indeed some kind of paradise. Although today's experts differ on the actual figures, Tahiti and the other high islands were well populated. When the Europeans arrived, they encountered a healthy-looking people whose way of life was surprisingly complex, vital and sophisticated. Archaeological evidence suggests that the emergence of this rich culture on Tahiti had not been a recent phenomenon. For centuries, maybe more than a millennium, it had been their everyday way of life.

From the descriptions of those first Europeans to visit the Society Islands and from the subsequent scientific research, we can begin to visualize the daily routine of a Tahitian family. Most would wake with the dawn. In the tropics, this is the finest time of the day. The night has refreshed the air and there is an expectancy about the rising sun. All Polynesians have an affinity with sunrise which is almost spiritual. The rays of the new day fill the mind with hope and the body with energy. Those first few hours before the sun reaches its zenith are the most productive. No work can start until the body is cleansed. Tahitians are fastidious about personal cleanliness; even today three baths or showers are an essential minimum to ensure that the skin is pure and the body free of odours. Beauty is not simply visual but embraces all of the senses. When the Europeans came to Tahiti, the odour of their bodies, strengthened by many weeks at sea, announced that they came from quite a different world.

Tahiti is blessed with countless springs, streams and waterfalls. From every fold in the mountains, pure water tumbles down towards the sea. Homes were sited near fresh-water pools where the family could bathe. It was often a communal event at which neighbours were greeted and joint plans were made for the day. Some men shaved their faces, using mollusc shells or sharks' teeth as razors and tweezers, but others sported chin whiskers and moustaches. Men and women trimmed their hair, sometimes closely cropped for cleanliness. Others had a thick head of hair which they grew long and held in place with plaited strands made from the veins in the leaves of the *ti* plant. Other plants, such as the flowering ginger (*Zingiber zerumbet*), were picked on the way to this early morning bathe and their sap used as a shampoo and conditioner for the hair. Tahitians love fresh-water. The final stage of their daily toilet was spent sitting at the edge of the clearest pool. Monoi oil, derived from the coconut and perfumed with sandalwood, was used to anoint the clean dry skin and to dress the hair. It moisturized the skin and perhaps also helped repel insects. Although there was, and still is, no malaria in Tahiti, mosquitoes and other tiny biting flies plagued the ancient Polynesians just as they do the islanders today.

Sap of the wild ginger plant conditions the hair, and its flower is a source
of perfume for the skin.

Clean and smelling faintly of coconut oil, a Tahitian might glance at his or her reflection in the pool before heading back to start the tasks of the day. On the way home, each would instinctively pick a flower for the hair. Traditionally it would have been the small fragrant bloom of a gardenia, the flower every Tahitian knows as the *tiare*. Gardenias are members of the coffee family and are widespread throughout the western Pacific, but the Tahitian form (*Gardenia taitensis*) seldom produces fertile seeds. It can only be propagated from runners, and was almost certainly brought to Tahiti by the first Polynesians. It was commonplace when Captain Cook first voyaged to these islands; the ship's botanists recorded it and the expedition's artists made drawings of Tahitians with *tiare* flowers in their hair. Then, as today, wearing flowers was not the sole prerogative of women; men also used the simple image of a flower as an expression of their contentment with the day.

For the ancient Tahitians, to enjoy today was more fulfilling than toiling for tomorrow. Many people, because of their position in society, could command the services of others. Some households had slaves, who were prisoners of war or hostages from skirmishes with neighbouring island groups. These earned their keep by performing the more menial tasks of everyday life, such as collecting firewood and building materials, tending the livestock, tilling the soil and perhaps fishing. Other activities were considered far too important to be left to women or to slaves. It was a man's job to build houses and make boats, and the making and use of tools was almost an art-form. Skilled craftsmen commanded great esteem. Some specialist boat-builders even had their own guild and exclusive places of worship. The skills, knowledge and honour were passed down from father to favoured son.

Timbers were split into rough planks by stone and hardwood wedges driven along the grain. Then began the laborious and highly skilled task of shaping and smoothing with a stone adze. Fire was sometimes used to speed up the process, especially when hollowing out the hull of a canoe. Chiselling, gouging and drilling were all achieved with tools fashioned from bone, shell or sharks' teeth, while the finishing was done with coral rock and sand. Even the simplest of canoe hulls would have taken many man-hours. It is not surprising that such craftsmen were admired for their dexterity and patience.

Only the finest hardwoods, such as *ati* (*Calophyllum inophyllum*) and *mara* (*Neonauclea forsteri*), were used for seagoing canoes. These trees often grew in the island's interior. For more routine work, Tahitians found ways of using

Dressed in a simple *pareu* and with a crown of leaves, today's Tahitian
vahine is as beguiling as those that captivated the artist Gauguin. The hibiscus,
or any flower, worn behind the right ear is a traditional sign that the wearer
is unmarried and available.

timber with coarser grain. The bread-fruit tree (*Artocarpus altilis*), which the Tahitians call *uru*, not only produces an almost year-round crop of nutritious fruit but also grows tall and sturdy. When its fruiting days became numbered, it was pressed into service to make planks for smaller canoes. The boards were fitted edge-to-edge and sewn together with sennit cord, which was deftly twisted from the fibres of coconut husks and threaded through holes drilled along the edges of each plank. The joints and the holes were then caulked with coconut fibre and a pitch made from the gum of the bread-fruit tree. The wood of the coconut palm also made workable timber, as did that of the *tou* tree (*Cordia subcordata*). Even hibiscus and barringtonia, renowned mainly for their colourful flowers and medicinal fruits, were fashioned into parts for boats and buildings. The attraction of these coarse-grained trees was that they grew relatively quickly and flourished in the more accessible valleys and along the coast. As the harder woods became scarce, groves of trees were planted as sources of timber as well as food. Famous in Tahiti, where it is found alongside streams and in other wet soils, is the Tahitian chestnut (*Inocarpus fagifer*) known as *mape*. The mature nut is flat and kidney-shaped and about three inches long. When the ripe nuts fell in October and November, Tahitians would let their pigs forage for this nutritious wild harvest. Roasted or baked, the Tahitian chestnut is delicious.

As the sun reached its peak, those working on the soil or out on the lagoon would head back towards the settlement. Others gathered with friends beneath the shade of *mape* trees. Men and women kept very much to themselves during the day; they were even segregated at meal-times. Preparing Tahitian food took a long time, often most of the day. Predictably, it seems to have been women's work. The staple root crops of taro (*Colocasia esculenta*), wild yam (*Dioscorea nummularia*) and arrowroot (*Tacca leontopetaloides*), together with bread-fruit, were brought to Tahiti by the first settlers. In time they also adopted the sweet potato (*Ipomoea batatas*) as an important carbohydrate. Over the centuries they learned how to utilize wild food plants which grew in the forest. As well as *mape*, they harvested the Malay apple (*Syzygium malaccense*) and the small fruit of the nono tree (*Morinda citrifolia*), the large shiny leaves of which were used to wrap fish for baking. The nono also had several medicinal properties and provided a brilliant yellow dye. Even the root of the *ti* plant was palatable when cooked but no amount of preparation could soften the root of tree-ferns; only on long expeditions into the mountains would a Tahitian resort to eating it, or perhaps in time of famine.

Shortage of food does not seem to have been a hallmark of life on Tahiti, certainly not at the time when Europeans first arrived. Joseph Banks, the botanist with Captain Cook, was renowned as being something of a gourmet.

He was so impressed with the quantity of food consumed at a typical Tahitian meal that he devoted several pages of his journal to describing the fare. One man apparently devoured three bread-fruit, each bigger than two fists. This appetizer was followed by a main course of two or three substantial reef fish, and for dessert, the Tahitian gourmand demolished a dozen or so ripe bananas. All this was washed down by the contents of several large coconuts. Banks also commented on the large size of many Tahitian men and women, a characteristic shared by some of their descendants.

Fish was cooked or marinated before eating, but shellfish was often consumed raw, straight from the lagoon. Although meat was not as plentiful as the tropical fruits and root-plants, the Tahitian diet included the flesh of pigs, dogs, the domestic jungle fowl (*Gallus gallus*) and wild birds such as the *upu* or Tahitian fruit dove (*Ptilinopus purpuratus*), which has a call just like its Tahitian

The wild jungle fowl (*Gallus gallus*), from south-east Asia, became the Polynesians' most domesticated stock. They called it *moa*.

name. The Polynesian rat (*Rattus exulans*) was considered a delicacy. This quite graceful rodent is essentially a vegetarian and consequently its flesh is sweet and palatable. So was that of dogs bred by Tahitians for eating rather than as companions on the hunt. Fed on the peelings from root vegetables and on coconut flesh, they made a useful and appetizing addition to the Tahitian daily diet.

Each family had its own earth-oven or *umu*. The ovens have survived as depressions in the soil, providing intriguing finds for archaeologists, who can estimate the size of settlements by their presence. Each pit was one or two feet deep and five to six feet in diameter. Layers of firewood and stones were stacked in the pit and the wood then burnt to ash. The food to be baked was laid on the hot stones, protected by fresh leaves. Fish and meat were often wrapped in larger leaves to separate the flavours and keep in the juices. Hot stones placed inside the carcases ensured that the flesh cooked right through. This simple but very effective oven is still widely used throughout Polynesia.

No description of Tahitian eating habits and day-to-day life would be complete without a celebration of the humble coconut. It is difficult to visualize how the islanders could have survived without this adaptable companion. Of all their plants, it had the widest variety of uses and travelled farthest across Polynesia in tandem with its cultivators. The timber of the palm was used to build houses and to make fence posts; the tough, conveniently shaped leaves were ideal for basketwork, interior walls and thatch; the fibres of the dried husk were plaited to make cords which could be fashioned into rope for boats or into sandals to protect the feet when walking on coral. The hard shells of the nuts were used as containers and bowls or, when blackened and filled with water, served as mirrors for the face. The liquid inside the ripe nut made a refreshing salt-free drink; the flesh could be eaten raw, or cooked and creamed; and its oil extracted for use as liniments and ointments. The Tahitians cultivated some sixteen different varieties and gave each one a special name according to its most important use. The image of the coconut palm near a blue lagoon now symbolizes the South Seas paradise. No plant could be more appropriate.

By the time the sun has begun its descent into the afternoon, the air on Tahiti is hot and often oppressive. Today's office workers in Papeete take as long as possible for lunch; even with air-conditioning, the afternoons are not the most productive time, particularly in the wake of a French-style midday meal. It must have been the same for the ancient Tahitians. *Avatea* was the term they gave to the part of the day that runs up to noon and *ahi'ahi* to the afternoon, when the air continues to heat up. By mid-afternoon, when temperatures reach their peak, work became impossible and it was time to eat and then rest. The women who had laboured to prepare the root vegetables for the earth-oven now had time to themselves, as their menfolk slept off the excesses of their main meal. There was time to sit in the shade talking with other women whilst they put their own manual skills to good use, making articles for the home.

Throughout Polynesia, plait-ware is one of the commonest textiles. The plentiful supply of fibrous plants that grow rapidly in the tropical climate provided them with an endless, renewable supply of materials for weaving baskets, mats, screens, bedding and other household articles, as well as fish-nets and sails for canoes. The leaves of pandanus and the coconut palm were used for almost all of these day-to-day objects. Stalks of bamboo and arrowroot and the stems of grasses and ferns have different textures which were ideal for specialized work. It is captivating to watch a contemporary Tahitian woman, attired in modern clothes, dextrously plait a basket or a sun-hat from a few strips of pandanus; in minutes a work of art is ready to be used. Surprisingly, in an age of plastic bags, it is a skill which few Tahitians have lost.

Much of the plait-work was very fine and the best was so admired that it was often used as gifts, sometimes as payment. Wraparounds made from thin, bleached strips of the inner bark of the hibiscus plant were particularly prized. They were light and elegant and remarkably durable. Because such material took months to make, it became the attire of chiefs rather than clothing for commoners.

The ancient Polynesian mariners who first discovered Tahiti probably cared little for sartorial elegance. *Ti* leaves and pandanus braid kept off the sun and rain, and served as guardians of modesty. Contrary to popular belief, Tahitians did not go about naked; covering more personal parts of the anatomy had been the fashion long before the Europeans came and imposed their cultural values. Even the members of Cook's expedition differed in their observations as to whether the Tahitian women routinely went topless. Banks, a ladies' man by all accounts, noted that at sunset they always 'bared their bodies down to the navel'.

The Tahitians had no cotton or flax; nor did they have wild or domestic animals from which they could spin wool or cure skins. Their clothing was made of bark-cloth called *tapa*. This textile was prepared from the soft inner bark of several kinds of trees, notably the *aute* or paper-mulberry (*Broussonetia papyrifera*), a variety of bread-fruit tree and a kind of fig tree. The art of making cloth from the fibrous bark of plants had been brought with them, and no doubt the essential plants as well. The *aute* trees were cultivated on plantations near the settlements to ensure a constant supply of this vital natural resource. Every settlement would resound to the beating of wooden mallets on boards as the strips of moist bark were matted together into a pliable cloth. Sun-bleached or dyed with the pigments from wild plants, this bark-cloth was fashioned into simple clothing and provided bedcovers and the basis for decorative screens.

In the late afternoon, life quickens on Tahiti. The heat of the sun's rays begins to wane and there is a mild urgency to complete domestic tasks before the end of *ahi 'ahi* and the coming of the night. For those who have woken from their siesta, it is an opportunity to bathe again, to feel clean and refreshed for what might lie ahead. For young and old it is a time for visiting friends, playing games and making love. Tahitians had a forthright view of their own sexuality, which is shared by their descendants today. Their well-deserved reputation for this stems from the uninhibited generosity with which Tahitian women shared

their bodies with travel-weary European sailors. To them, it was a very natural way of life. As one of Captain Cook's younger chroniclers romantically observed: 'After their meals they resume their domestic amusements, during which the flame of mutual affection spreads in every heart, and unites the rising generation with new and tender ties.'

Finally night clouds gather behind the silhouette of distant Moorea to the west. Tahitians have a fear of the dark. Inside the houses some gather to talk or to play music while others go to bed. *Ao* is the name given to that period of the day which is illuminated by the sun; the night is called *po*. It is the period of darkness when humans stay indoors and spirits haunt the world outside. The day was for the people of ancient Tahiti; the night was for their gods.

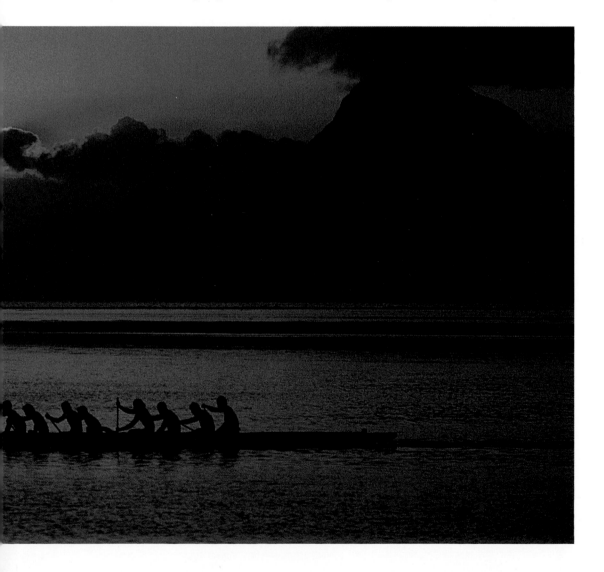

CHAPTER TWO

BIRTH and DEATH of the NOBLE SAVAGE

For the Polynesians, gods and spirits were their ancestors. They had no concept of distinct natural and supernatural worlds. Their gods had created the universe and everything in it, and therefore people and nature were related as one. The land and the sea, the sun and the sky, the plants and the animals were all part of that heritage to which they and their ancestors belonged.

Spirits and humans were members of the same society; they had the same ambitions and motives and even the same needs. What set spirits apart from humans was that they took on versatile forms, were more mobile than people and certainly more powerful. This made them sacred and endowed everything associated with them as sacred too. Because spirits and humans occupied the same world, parts of that world were deemed taboo.

The word taboo itself is Polynesian: *tapu* or a very similar word is a feature of every Polynesian language. The exact meaning may vary across the Pacific islands, but the sentiment is always the same. It implies 'restricted', 'dedicated' and very often 'forbidden'. Chiefs were nearest to ancestral spirits and, depending on rank, often just as sacred. This accorded them the privilege of declaring things *tapu*. It was a power which they often exercised to their personal advantage. In this respect, the leaders of Tahitian society were no different from chiefs the world over. Taboos were imposed on the natural resources of the Tahitian world, on fruit, fish, pigs, trees, water or any commodity essential to life. It was the Tahitian way of restricting their own consumption

The 'Stone of Investiture' at the mystic *marae* of Taputapuatea on the sacred isle of Raiatea – ancient site of secret rituals.

of the physical world to which they and their ancestral spirits belonged. *Tapu* commanded fearful respect and violation brought spiritual and social reprisal. In this way, the ancestral spirits, through their earthly descendants, controlled the use and abuse of nature. It formed the basis of a natural order to which every Tahitian was born and which he or she followed to the grave.

For our small group of pioneering Polynesians who first settled Tahiti or one of the neighbouring high islands, the birth of the first child in their adopted home was a historic turning-point in their new life. The addition to their number symbolized for all of them the purpose of the long and hazardous voyage that had brought them to this faraway place. In the nearby forest, suckers of bread-fruit, which they had planted when they first arrived, were now well established. By the time the child was five, they would bear fruit. In a human lifetime, a single bread-fruit tree produces sufficient sustenance to meet the basic needs of a Tahitian.

Above The bread-fruit tree – called *uru* or *maiore* – yields up to
150 heavy fruit each year; roasted or steamed, they are still an
important and delicious part of the Polynesian diet.
Left The village at Matavie, painted soon after European encounter
with Tahiti.

Within a few generations, the new colony had grown to a substantial size.
Settlements were established all around the island, wherever there was fresh-
water, a fertile valley and access to the lagoon. Family or other kin-groups
declared ownership of these tracts of land, which often included stretches of the
more mountainous interior. Just as today, the most popular parts of the island
were near the coast where fresh-water meets the sea. Here the Polynesians could
fish and sail their canoes to reach less accessible parts of the coast. Along the
coastline were many of the trees which provided timber and leaves for construction, and fruit and nuts for their daily diet. As the population expanded, the
prime areas adjacent to the lagoon became the province of the chiefly people;
lesser mortals moved further inland to set up home on the more difficult terrain
that flanked the valleys. Access to the fish-rich lagoon became controlled by
those who, for reason of status or influence, had staked their claim on the
shoreline. In exchange for granting permission for others to exploit this once

communal natural resource, the owners of coastal land extracted payment in the form of gifts or labour, or simply demanded a substantial part of the commoners' catch. Very soon, the entire resources of the island, whether natural or man-managed, came under the control of a small select group of society. Their authority was usually inherited but could be won by coercion or force. Once secured, it was protected by the prudent imposition of taboos.

Most privileged were the chiefs themselves, the *ari'i*. They wielded considerable power over their subjects, who were required to bare the upper parts of their bodies when in their presence. If a chief entered a commoner's house, it was declared *tapu* and was burnt afterwards. Tithes were paid to chiefs in the form of food, bark-cloth or other manufactured goods, such as finely woven mats. The chief's own immediate family formed an aristocracy who were distinct from ordinary people. Such status was carefully protected and marriage outside the circle was prohibited. Some chiefs were required to take two or three wives to ensure that they produced sufficient heirs to carry on the exclusive line.

The lesser chiefs and major landowners formed their own distinctive class, the *ra'atira*. They had minor privileges but enjoyed a special position in Tahitian society, one that meant that they, too, seldom had to work. That business was left to the *manahune*, the commoners. Far from being democratic, Tahitian society was class-conscious and feudal. Like its medieval counterparts in Europe, it was clearly open to abuse. What made it work was the fact that Tahiti, like all the Polynesian islands, was a small place. There were several chiefs and each could walk round his chiefdom in a day. He ruled only a few thousand subjects, all of whom were related to each other, if not to him. He knew every family and made it his business that complaints were heard as fairly as possible. It was in his interest for the system to be seen to work. Tahitian chiefs were more aware of their dignity than their power. They were, as everyone knew, descended from gods and had an obligation to respect their ancestry. Fear of spiritual retribution governed the lives of chiefs as well as commoners.

For their part, the peasant class, the *manahune*, were content to support their rulers with labour and provisions. It was no great burden for a community which was blessed with plentiful food and natural resources. Envy and jealousy were not hallmarks of the Tahitian way of life. Allegiance to chiefs was as natural as respect for ancestors, who long ago had established this strict hierarchical and confining system.

Tahitian laws, like those throughout Polynesia, were straightforward and effective. In place of a formal written code of practice, there was a strong sense of what was right and what was wrong. Those who infringed *tapu* were rebuked by priests and other elders, and the whole family shared the shame. It seems that any other kind of retribution was unnecessary and that physical punishment was rarely, if ever, inflicted. Public disgrace was often punishment enough. It was the fear and shame of what might happen if a taboo was broken that controlled people's actions.

Such taboos were probably descended from ancient beliefs handed down from times when life was not so easy. Before the first Polynesians fashioned the landscape of these islands into a productive natural system, there must have been great hardship. By the time the Europeans first encountered Tahiti, most people seemed content with what they had and they made sure that family and friends were never in need. A Tahitian would give food to anyone who was hungry; it is a generous trait that is still found all across Polynesia today. Nothing is immediately expected in return, except the knowledge that if there were ever such occasion, the gift would be willingly reciprocated. Society was held together by a network of obligation. Nobody thought of him- or herself as the permanent owner of anything; there was no need for the concept of private property. If a man needed the use of a boat, he took the one nearest to hand; everyone would understand. If he desired his friend's wife or his friend's daughter, the same understanding applied, and the gift would be reciprocated whenever the need arose. It was this simple approach that the Europeans were to find so perplexing. What they saw when they first encountered this uncomplicated way of life was a naivety and lack of worldliness. This presented them with a dilemma about how they themselves should behave now that Europe had discovered that the 'noble savage' did indeed exist.

What confounded the European mind was the Tahitian attitudes to religion, life and death. It may be because of their prejudiced view that early accounts of Polynesian religion leave so much tantalizingly vague. In common with other Pacific islands, the people of Tahiti believed in Te Atua, the one supreme 'creator of life' who had no earthly manifestation. Other lesser gods were more like folk-heroes and were associated with particular human activities. Ta'aroa was the god of the sea; Rongo was god of horticulture; Oro was god of war; Tane was god of sex and procreation. Still further down the godly pecking order came a number of local gods with specialized powers that met the needs of that community.

The spirits communicated with people in all kinds of ways. Trees were a favourite medium, especially sacred trees such as *miro* (*Thespesia populnea*), *aito* (*Casuarina equisetifolia*) and *ati* (*Calophyllum inophyllum*), which were most frequently planted near places of worship where the rustling of the wind in their leaves was taken as a sign of the presence of spirits.

The more usual medium through which spirits interacted with people were tiki figures, known in Tahiti as *ti'i*. Someone requiring the services of a spirit would carve or commission the carving of a human-like image in wood or stone.

Then, with offerings and entreaties, the spirit would be persuaded to enter the *ti'i* and remain there in service on a more or less permanent basis, to protect property and people from evil spirits and sometimes to assist with sorcery against other people who had caused harm in some way. Such carved images were commonplace in the houses of most families and afforded protection to them as they went about their domestic tasks. The figures were not worshipped, but were simply there to bring good fortune.

The images that harboured the principal gods were the *to'o*. Larger than domestic tikis and sometimes constructed of tressed coconut fibre, these were often of simple design and were intended as 'receptacles' into which a god would temporarily enter so that it could be worshipped and consulted. A conspicuous feature of *to'o* were red and yellow feathers attached to the image. These feathers were much prized in all Polynesian societies and in Tahiti were taken from native parakeets. The male of the now extinct Society Island lorikeet (*Cyanoramphus ulietarius*) had a yellow breast and both sexes had a bright red rump-patch. Tahiti also had a species of lorikeet (*Vini kuhlii*) which is now confined to the Austral Islands a long way south of Tahiti. It too has spectacular red plumage.

When the European explorers arrived, they witnessed religious ceremonies at which long, feathered girdles were worn by the highest chiefs as a mark of their godly ancestry. These belts were made of strengthened bark-cloth or *tapa* to which were attached countless brilliantly coloured feathers, mostly red. The largest girdle seen in Tahiti was more than twenty feet in length and would have required the feathers of thousands of parakeets. It is no surprise that the bird became extinct in Tahiti, probably by the eighteenth century. Some enterprising European seafarers soon discovered the worth of red feathers in Tahiti and brought them from other Pacific islands to use as payment for trade and favours.

The *to'o*, complete with feathers, became focal points of religious ceremonies at Tahiti's most sacred sites, the *marae*. These hallowed places were the pride of the people, an expression of their cultural and religious wealth, and at these temples they presented their verbal and physical offerings to their gods. The god Ta'aroa, as Tangaroa was called in Tahiti, had created the universe, but before it became inhabited by gods and spirits and people, chaos and darkness had prevailed. The sky was raised from the earth and the sun made to sweep daily across the heavens, thereby establishing the two worlds of *po* and *ao*. The final order could not be complete until the proper links were initiated between the spiritual sphere and the world of humans. For this it was deemed necessary to establish places where people and gods could come together in a befitting manner.

Today, the *marae* of Tahiti and her neighbouring islands are the most enduring monuments to have survived from pre-European times. They are witness to an extraordinary religious culture that developed over hundreds of years here in the middle of the Pacific. After the coming of the European with his compelling alternative religion, most *marae* were abandoned and fell into ruin. It was not until the 1950s that archaeologists began systematically to excavate and restore some of these ancient sites. A few may date back to the eighth century AD, but many were built during the height of Tahitian culture, which started around AD 1200 and was still flourishing when Europeans stumbled on Tahiti towards the end of the eighteenth century.

A great number of *marae* ruins have been discovered hidden beneath dense tropical vegetation throughout all the islands of eastern Polynesia. This gives us some idea of the extent to which people's lives were governed by the all-embracing political and religious system that centred on the *marae*. If you walk through the stands of coconut palms that now shade the silent ruins, you cannot fail to feel something of the atmosphere that pervades these places. Many Tahitians will never go near them; since the coming of Christianity, they are fearful of the consequences. Like their dread of night, they see these ruins as relics of *po*, places of demons and the anti-Christ. It is true that the *marae* of Tahiti were the centres for much that, in our contemporary terms, is bizarre and savage about ancient Tahitian life.

Many *marae* were small, discrete areas set aside essentially for family worship. Here groups of people would assemble, often with their *ti'i*, to commune with their favourite spirits and to bring gifts as tokens of their gratitude to the higher gods. The appearance of wild birds such as herons and kingfishers indicated to the participants that the spirits were there too. At one end of the *marae*, a stone platform, the *ahu*, served exclusively as a place for the spirits and gods. These platforms were not altars for offerings but were the focal points for worship, since it was within them that the gods, when summoned, took up temporary residence.

Sometimes the *ahu* consisted only of a small pile of boulders. On more elaborate *marae*, the *ahu* was carefully constructed of worked stone and coral slabs that fitted together to create a multi-level platform. The largest was the mighty pyramid of the Mahaiatea *marae* at Papara on Tahiti. Its base measured 260 feet long by 78 feet wide, and it rose in ten steps to a height of 45 feet above the level of the *marae* precinct. This remarkable structure was built in 1767 on the instructions of a powerful female chief named Purea. Captain Cook's party saw the completed edifice and it became a feature of subsequent South Sea sightseeing voyages until destroyed in the wake of missionary zeal. Such elaborate *marae* with stepped *ahu* were rare and were all probably built in the

The Mahaiatea *marae* at Papara, the largest ever constructed on Tahiti;
drawn from the original sketch by James Wilson, 1797.

eighteenth century. They represented an extravagance of design and achieve-
ment which paralleled the rise in Tahitian hierarchy; the bigger and more
elaborate the *marae*, the more powerful and influential the society that
commissioned it. The *marae* shown proudly to European visitors had been
developed from more humble origins.

Typically, the entire precinct of the *marae* was oblong with the raised *ahu*
at one end. Nearby was the *ava'a*, the 'gods' bed', a stone platform on which
were rested the *ti'i* and *to'o* by which the spirits and gods would enter the *marae*.
Stone slabs were sunk vertically into the stone paving of the court. Facing the
ahu, they served as backrests for high officials and maybe even for the
participating spirits themselves. On each major *marae*, there was also a sacrificial
table on which offerings were presented to the gods. Usually made of wood,

these tables were elevated on tall legs which were skilfully carved in such a way as to deter rats from climbing onto the offering table itself. The fruits and flesh laid out in full view of all were intended for godly consumption.

Many *marae* were overshadowed by giant trees such as the banyan (*Ficus prolixa*). Their curtains of aerial roots sometimes embraced the skulls of the celebrated dead and their sprawling branches cast a gloom over the *marae* which together with the rustling of wind through their leaves contributed to the atmosphere of superstition and terror that was said to pervade such places. By all accounts, such a reputation was quite justified. The building of an important *marae* took its toll on the community. For two or three years prior to starting work, religious taboos were imposed on the area to conserve pigs and fowls, fish and plant produce, so that everything could be invested in the construction of the important new monument. The population was then required to observe the greatest solemnity while the *marae* took shape. Men withdrew from family life to help with the construction. All other living creatures were banished from the selected site. No fires were kindled along the nearby shore, nor were people allowed to speak except in hushed voices. Those not directly involved in the construction were deployed to catch and prepare food for the artisans and to bring the giant stones from the mountains and the slabs of coral from the lagoon. It was an enterprise that consumed the energies and emotions of the entire community. For those working on the site, it was an honour which would never be repeated in their lifetime.

For one participant, the end of that time was imminent. When all the new stones for the *marae* had been transported to the cleared site, the ground was sprinkled with sea-water by the priests. A long rock slab was then brought from another royal *marae* to act as the chief cornerstone of the new place of worship. Before it was set in place, a gruesome ritual was performed. A man was chosen and killed. His warm body was then lowered into the waiting hole and, to the chanting of the high priest, the sacred stone was set firmly upright on the corpse. The spirit of the slaughtered man would become the guardian of the new *marae*. That was his great honour.

Away from the solemn business of their *marae*, Tahitian people were a carefree and healthy breed of Polynesians. Their ancestor-gods had delivered them to this land where, by proven skills in horticulture and the astute management of limited resources, they had created their Garden of Eden. Their culture had been determined by the nature of the land. Island life is finite; it is a closed system which must sustain itself or perish. The Tahitian way of life may not have been perfect, but the island was a paradise for a people who saw themselves as fortunate to be at the centre of a world that to them was an endless ocean.

Above The *fei* banana tree (*Musa troglodytarum*), characterized by its erect
fruiting bunches, produces only one crop in its lifetime; it was a luxury food
reserved for Tahitian nobility.
Right A Tahitian boxing match, seen on Captain Cook's second voyage, 1778–9.

In Tahiti, no-one went short of food or housing, and there seems to have
been very little sickness. As in the Bible's Garden of Eden, fruit grew in
abundance at all times of year, plants took root and flourished, birds called from
flower-laden trees and, unlike the biblical paradise, there were no snakes. Other
than the ubiquitous mosquito and other minute biting insects, dangerous
creatures lived only in the sea. It seems that the entire social and ecological
framework established by the Tahitians made it unnecessary for people to toil
for much more than an hour or two a day. The rest of their time was spent
pursuing more enjoyable activities which we would consider to be hobbies and
pastimes.

Tahitians spent as much time in and on the water as tilling the land. Before
a child could walk, he or she could swim and was introduced to the cleansing
qualities of fresh-water and to the richness of life in the salty lagoon. Every child
was at home in a canoe and knew the rudiments of sailing and the dangers of the
sea beyond the embracing reef. When strong enough, children would practise

surfing, using a canoe paddle as a board. Adults used the split timbers of lightweight trees such as palm and hibiscus. Their skill at riding the surf on the windward side of Tahiti impressed the first European visitors; here in the warm blue water of the South Seas was the natural home of surfing as a sport. It was equally popular with both sexes; indeed women were often the more skilful and could stand on a short board as they surged on the crest of a large wave.

Sports similar to boxing and wrestling were also the province of both men and women. Often violent, these combats attracted large audiences. William Bligh was a spectator at several matches when the *Bounty* spent five months on Tahiti at the end of 1789. In his view, women's wrestling was far more savage than men's, and included such unrestrained tactics as eye-gouging. After the victor was declared, the combatants would embrace like old friends. Champions were loudly applauded and greatly esteemed.

Other popular athletic sports included sling shooting, javelin throwing and a variety of ball games using nuts and inflated pigs' bladders. Tahitians also practised a sophisticated form of archery. Although sometimes used in hunting, bows and arrows were not employed in Tahitian warfare at the time when European accounts began. In place of combative skills, a highly stylized sport had been developed which had become the principal pastime of the upper classes. Bows, about five feet long, were fashioned from the strong but flexible wood of *purau*, the beach hibiscus (*Hibiscus tiliaceus*), and strung with fibres of *ro'a* (*Pipturus argenteus*). Arrows were of bamboo, about three feet in length and tipped with hard points made from sharpened *aito*, the ironwood tree (*Casuarina equisetifolia*). No feathers were used to help guide flight, as distance rather than marksmanship was the object of the exercise.

The sport was practised from special stone platforms, three or four feet high and triangular in shape. The archer, robed in special *tapa*-cloth, took up position at the centre of one convex-shaped side of the platform. Poised on one knee, he drew back the bow with all his might before firing the arrow in an arc that was calculated to take it furthest. Spotters reported on the individual's performance and champions were greatly revered. Very often the ceremonial archery platforms were sited near to a *marae*, and the arrows were respectfully fired towards that sacred place.

It was, however, at the Tahitians' prowess with canoes that the Europeans marvelled most. From modest dugouts to plank-built double-hulled ocean-going craft, all were collectively known as *va'a* but each design had a different name to match its use. Some *va'a* were for fishing and had simple outriggers and were propelled by pole or sail; others had keels and could tack close to the wind. The craft most admired by the European explorers, who were themselves no novices to the art of seamanship, was the Tahitian war canoe. The largest were of double-hull construction and could carry at least forty men, who propelled the craft at great speed by paddling in unison. It was an impressive sight.

When Captain Cook and the other European seafarers encountered Tahiti, all the Society Islands were preoccupied with warfare. It was an era in the history of their culture which had started before contact with Europeans and which, perhaps not surprisingly, continued afterwards. Against the backdrop of their Garden of Eden, the ferocity with which island fought island and cousin killed cousin seemed, to outsiders, a contradiction of the Tahitian way of life. From his own vessel, in April 1774, Captain Cook watched one Tahitian war fleet assemble in readiness to launch an attack against neighbouring Moorea, which is well in sight, just to the west of Tahiti. He estimated that there were 160 large double-hulled war canoes and 170 smaller craft. In all, the armada carried more than 7000 men. It was from this observation that Cook calculated the

William Hodges, the chief Admiralty artist on Captain Cook's second
voyage, recorded the grandeur of the Tahitian war canoes.

total population of Tahiti to be in excess of 100000 people, but it is more likely
to have been less than half that figure at the time. Whatever the real total, the
island clearly supported a large and well-provisioned seagoing force.

Most naval engagements were preceded by verbal battles as the warriors
worked up their passions. The two opposing sides each fastened their canoes end
to end and then the two lines were lashed to each other. What followed was a
hand-to-hand battle of the most terrible kind which resulted in great maiming
and slaughter. One side eventually emerged victorious and took hostages and
slaves, many of whom were friends or even relatives. The rest fled to nurse their
wounds and bury their dead.

To us this rivalry seems barbaric. To the Tahitian, politics and religion were
inseparable and both were linked to the constraints of island life. There was no
escape from the physical and ecological confines of each speck of land, except
by expansion into the next. During the centuries before European contact, each
of the Society Islands had been developing its own distinct way of life and had
great pride in its own island. Linked by a common ancestry, the islanders had
developed their own loyalties, their own chiefs and their own gods. Competition
for resources such as hard timber and marine life may have sparked inter-island
conflict, but it was in defence of their own gods and the prestige of their own
island that they were prepared to shed blood.

Although Tahiti was the largest and most populated of the Society Islands, Raiatea was the most sacred. It was here that the war god Oro, son of the great god Ta'aroa, was born. Backed by a powerful priesthood, the cult of Oro grew strong in Raiatea until, by the late sixteenth century, Tahiti became eclipsed in religious influence. The great *marae* at Opoa on the south-eastern side of Raiatea is perhaps the most ancient of all the surviving royal *marae* in the Society Islands. It was given the most sacred name, Taputapuatea, and its reputation spread to distant islands far beyond the horizon. Its former name had been Vaerai and archaeological evidence suggests that it was first built in the mid-fourteenth century but found fame when Raiatea became the focal point for a religious sect known as the *arioi*. This strange brotherhood recruited members from all classes of society and travelled from island to island giving theatrical performances in which lascivious dancing was a provocative feature. They also hired themselves out to wealthy families at times of bereavement. Like mummers, they would noisily terrorize the neighbourhood, until their client called an end to the wake and the spirit was finally permitted to depart from the corpse. The *arioi* were given certain immunities but in return they were required to serve their ruler as warriors and kill their own newborn children, thereby reserving their energies and resources for the cause. Their reputation and the compelling cult of Oro made Raiatea a centre of religious and secular power.

Raiatea today has 7000 inhabitants. Its district capital, Uturoa, is a town of great charm, despite being the second largest in French Polynesia. Most of the islanders live there and the rest of Raiatea's coastal plain is a scantily spread mosaic of coconut groves, vanilla plantations and hamlets with a generous ratio of churches of various denominations. Inland looms the two-million-year-old volcano of Mount To'omoro and the sacred summit of Mount Temehani. If you hire a car and follow the long coast road, or take a short cut by boat across Fa'aroa bay, you will discover the relics of Taputapuatea. Until you set foot on the promontory, you will see little sign of its epic history. Coconut palms, banded with strips of tin to deter rats, have been allowed to grow through the ruins and block out the sun. Everywhere there are holes in the ground made by land-crabs, which emerge at dusk to scavenge the once magnificent *marae*. These crustaceans are known in Tahiti as *tupa* and were considered to be messengers of spirits. Those from anywhere near *marae* sites were never killed.

The best time to experience the mystery and power of Taputapuatea is at dawn. As the brilliant sun-ball first appears on the horizon out to sea, it casts slanting rays beneath the palms and strikes the upright stones with fire. By the water's edge is a small 'navigators' *marae*' with its own *ahu* where Polynesian seafarers would worship their gods. Nearby is the Havuiri *marae* which was the landing place for canoes arriving with sacrificial offerings. Just inland is a massive

The Blue land crab (*Cardisoma bircipes*) is widespread throughout
the coastal forests of south-east Asia and the Pacific islands; its larvae are
carried by the ocean currents.

white rock impaled in the ground. This is the 'Investiture Stone' at which
visiting dignitaries were greeted by Raiatea's chiefs. Local people will tell you
that beneath this massive rock, which was brought from a distant part of the
island, are the remains of four men, one supporting each corner of the stone.
When you turn your back on this gruesome thought, you will see the main *ahu*,
overshadowed by a giant banyan tree. A few upright slabs survive to indicate
where the chiefly people once sat to view the rituals of Taputapuatea.

Joseph Banks, on Cook's first voyage to Tahiti, visited this sacred *marae* and
described how he discovered the remains of a giant hog that had been sacrificed
and left as an offering to Oro. Although he and Cook witnessed human sacrificial
ceremonies at other Tahitian *marae*, they never witnessed the solemnity and
power of ritual at Taputapuatea. The most vivid description was recorded by

Teuira Henry in her account of ancient Tahiti. Her grandfather lived on Moorea in the early nineteenth century and left manuscripts describing Tahitian legends and customs that dated back centuries. She, too, describes the scene at dawn.

At sunrise, the canoes approaching Tearamoa Pass would line up two by two, each representing a kingdom. They would draw closer, slowly paddling to the rhythm of the drums and the call of the conch-shells. Numerous high-ranking visitors would appear, bearing no weapons and without women or children. The double-hulled canoes were lashed together by a plank bridge

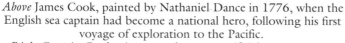

Above James Cook, painted by Nathaniel Dance in 1776, when the English sea captain had become a national hero, following his first voyage of exploration to the Pacific.
Right Captain Cook witnesses a human sacrificial ceremony at a *marae* on Tahiti. At the far right stands local guide and interpreter, Tupaia, wearing a European uniform.

under which were shelters containing idols, drums, conch-shells and other treasures for the gods and for the population of Raiatea. On a wooden platform lay rows of human sacrifices, newly killed, as well as large fish caught off neighbouring islands. These rows were aligned as follows: one human corpse, one trevally, one corpse, one shark, one corpse, one turtle, etc., with a corpse at the far end of the row. The king and the priests proffered words of welcome in a slow, deep voice. Afterwards, everybody got to work to prepare the sacrifices offered by the visitors as well as those provided by the local inhabitants.

A human being was the highest offering that could be made to the gods, in particular to Oro, who delighted in war and presumably in the death of a human. The victim was usually male and elderly, but in times of peace the offering was required to be physically unblemished with no wounds or disfiguring scars. After being despatched at some place away from the main *marae*, the corpse, wrapped in plaited coconut leaves, was brought to the offering table. At this stage, the human offering was euphemistically referred to as 'the fish' or as 'the man-long banana'. It was probably the soul rather than the flesh that was thought to be consumed by Oro.

The last human sacrifice was offered at the Taputapuatea *marae* about the year 1815. By then Captain Cook had come and gone, and in the wake of those first pioneering European seafarers had come opportunist venturers in search of fortunes and missionaries in search of souls. Nowadays, few Tahitians ever visit Taputapuatea; for them it is a self-imposed taboo. Such places represent a part of their culture which is at variance with what they now know of the world outside. The eighteenth-century European explorers may have 'discovered' Tahiti but, more significantly, Tahiti 'discovered' Europe. News of this faraway heaven in the South Seas spread through Europe and America like fire. Everyone yearned to see it for themselves, to find out whether the 'noble savage' really lived in paradise. Soon the bitter-sweet nature of the Tahitian way of life engendered mixed feelings of admiration and revulsion. Europe was primed to discover 'paradise' but was not ready for the realities of the encounter between these two worlds. Neither world would ever be the same again.

Captain Cook, in particular, lamented the magnitude of the social encounter. 'We debauch their morals,' he wrote in his log, 'and introduce among them wants and diseases which they never had before, and which serve only to destroy the happy tranquillity they and their forefathers had enjoyed. I often think it would have been better for them if we had never appeared among them.' His crew clearly felt little guilt. For them, this was the faraway heaven of their dreams. Where else in the world could you buy a share in paradise for the price of a ship's nail or a bunch of red feathers?

The primary purpose of Cook's expedition of 1769 had been to transport scientists from the Royal Society to observe the transit of Venus across the face of the sun, an event that would not happen again for another hundred years. Tahiti, which had been 'discovered' and charted by Captain Wallis just two years earlier, was ideally placed for their observations. Not only could scientists perform their astronomical studies but they could observe and collect

For the people of Raiatea, the ancient *marae* of Taputapuatea is still a
fearful place of mystic power.

specimens of the island's native plants and animals. For Daniel Solander, Joseph Banks and the other botanists and zoologists on board HMS *Endeavour*, the encounter with Tahiti presented them with important questions about the natural history of these remote Pacific islands. How could these plants and animals have developed here in such isolation, or, if they had reached here from distant continents, how had they arrived and from which direction?

Captain James Cook was not a scientist by training; his passion was the exploration of the world and its people. For him the overriding question concerned the origins of the Tahitian people themselves. From where had they come and how had they crossed the vastness of the Pacific Ocean? When Cook asked such questions on Tahiti, his guide and interpreter, a man called Tupaia, told him about the island of Raiatea to the west of Tahiti. That is the island to which Ta'aroa, the great god of the sea, came in his ancestral canoe. It was on Raiatea that he died and his spirit inhabits the sacred mountain Temehani, together with all the other founding ancestral spirits. Not everyone's spirit achieved that heavenly paradise; but in ancient, innocent Tahiti, there was no concept of hell. Faraway to the west of Raiatea, there was a greater spirit-land where the air was salubrious and the forests were filled with sweet-smelling red flowers and red-feathered birds. Fish abounded in the sea and on land there was food for everyone. There was no sickness or ageing and the women remained eternally beautiful. Such was the Tahitian view of their ancestral homeland far beyond the setting sun.

CHAPTER THREE

CROSSROADS of the PACIFIC

Ever since Captain Cook's epic first voyage to the islands of the South Pacific, scholars have argued over the origins of the people who were living there. The naturalist Joseph Banks came to a firm conclusion, even before HMS *Endeavour* had left New Zealand to head for home. 'From the similarity of customs, the still greater of traditions and the almost identical sameness of languages between these people and those Islands of the South Seas, there remains little doubt that they came originally from the same source; but where that source is, future experience may teach us. At present I can say no more than I firmly believe that it is to Westward and by no means to the East.'

When he came to that conclusion, Banks had encountered the people of Tahiti and the other Society Islands, the islanders of the Austral Islands to the immediate south, and the Maori of New Zealand. It was on two subsequent voyages that Captain Cook made contact with Easter Island and Hawaii, the other two corners of the Polynesian Triangle. Sadly for science and for us, Banks did not join those later expeditions; had he done so, he would have been even more impressed by the similarity in physical and cultural characteristics that unite the far-flung oceanic people whom we now refer to as 'the Polynesians'.

Although of sturdy build, the Polynesians have an 'oriental' look; but so do many of the native peoples of North and South America on the opposite side of the Pacific. It was this, together with some striking cultural similarities, which prompted Thor Heyerdahl and others to propose that the Polynesians had originated from the Americas and that they had moved westwards from there into the Pacific. Heyerdahl's famed *Kon-Tiki* raft expedition from the coast of Peru to the Tuamotu Islands east of Tahiti showed that South American Indians might have reached the islands of eastern Polynesia. The native peoples of the American continents were described as 'Indians' because they looked very much like the inhabitants of the Indies, the islands we now know as Indonesia. In fact Christopher Columbus believed that his own epic voyage across the Atlantic in 1492 had taken him straight there.

When Captain Cook set out for Tahiti in 1768, most of the world was known to Europeans. The Americas had been colonized for two and a half centuries and, to the east, the world had been mapped as far as Australia. The Pacific remained a puzzle. There were still thousands of islands to be sighted and charted, and the possibility of an entire new continent to the south. During the year after leaving Tahiti, Cook's team mapped New Zealand with amazing accuracy, and then did the same for the east coast of Australia. Having experienced one misadventure with the Great Barrier Reef, they hugged the coast to the most northern tip of the Australian continent and then headed due west towards the relatively well charted waters of the Indies. It was there in Batavia, the cosmopolitan port now called Jakarta, that his crew, which had so far remained healthy, fell sick from fever, dysentery and malaria. Tragically, many of them died, including Cook's native guide from Tahiti, Tupaia, who would otherwise have become the first Polynesian to see Europe.

From the Dutch East Indies, the run home westward across the Indian Ocean, around the Cape of Africa and into the Atlantic was a long but familiar haul. The loss of friends marred a homecoming which hailed Cook's voyage in the *Endeavour* as a milestone in the mapping of the globe. It would take Cook two more expeditions to complete his exploration of the Pacific. In little more than a decade, European geographic knowledge of the inhabited world was complete. Now attention focused on the mysteries surrounding the origins and migrations of the native peoples and wildlife of the newly discovered lands.

The Pacific islands can be grouped into three regions defined by their ethnic peoples. Melanesia, meaning 'black islands', embraces the islands from New Guinea to Fiji, where the people are predominantly dark-skinned. Micronesia describes the archipelagos of the Caroline Islands and a multitude of other very small islands to the north of Melanesia; they are inhabited by people of more Mongoloid size and appearance. Polynesia, meaning 'many islands', takes its identity from the remarkably similar linguistic, cultural and physical character- istics of its widespread people. From native Hawaiians in the far north to the Maori of New Zealand in the south-west and the original inhabitants of Easter Island in the remote eastern Pacific, all Polynesians identify with each other as being part of the same racial culture. The name is European but the concept of Polynesia comes from a shared tradition which stems from the people's common ancestry and fashions their collective spirit.

Although darker skinned and curly-haired, the people of the Fijian islands have
much in common with their Polynesian neighbours on Tonga and Samoa.

The Polynesian Triangle is best visualized as having Rapa Nui, the island we
call Easter Island, at its apex. Piercing the sunrise, this point is the most easterly
outpost of the Polynesian culture. Hawaii to the extreme north-west and New
Zealand to the south-west form the two corners of the base of the triangle. To
the west of this base-line of Polynesia lie the other ocean realms of Micronesia
and Melanesia, beyond which are the continents of Asia and Australia. When
picturing the story of the Polynesians, it helps to see their world like a spearhead
laid out across the Pacific, with its tip pointing east and its shaft reaching back
towards south-east Asia.

For Polynesians, the sunrise is a symbol of life, hope and new lands, while the sunset represents death, their spirit ancestors and the lands from which they came. If the ancestors of today's Polynesians did indeed come from the west, their homeland could well have been the islands on the continental shelf of south-east Asia or even the coast of the Asian mainland itself. Who these people might have been and how they came to settle the entire Polynesian Triangle are questions that have fascinated experts and amateurs ever since the days of Captain Cook. The route which they might have taken, island-hopping eastward into the Pacific, may have followed more or less the same path taken by the wildlife that settled Polynesia long ago. Other plants and animals, carried as domestic stock, came with those first ocean venturers. The courses of man and nature into Polynesia were interlinked, each paving the way for the other.

Where the two great archipelagos of Melanesia and Micronesia converge to form a 'shaft' for the Polynesian spearhead are three distinct groups of islands. Lying at the very base of the triangle, the islands that now make up Fiji are traditionally deemed to be the eastern limit of Melanesia, while those of Samoa and Tonga are unmistakably part of Polynesia. The three groups are separated from each other by only two or three hundred miles, a small distance on the Pacific scale. Fijians are mainly dark-skinned people with physical characteristics quite distinct from the Polynesians on Tonga and Samoa. Experts have long pondered on why there is such a marked divide and when it took place.

At the last count, there were more than 400 islands belonging to the Republic of Fiji. They lie on the same latitude as Tahiti, which is more than 2000 miles to the east, and like Tahiti, the main islands are high and of volcanic origin. Well within the tropics, they have a warm climate which, when the south-east trade winds blow from May to October, is also very wet on the windward coasts. The largest and highest island, Vitilevu, is substantial compared to most islands further east. You would be hard pushed to drive round it in a day, and the mountainous interior rises to 5000 feet.

More than half a million people live on Vitilevu, most of them in and around the capital, Suva, on the wet south-eastern corner. The port at Suva is an exuberant mixture of Melanesians, Indians, Micronesians, Polynesians, Chinese and Europeans. Few places in the South Pacific have a greater ethnic mix, one that has developed from Fiji's key position at the crossroads of the Pacific. On the drier western coast, the international airport at Nadi (pronounced 'Nandi') has direct links to Sydney and Auckland, Tokyo and Hawaii, as well as to the other island countries of the South Pacific, for which Fiji is a focal point for their commerce. For those visitors who have shared in the vibrant atmosphere of Fiji's busy capital, it comes as no surprise to discover that Vitilevu and the other Fijian islands have been a centre of Pacific life for thousands of years.

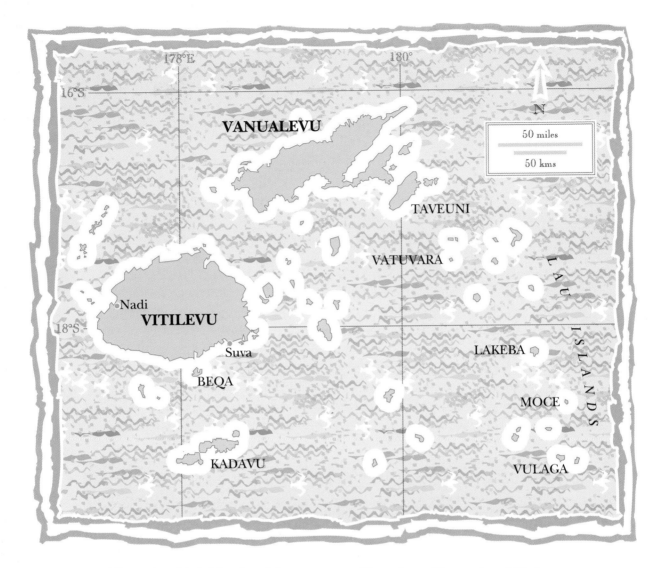

The other high islands of the group are Vanualevu, Taveuni and Kadavu. Together with Vitilevu they make up more than ninety per cent of the land mass, parts of which have been in existence for more than fifty million years. Although young by 'continental' timescales, this makes Fiji older than most of the other oceanic islands of the Pacific and there is an ancient quality to the rainforests of the interior. Almost half of the land is forested and some species, such as the dakua (*Agathis vitiensis*) are related to trees which evolved on New Zealand 200 million years ago. Other plants, such as the handsome cycad ferns (*Cycas* spp.) which grow to twenty feet or more, have origins in Australia, but most of Fiji's 6000 plant species derive from mainland Asia. It was on that vast and varied continent that the immense diversity of oriental wildlife first evolved.

Considering how far Fiji is from that natural powerhouse of evolution, it has acquired a richness of flora that astounds botanists. There are 300 species of fern in its lush forests, the most striking of which are the large tree ferns known as *balabala* in Fijian. From every tree in the rainforest hang orchids and other colourful epiphytes, and the trunks, root buttresses and forest floor are carpeted with lichens, mosses and spectacular fungi. If you travel west from Tahiti, the variety and colour of Fiji's plant life is captivating. In the forests, some trees would be familiar. As in eastern Polynesia, many are valued for the special qualities of their timber. Nokonoko (*Casuarina equisetifolia*), called *aito* in Tahiti, is the ironwood of Polynesia used for making clubs and weapons. Dilo (*Calophyllum inophyllum*) is a hardwood used for house-building, while oil from its fruit serves used as a liniment. In Fiji, there are several other species locally called *damanu*; interestingly, it is this name which arrived in Tahiti, where the tree is called *tamanu*. Vau (*Hibiscus tiliaceus*), called *purau* in Tahiti, is the hibiscus used throughout Polynesia for its fibrous bark; ivi (*Inocarpus fagifer*) is the Tahitian chestnut, *mape*. It seems that the forests of eastern Polynesia have their roots here in Fiji.

Many other species are endemic, found only in Fiji, and their great number and variety is a sure indication that Fiji has been physically separated from the other islands for a long time. The plants and animals which managed to bridge the ocean gap are most likely to have been those which, by nature of their seeds or their own ability to fly, were wind-borne and they have developed here, some

Above The two sexes of the Golden orb-weaving spider (*Nephila maculata*) are of very different shapes and sizes; here the diminutive reddish-coloured male can be seen performing his courtship on the back of the giant female.
Left Fijian stick-insects can grow to a foot in length and are well camouflaged in the verdant bush. This species is *Hermachus appolonius*.

for millions of years, in their own splendid isolation. More than 3500 different insects have made a home on Fiji and half of them cannot be found on any other island group, neither to the west nor to the east. One endemic longhorn beetle (*Xixuthrus heyrovski*) is claimed to be the largest insect in the world, measuring more than six inches from head to tail. Other giants in Fiji include monster stick-insects (*Cotylosoma* sp.), a foot-long, inch-thick millepede (*Salpidobolus* sp.) and a spider with shiny black legs which spans more than six inches. This spider (*Nephila* sp.) spins an enormous web with silk so thick and strong that it has been known to trap small birds in flight. It belongs to a genus of spider which is common throughout New Guinea and the Solomon Islands, where the tough web was used as a fishing net.

As with insects and spiders, it was from those large islands to the west that most of Fiji's airborne creatures made their way. Sixty land-based birds are now part of Fiji's native fauna, together with some recent introductions. Many are exotically coloured and all belong to avian families that derive from tropical south-east Asia. Their bright colours and noisy vocalizations bring to the Fiji bush a very distinctive 'jungle' character. In spite of their powers of flight, birds have been dissuaded from reaching Fiji by the daunting expanse of water that separates this group of islands from points west, and also because the prevailing winds blow in the opposite direction. Those few birds that, by chance, made landfall have evolved into distinct Fijian species and today no less than twenty-three of Fiji's bird species are found nowhere else.

Amongst the more spectacular birds you will find in Fiji are the parrots and fruit doves. The red-throated lorikeet (*Charmosyma amabilis*), which the Fijians call the *kulawai*, is a tiny green parakeet with a long tail tipped with brilliant yellow. The feathers on the underside of its head and on its thighs are almost scarlet. Darting in small groups, often high in the canopy of Vitilevu's mountain forest, they feed on pollen and nectar. Much larger and more conspicuous is Fiji's red-breasted musk-parrot (*Prosopeia tabuensis*), a substantial, blunt-headed parrot with a long tail. Its wings and tail-feathers are brilliant green and its head and underparts mostly red or maroon. Called *kaka* by Fijians because of its call, this handsome, robust bird has established five distinct races in Fiji. Each differs slightly in its plumage, the one on the island of Kadavu being considered by Fijians to be the most splendid. It is the vividness of the red feathers which delights the Fijian eye, for, like their fellow islanders in Polynesia, Fijians prize red feathers highly. Not surprisingly, the *kaka* has learned to keep alert. Finding safety in numbers, they will noisily mob even the most discreet

The Yellow-breasted musk-parrot (*Prosopeia personata*), now found only on the main Fijian island of Vitilevu.

bird-watcher. With loud squawks and high-pitched shrieks, the flock boldly announces the intruder and gathers inquisitively in the branches just out of reach. Sadly, this striking, characterful parrot has become the object of an illegal trade in cage-birds. Their cunning may not defeat the modern dealer.

The red bird of Fiji, *par excellence*, is the *kula*, whose very name has come to have the same connotation for Fijians as 'gold' does for us. Known to non-Fijians as the collared lory (*Phigys solitarius*), this chunky little parrot has long been a favourite of Fijians on account of its brilliant red feathers, which were eventually so prized as decorations, particularly as a colourful fringe to finely woven ornamental mats, that they became exchanged like currency. Even today, Fijians refer to the coloured fringes of their day-to-day matting as *kula*, although the material is now strands of wool and the colours need not be red.

Fortunately the bird still finds sanctuary in Fiji. The highlight of a trip to the bush is to encounter a flock of these charming, chattering birds. They nomadically glean the forest for pollen and nectar, and eagerly devour soft ripe fruits and caterpillars. With whirring wings, a gang of maybe ten or twenty of them will dart into view from nowhere and take possession of a tree in bud or fruit. One of their favourites is the drala tree (*Erythrina variegata*) which in August and September bursts into brilliant red bloom. The flowers are rich in pollen and have nectaries at their bases which the *kula* attack with great enthusiasm. They use their paintbrush-like tongues to extract the riches but often rip straight into the nectaries, scattering petals to the ground. These gregarious birds take no notice of their specific name, *solitarius*, but revel in each other's company. Hanging upside down from the flimsiest of twigs, they chase each other through the canopy. Some fall to the ground as they playfully grapple with their companions; others acrobatically dangle by one foot and 'shake hands' with their mate. Pairs huddle together, affectionately ruffling their partner's flame-red neck feathers. When the defenceless tree has been worked over, the flock takes off as one, chittering and squeaking, and within seconds the bandits are gone.

No less magical are the fruit doves of Fiji. Though less acrobatic than the parrots, they are equally colourful and characterful in their own way. Living up to its name, the many-coloured fruit dove (*Ptilinopus perousii*), known as *kuluvotu* to Fijians, is found wherever there are wild figs. It is astonishing that such a brilliantly coloured bird can remain so inconspicuous. Often heard but seldom seen, they live at the top of the forest canopy. Here with pugnacious confidence they cannon into fruiting trees, which they monopolize by beating

Collared lory (*Phigys solitarius*), the spectacular red *kula* of Fiji, feeding on the blooms of *drala* (*Erythrina variegata*).

off competitors, large and small. Not only widespread through the islands of Fiji, this successful bird has also spread to Tonga and Samoa where it wreaks similar havoc in fig and banyan trees.

The sound that most visitors associate with Fiji's forests is that of the barking pigeon (*Ducula latrans*). This massive imperial-looking bird announces its presence with a truly hound-like bark. It often calls at night and has fooled many newcomers to the Fiji bush. More heavily built than the familiar Pacific pigeon (*Ducula pacifica*), it can be immediately distinguished from its relative by the lack of a fleshy knob on the top of its bill.

All these pigeons and fruit doves have few natural predators on Fiji. Swooping through the forest canopy, there is however the Fiji goshawk (*Accipiter rufitorques*), which is a bold hunter. Although small, this very handsome hawk is tenacious in pursuit of its quarry and will confidently take birds larger than itself, such as the barking pigeon. After feeding, it often sunbathes spread-eagled high in the canopy or on open sunlit ground. For many Fijians, this fearless bird is their family totem, a creature which they respect and would never harm.

Many smaller, less aggressive birds have not fared so well in recent times. The introduction of the mongoose in 1883 to control rats on sugar-cane plantations has taken its toll of Fiji's birds, particularly those that nest on or near the ground. Eight species have already been lost from the two main islands. The island of Taveuni, however, famed as the 'Garden Island' of Fiji, is free of the mongoose and boasts a particularly rich bird-life. Taveuni is Fiji's third largest island, lying to the east of the other two, and much of it, including steep cliffs that plunge into the sea, is cloaked in dense tropical forest. The lushness reflects the island's high rainfall; numerous waterfalls tumble from the high interior, often gushing directly into the ocean. Although some of this fertile island is given over to cash crops, you can clearly see and feel its original nature which is very different from Tahiti. Here there is a natural diversity of life.

Volcanoes were still erupting less than a thousand years ago. Since the heat and dust subsided, a rich flora has colonized the new landscape. As with distant Tahiti, the combination of volcanic soils, warmth and high rainfall produces an explosion of life. The differences between the two islands, 2500 miles apart on the same latitude in the tropics, are a measure of their respective isolation. The further east away from the biological warehouse of south-east Asia, the more impoverished is a Pacific island's natural fauna and flora. Tahiti looks lush and green, but it has few land species of plants and animals. By comparison, the island of Taveuni is a real Garden of Eden.

Taveuni deserves its reputation as the 'garden island' of Fiji.

As if to reinforce this claim, Fiji's special island is the home of two extraordinary birds which attract bird-watchers from all over the world. Both are common but extremely elusive. Velvety black plumage with metallic-blue spangling gives the silktail (*Lamprolia victoriae*) an entirely exotic appearance. Supremely beautiful when caught in pools of forest sunshine, this iridescent bird could be mistaken for a bird of paradise; indeed for many years it was. It is probably related to the monarch flycatchers of south-east Asia, but its uniqueness sets it aside as an enigma of Fiji. The other jewel of Taveuni is the orange dove, which is also endemic to a few Fijian islands. The male is brilliant to behold; it is so fiery orange all over that it seems unreal. Some Europeans call it the 'flame dove'; to the Fijians it is simply *bune*. Foraging for small fruits and insects in the forest canopy of Taveuni, the male gives its presence away by a single penetrating 'tock' but it is a master of ventriloquism and seems to throw its call from every corner of the canopy. If you can home in quickly enough on the sound, you might be rewarded by a glimpse of this fabulous bird, invented by nature to celebrate the uniqueness of Fiji. Here is a group of islands which are near enough to the hub of evolution to be enriched, but far enough away to be distinctly different.

Fiji today is such an ethnic mix that it is hard to tell what kind of people the Fijians were before the days of Captain Cook and Captain Bligh. Both of these English seafarers made brief contact with the islands, then called the Cannibal Islands, a reputation which, by all accounts, they well deserved. Perhaps because of this, half a century passed before Fiji was properly explored by Europeans. In 1840 an American expedition led by the headstrong Lieutenant Charles Wilkes spent three months there with an excellent team of surveyors, geologists, naturalists, philologists and artists, who put the islands on the world map. A steady flow of Europeans had begun to brave this 'land of savages' in search of wealth or souls. A remarkable account was published in the middle of the nineteenth century by a young Methodist missionary from Lincolnshire, the Reverend Thomas Williams, who arrived with his wife at the islands of 'Feejee' to convert the cannibals to Christian ways. Not only did he have a stomach strong enough to witness and describe some of the less attractive aspects of Fiji's ancient culture, but he was also perceptive about the Fijian people and their special place in the Pacific.

'In considering the origin of the present inhabitants of Fiji,' he writes, 'the period of the Fijians' residence in their islands is to be placed far back at a very early date, probably as remote as the peopling of the American continent.' He points out that across the group of Fijian islands, the distinguishing features of the Polynesian and Melanesian peoples seem to meet. 'Many of them blend,' he observes, 'thus betokening a confluence of the two races. At the east end of the group the Asiatic peculiarities are found marked, but die away as we go westward, giving place to such as are decidedly African, but not Negro. Excepting the Tongans, the Fijian is equal in physical development to the islanders eastward, yet distinct from them in colour . . . although he is by language united to them all.'

The Reverend Williams was impressed by the farming and horticultural prowess of the Fijians, which he said distinguished them from the people of nearby Pacific islands. 'Side by side with the wildest savageism, we find an attention to agriculture and a variety of cultivated produce.' Yams were then the staple diet. These tuberous vegetables are so suited to the soils and climate of tropical volcanic islands that, like potatoes, almost any piece of tuber will sprout into a new plant and produce an abundant root crop with very little further attention. Hundreds of cultivars have been created from the greater yam (*Dioscorea alata*) which is a native of south-east Asia. In Fiji they call it *uvi*, and traditionally the Fijian calendar revolved around the yam season. The time to plant was in the hot wet season and the tubers would be respectfully buried in specially heaped mounds of soil on which the owner would spit once as a gesture of good luck to his crop. A single tuber typically grows to a weight of five to ten pounds and some prized specimens have topped 100 pounds. The appeal of the yam was that it could be stored for months without the need for any elaborate processing. In a part of the world plagued by hurricanes and famines, life revolved around its cultivation. Just like the bread-fruit of Tahiti, the yam was indispensable for island life.

Like the Tahitians, the people of Fiji also grew taro (*Colocasia esculenta*), the all-purpose root vegetable of Pacific islanders which Fijians call *dalo*. Recent archaeological work by the Fiji Museum revealed that *dalo* was often intensively cultivated in highly engineered gardens which must have required great man-power and social co-operation to construct. The land was meticulously terraced and irrigated by diverting mountain streams and regulating the flow, so that every bed of *dalo* was evenly watered. As on the islands of Indonesia and Melanesia, this technique is highly productive even in periods of drought. It uses land efficiently with little fear of erosion.

Fijians cultivated more than thirty varieties of banana which, together with the bread-fruit tree, were among the most useful food-plants of the islands. Sugar-cane was also grown in large quantities, just as it is today. The canes could grow to six inches in girth and the juice would satisfy both hunger and thirst. It was, however, the cultivation of the *kava* plant (*Piper methysticum*) that provided Fiji with a beverage that for centuries has been their national drink. Known locally as *yaqona* (pronounced 'yanggona'), this plant is also a native of south-east Asia. Recent research suggests that it was first cultivated in Vanuatu,

Planting yams, *uvi*. Traditionally the Fijian calendar revolved around the
seasons of this robust and adaptable root-crop.

from where it must have been brought as a treasured crop by the first Fijians. The root is what is relished. It is sometimes used green, when it is referred to as *yaqona droka*. The fleshy part of the root is scraped and ground into a pulpy mess, a task that it is said would traditionally have been performed by young men or women who would chew the roots for the older men. Apparently the saliva of young virgins, male or female, added a powerful ingredient. *Yaqona madu* was prepared from roots that had been washed and then dried in the sun. This is the usual practice today and the sound of the roots being pounded in a *tabili*, a specially hollowed log of hardwood, is something which visitors to rural Fiji never forget. The pulp or powder was then mixed with a little cold water in a special wooden bowl, the *tanoa*, and strained through a mesh made of strips of vau bark (*Hibiscus* sp.). Today Fijians have succumbed to using a muslin bag, but the principle is the same.

To Europeans, the end product looks most unappetizing but Fijians treat *yaqona* with reverence. The muddy-coloured drink is not alcoholic, but is mildly intoxicating due to the release of narcotic chemicals from the pepper roots. The effects range from a fuzzy head to mild euphoria. The most important aspect of *yaqona* drinking is however its social value. Sharing a bowl with Fijians, sitting barefoot and cross-legged on the floor of their home, is an honoured mark of acceptance. Drunk from a polished half coconut shell, passed with great ceremony from host to guest, the foul-looking, strange-tasting liquid soon takes on a special significance. Ceremonial drinking of *yaqona* links Fiji with the islands of Tonga where long ago it became inextricably woven into the fabric of their Polynesian culture. The custom spread to Fiji, where it is now part of their way of life. At every important meeting, whether to discuss some point of village life or to determine national politics, the *yaqona* bowl is a central feature. The rituals have origins which are lost in time but the spiritual power that surrounds the *tanoa* is very real.

Like many of the other plants brought to Fiji from islands to the west, *kava* also spread into Polynesia. Although not treated with such reverence, it was a feature of Tahitian life when Cook was there. Its use is documented in many other Polynesian islands, as far east as the Gambier Islands and to the far north in Hawaii. Perhaps because of climate, *kava* was not established on Easter Island or in New Zealand, the other corners of the Triangle, although the peoples there discovered alternative plants which produced a similar effect.

Spiritually, Fijians also have much in common with the distant island communities of Polynesia. Their ancient religion, the one the missionaries endeavoured to sweep away along with cannibalism, featured a galaxy of gods and spirits. The central feature of their beliefs was the worship of ancestors, particularly those who in their lifetime had been illustrious in war. Each clan had its own deities and built its own temples at which they communed with the spirits of the dead. Each ancestral spirit had its specific role. One might be descended from a great warrior and would be consulted in times of war; others were linked by heredity to crops or fishing, house-building or canoes. As in Tahiti, the gods of Fiji reflected the society from which they originated.

Vanua means the land, the place. The word has a physical, social and cultural dimension for all Fijians. It does not simply mean the rocks and the soil, the water and the wildlife, it embraces the whole of their social, cultural and spiritual beliefs and values. It provides a sense of identity and belonging which was established by ancestors. In its spiritual sphere, *vanua* is a source of *sau*. This is the Fijian equivalent of Polynesian *mana*, the power to effect the day-to-day business of living. To most Fijians, the idea of parting with one's own *vanua*, one's own land, is tantamount to parting with one's life. The concept of *vanua* came to Fiji long ago, presumably with its earliest settlers, and issues surrounding land use and ownership have been at the heart of Fiji's turbulent and often violent history.

Those ancestors brought another notion that was central to their lives, the concept of *tabu*. The word, although pronounced more like 'tambu' in Fijian and *tapu* on other islands, has almost the same significance here as throughout Polynesia. *Vanua tabu* is a sacred place, such as the burial site of paramount chiefs or the abode of gods and spirits. All spirits form part of the mortal world and watch over people's earthly lives. After death, people's souls depart to the spirit world of *bulu*; from there they continue to affect the lives of those they have left behind. A chief who is feared and respected in this world for his *sau*, will continue to be feared after death, when his *sau* may become more powerful because he has achieved supernatural status. In traditional Fijian thinking, *sau* and *tabu* complement and reinforce each other. Today no Fijian would publicly profess to be a follower of their ancient religion, but few would deny that it is still a powerful influence on the affairs of Fiji.

When you meet a Fijian, you establish an instant rapport. From childhood they learn that family and friends are more important than material success. Today it seems extraordinary that only two centuries ago, cannibalism was accepted as a perfectly normal part of life. As in ancient Tahiti, the sacrificial killing of human beings was a function of Fijian religion. The land, the *vanua*, would not be prosperous unless such gifts were made; the social well-being of the people depended on such sacrifice. The great warrior-gods delighted in this ritual human death. These gods were cannibals, consuming the *sau* of those that were offered to them. The victims were usually enemies taken in battle. To eat your enemy defiled his ancestral line and was the greatest wound you could inflict on him. To consume just his eye or his heart was the greatest insult and

All the houses of Navala village, in the highlands of Vitilevu, are built to the
traditional Fijian oblong design; further west in the Lau Islands and in Tonga,
they are usually oval in shape, a style typical of Polynesia.

ornately carved wooden forks with four prongs were so designed that such
delicacies could enter the victor's mouth without the victim's flesh touching his
lips. Not everyone ate human flesh. For some clans it was *tabu*. It was however
eaten at feasts as a welcome addition to the normal fare. The dead victim selected
to be eaten was referred to as the *bokola* and today, if extremely provoked, a
Fijian might inflict ridicule on his adversary by calling him by the ancient name
of *kaisi bokola*, an insult of considerable force.

It is in the mountains of Vitilevu that you encounter some of the most
traditional Fijian villages. Many of them take a particular pride in maintaining
their physical and spiritual character. In a way unique to Fiji, their ancestral
beliefs exist side by side with their devout Christian faith. Some villages have

both a church and 'ancestor-houses' where offerings are made to the spirits of the departed. There seems no problem in reconciling the two religions. It is a strength of Fijian society that traditional values and rules still shape their way of life. As in Tahiti, personal cleanliness is essential. Most villages are sited by streams and people bathe at least twice a day. Being dirty is shameful, so is an unkempt home. The entire community takes a pride in the look of their village which they maintain in a way that would please their forebears.

The fire is a symbol of life to Fijians. A house without smoke is a home without life. In former times, much of the cooking was done in earthenware pots and for feasts an earth-oven, the *lovo*, was prepared. The technique was almost identical to the *umu* of Tahiti and the diet was also similar, with pig as the great treat. What is different about Fiji is the traditional use of clay pottery for cooking and other domestic tasks. Fiji has plenty of suitable clay soils and the art of moulding and firing earthenware came to Fiji with the first colonizers more than 3000 years ago.

Throughout the islands of Melanesia and Fiji, pottery-making has always been the prerogative of hereditary clans. The men specialized in fishing and the women manufactured earthenware. Today, in Fiji, the technique is probably the same. The clay is kneaded together with sand as a temper to control shrinkage and improve the texture. The tools are simple. Pottery wheels were unknown to ancient Fijians and are still not used. In their place the potters use a large pebble to mould the inside of the pot and a wooden paddle to beat the outside into shape. Considering the simplicity of the technique, Fijian women achieve remarkable symmetry. The moulded pot is left to dry naturally for several days before being fired in a simple open hearth. Finally the piece might be glazed with gum from the dakua tree whilst still hot from the embers of the fire.

It is puzzling that traditional pottery skills have not survived on the nearby island groups of Tonga and Samoa where there are clay deposits but no potters. After a few centuries of settlement the craft died out. Nor, it seems, did the skill reach the other islands of Polynesia. Fragments of pottery have been unearthed on the Marquesan Islands several hundred miles to the north-east of Tahiti, but these seem to be the remains of pots made in Fiji and taken there by the first settlers. Some islands, like Tahiti, have little or no suitable clay, but others, such as Easter Island, Hawaii and New Zealand, have workable deposits which were never used by Polynesians. Maybe few, if any, of the clan of potters ventured to join the eastbound ocean voyages. By the time the most distant parts of the Pacific were settled, the skills of the potter had been lost in time.

Intriguingly, it is pottery which has given archaeologists the most tangible evidence that the first Polynesians did indeed come from the islands of south-east Asia. It also tells them when they did so and confirms that Fiji was a crucial staging-post for their migration into the eastern Pacific. This ancient pottery has been named *Lapita*, after one of the sites in New Caledonia where it was first unearthed in excavations. The pieces discovered were often not well made; they seem to have been moulded from a rather sandy-textured red-coloured clay, sometimes tempered with beach sand. What makes the pottery so distinctive is its decorative finish. Most pots seem to have been embossed with characteristic stamped designs and have notching and incised decoration on the upper surfaces and around the rims. It could well be that this dentate decoration was stamped into the soft pottery using tattooing picks. A few pieces carry designs which incorporate recognizable images of birds' heads, pigs and human faces. Compared to the plain earthenware familiar now in Fiji, *Lapita* with its often elaborate geometric forms must have had an artistic magnificence which was the pride of its potters. Whoever these people were, they carried their skills with them across Melanesia, through Fiji and into western Polynesia. Identified mainly by the trail of broken pots they left behind, they are known to archaeologists simply as the *Lapita* people. It is a rather misleading term, for it really refers to a style of pottery and not necessarily to the entire culture that used it. So far, however, this distinctive pottery is the best tangible guide we have to the origins of the Polynesian people.

Lapita sites have been discovered as far west as the Bismarcks, a group of islands near New Guinea. Other major finds have focused attention on New Caledonia and Vanuatu, two large island groups which lie more than halfway between there and Fiji. Some of the archaeological sites yielded remains of house timbers and thatch, storage pits, wells, fireplaces and earth-ovens. It was from carbon-dating these relics that a sequence of dates could be placed on the spread of the *Lapita* culture across the western Pacific. There is growing evidence that ancestors of the Polynesians lived in the coastal areas of island south-east Asia five or six thousand years ago. The *Lapita* trail does not yet extend back that far, but this may simply indicate that the *Lapita* pottery style emerged at a later date or that archaeologists have yet to discover the evidence. The oldest *Lapita* sites found so far are in the Bismarck Archipelago and date back 3600 years. Pottery very similar in design to *Lapita* has been found in the Philippines and on Borneo and other islands of eastern Indonesia. All the evidence indicates a west to east wave of colonization by a distinctive seafaring people which took them and their culture island-hopping towards Fiji and the other oceanic Pacific islands. In the wake of this pioneering surge, they left settlements which continued to flourish for centuries.

From studies of language and blood groups it is thought that these ancestors of the Polynesian people not only developed their distinctive culture during this period of expansion through Melanesia, but also retained their physical identity.

Above A human face and distinctive geometric decoration on a shard of *Lapita* pottery discovered in the Santa Cruz Islands almost 1000 miles north-west of Fiji. The motifs were stamped in the earthenware before firing, probably using a toothed implement like the widespread Polynesian tattooing chisel. Maybe the geometric tattoo designs on the skin of people in the Marquesas Islands and Tahiti had their origins in the artistic skills of potters many thousands of miles to the west.
Right An ancestor image – the Fijian equivalent of the Polynesian *tiki* – carved from the sacred *vesi* wood (*Intsia bijuga*).

Skeletal remains found together with *Lapita* pots and other artefacts show that these people were not typically Melanesian. They seem to have been tall and large-bodied, with very long fore-arms and slender hands and feet. Their skulls had small teeth but a wide lower jaw which often had the 'rocker' shape characteristic of many modern Polynesians. Their large, lanky physique was inappropriate to the land environment of tropical islands such as New Guinea; it was much more suited to life on the coast of small islands and ideally fitted for the demands of long voyages.

About 3300 years ago, some of these people crossed the wide ocean gap to Fiji. When they arrived, the islands were uninhabited. For more than a thousand years they had the high fertile land and tropical lagoons to themselves. In time they were joined by Melanesian people who came, or were perhaps brought, from the islands to the west. No doubt there was conflict, but also intermarriage. Many of the physical characteristics of the Polynesian people on Fiji were merged with the features of the darker-skinned newcomers from Melanesia. Height remained a distinctive attribute of the new Fijians, but they also held onto many of the cultural characteristics of the first pioneers. Today's Fijians trim both ways; outwardly they are Melanesian, but culturally and linguistically they are part of Polynesia.

Fiji's geographical position at the crossroads of the Pacific was instrumental in shaping the distinctive way of life of the Polynesian people. Here, away from the mainstream of south-east Asia, the first Polynesians were able to flourish. On the many islands of Fiji and on the neighbouring groups of Tonga and Samoa, they developed their independent, idiosyncratic way of life. Behind them to the west lay Melanesia with its great multitude of peoples and wildlife. Ahead lay the beginning of a new, unexploited world into which the first Polynesians could strike out on their own.

CHAPTER FOUR

The CRADLE of POLYNESIA

There is no link stronger than that which ties a Polynesian child to its *fenua*, its land. It supports him, feeds him and one day will claim him back. In Tahiti, after a child is born, it is customary for the placenta, the *pu fenua*, to be buried in the earth and then a tree planted there, to grow in harmony with the child. Trees symbolize the fruitfulness of life but they are also inhabited by ancestral spirits whose powers influence the life of the child. In Aotearoa, the Maori name for New Zealand, a child's umbilical cord, the *iho*, was often placed under a *kahikatea* tree, the native white pine which provided the Maori with plentiful timber and fruit. They too believed, and still do, that trees have souls. This respectful fear of the forest has been carried throughout Polynesia in the collective memory of the Polynesians. It is central to the identity and culture of that very distinctive island people who put down their roots in the western Pacific more than 3000 years ago.

On the western border of the great Polynesian Triangle lie the islands of Samoa, their rugged crests rising high from the brilliant aquamarine of their fringing coral reefs. To the south-west is another archipelago of much smaller low islands which now make up the Kingdom of Tonga. Together with the islands of Fiji, a little further to the west, this region of the Pacific became the cradle of the Polynesian world. It was here that the first Polynesians established a way of life that would take their descendants eastward to colonize the most remote islands of the Pacific. Their route echoed that taken long before by many of the plants and animals which had dispersed from the rich ecosystems of south-east Asia and had pioneered a new existence in the vastness of the Pacific Ocean.

The native wildlife on the islands of Tonga and Samoa is related to the fauna and flora of the islands of Fiji. Together the islands form a series of natural stepping-stones for land-based species for which the great expanses of water were formidable obstacles. Compared to Fiji, Samoa is less well endowed with plant and animal species. The islands are geologically young, some less than a million years old. They bear the evidence of recent volcanic activity and in some places the soils are still warm just beneath the surface. Samoa is close enough to Fiji to allow occasional colonizers to establish a foothold, but far enough away to make such events infrequent. Consequently, new arrivals had a chance to develop along their separate, evolutionary path. This combination of history and geography has given the forests of Samoa their distinctive character.

Today Samoa is a divided land. To the east are seven islands and a handful of rocky outcrops that make up American Samoa. They were once as Polynesian as their cousins to the west, but the influence of the United States since annexation in 1900 has masked their indigenous culture. Western Samoa has retained its independence and prides itself on being the true birthplace of Polynesia. Indeed, their legends suggest that the people of Samoa have been there ever since their god Tagaloa created these rocky islands from an expanse of empty space. If you explore the main islands of Upolu and Savaii, it is not difficult to believe that their creation was very recent. The evidence of volcanic activity is everywhere. The northern coast of Savaii is covered with lava flows

Blown in by the wind, spores of tropical ferns take root in the recent lava flows on the geologically young Samoan island of Savaii.

from eruptions earlier this century and is sparsely covered with vegetation struggling to gain a foothold on this newest stretch of land. Elsewhere Savaii's mountains are gentle and green. The south-facing slopes are wet throughout most of the year and covered with an almost impenetrable jungle. Fresh-water from the porous rocks emerges along the margins of the island, and for that reason, most people live there. In the high interior the heaviest rainfall nurtures huge tree-ferns and slow-growing hardwoods which, laden with moss and other tropical epiphytes, give the forests of Savaii their primordial feel. It is here, away from the coast, that wildlife is less disturbed and where you may discover some of Samoa's very distinctive creatures.

The large parrots found on Fiji never made the crossing to Samoa. In their place a pigeon has evolved to become the champion fruit-eating bird of these islands. The tooth-billed pigeon (*Didunculus strigirostris*) was given its scientific name on account of its massive hooked bill which in 1848 reminded its discoverer of that most formidable of all pigeons, the dodo. The similarities between the two birds are by no means a coincidence. Pigeons, as an avian group, are all strong fliers, very gregarious and highly adaptable. It is these qualities which have made them very successful island colonists. They have been able to cross wide expanses of sea in the company of mates for breeding and with the ability to take advantage of whatever fruits, buds and leaves the new home might have to offer. They are the super-tramps of the Pacific. The dodo once lived on the island of Mauritius, the same latitude in the tropics as Samoa, but in the Indian Ocean. Mauritius, like Samoa, is volcanic in origin and has a similar geographical relationship to ancient Madagascar as Samoa has to Fiji. Ancestors of the dodo and the tooth-billed pigeon each arrived at an island where there were no predators but a surfeit of plants with large tough seeds that could only be exploited by birds with powerful beaks. In time, the processes of natural selection encouraged both races of bird to increase their body size, develop formidable beaks and come down to earth.

On Samoa the tooth-billed pigeon has developed a partnership with a tree called *Dysoxylum*. This forest giant produces clusters of tough green fruits which the pigeon can open with a sawing movement of the two halves of its parrot-like bill. It then extracts and swallows the seeds by delicate manoeuvring of beak and tongue. Undigested seeds are spread through the forest and have a chance of germinating, thereby benefiting both the plant and the bird. Over on Mauritius, the dodo developed a similar relationship with a plant that lived on the forest floor. The bird no longer needed to fly to find food and, in the absence of predators, lost that ability. When hungry European sailors landed on its island, the dodo was doomed to extinction. Fortunately, when Polynesians set foot on Samoa with their dogs and pigs, the tooth-billed pigeon could still manage to

fly. When Europeans first discovered this bird, it mostly nested on the ground and, like the dodo, was easily caught by ship's rats and domestic cats. The tooth-billed pigeon almost followed the way of its now legendary counterpart and the species owes its survival to a handful of birds that retained a preference for nesting in trees. Once almost as dead as the dodo, this extraordinary pigeon has returned to its ancestral way of life.

Other birds which, over the millennia, have made the ocean flight to infant Samoa have come in tandem with the plants that could support them. The cardinal honeyeater (*Myzomela cardinalis*) is widespread in the western Pacific, but Samoa is the most easterly limit of its range. It is a tiny bird and could easily be swept by winds from island to island. It probably arrived direct from the islands of Melanesia after nectar-bearing flowers had taken a hold on the scant soils. Since then, Samoa has evolved its own giant honeyeater (*Gymnomyza samoensis*), which Samoans call *mao*. It is probably a direct descendant of its Fijian counterpart (*G. viridis*).

Above Cardinal honeyeater (*Myzomela cardinalis*).
Top left Young Brown boobies (*Sula leucogaster*).
Left Adult Red-footed booby (*Sula sula*) with chick.

As the ancestor of the tooth-billed pigeon discovered, Samoa is a land of ecological opportunity. Even the new volcanic soils provide a novel niche for birds. Megapodes are birds named for their big feet. They are found in Australia, New Guinea and some of the islands of Melanesia where they have evolved into many different species. Their outsize feet are designed for excavating mounds of rotting vegetation in which to incubate their eggs, which are large to ensure that the offspring can fend for themselves when they hatch. What is extraordinary about the megapodes which have reached volcanically active islands is that they have adapted their nesting behaviour to take advantage of the warmth of the soils. Instead of incubating the clutch in heaps of decomposing vegetation, they employ their large feet to bury their eggs in the naturally heated soil and leave them to emerge into this strange new world on their own. The large eggs make good eating for all kinds of creatures, including man. Once widespread across the islands of western Polynesia, megapodes were soon eaten to extinction when the Polynesians arrived.

The exception today is the island of Niuafo'ou, which is off the beaten track between Savaii and the most northern islands of Tonga, to which it now belongs. Here a shy, slate-grey bird with orange legs and big feet still scrapes in the warm soil of volcanic vents to lay its eggs. *Megapodius pritchardii* is the sole surviving megapode in the entire expanse of Polynesia. It owes both its individuality and its survival to the remoteness of this tiny island where, by accident or fate, it made its home.

The only mammals to have reached Fiji, Samoa and Tonga on their own are bats. Their power of flight is clearly the key to their success as island colonizers, but, even for them, the various ocean crossings have been a daunting barrier to their spread into the Pacific. Bats are confirmed landlubbers and do not fly willingly for great distances across the sea. Their dispersal from the large islands of south-east Asia must have been by accident of hurricane winds that swept them helplessly out to sea and, if they were very lucky, make safe land-fall on a distant island. Fiji has collected six species of bat this way, three of which have also managed to reach Samoa. For bats, this is the end of the line. None has naturally colonized further eastward.

The smallest of Samoa's bats is the insectivorous sheath-tailed bat (*Emballonura semicaudata*), which, like so many of its relatives, spends the day roosting communally in caves. These bats emerge at dusk to hawk across the forest, using their sonar senses to hunt insects on the wing. Far more conspicuous are Samoa's two species of fruit-eating bats, known as flying foxes. Common throughout the islands of the western Pacific, flying foxes are the largest bats in the world. West of Fiji, they compete with a multitude of birds for the fruits of the tropical forest and rely on the advantage of their nocturnal hunting skills.

After hatching in its mound, the chick of the incubator-bird, *Megapodius pritchardii* burrows upwards through the soil and emerges, fully fledged, ready to fly.

Here in Samoa there are few rivals and no predators, except man. The Samoan fruit-bat (*Pteropus samoensis*) has taken to being active by day, either tending its young or flapping leisurely over the forest canopy in search of fruiting trees. Its wing span can measure almost five feet and allows these magnificent creatures to soar like birds of prey. To see them at sunset circling over the pristine forest of the Falealupo peninsula, the north-western tip of Savaii, is awe-inspiring. Here is pristine Polynesian wilderness. Cyclones have left their mark, but there is little sign of man. A dirt track circles the promontory, linking friendly villages which huddle by the shore amongst a landscape of lava. It is here, according to ancient Samoan tradition, that the spirits, the *aitu*, have their gateway to the underworld. There are two entrances, one for chiefs and one for commoners. One leads to a deep, dark cave in Cape Mulinu'u; the other follows the blood-red trail left by the setting sun. Here at the most western tip of Savaii, the giant bats take on the guise of unearthly ghosts as they wheel in slow motion against the reddening sky.

The first Polynesians, the *Lapita* people, probably arrived in Samoa and Tonga very soon after they reached Fiji. They came from the west across perilous expanses of ocean in search of new lands. Some, like the fruit-bats, may have been driven here by storms and cyclones, but in their wake came others who by choice set out to make a new life. In this respect, the colonization of Polynesia by people is quite different from the spread of wildlife. What they were searching for were high fertile islands which had substantial tracts of relatively flat coastal land with good soils and sufficient fresh-water. Given those conditions, the first Polynesians could put their fishing skills to good use in the lagoons and surrounding sea, while on land they could establish their crops and rear their domestic stock. Within their social organization were people with the traditional skills of pottery-making, mat-weaving and the use of stone adzes and shell knives. Then, as later, Polynesian society relied on the interdependence of different clans, each of which had their specialist, hereditary skill. Only a competent, well-organized and highly motivated people could spread this far across the Pacific. Central to their success in colonizing these oceanic islands were the skills of their boat-builders and the men who sailed them.

The slow but persistent rising of the sea in relation to the land was a powerful factor in the spread of the ancestral Polynesian people across island south-east Asia and into the western Pacific. The last Ice Age reached its peak 17 000 years ago. As ice-caps locked up more and more of the planet's water supply in vast mile-deep ice-sheets, the seas of the world dropped in level. At the height of the glaciation, all the oceans were nearly 400 feet lower than they are today. Although the Ice Age climate did not markedly lower air and water temperatures in the tropics, it did dramatically change the size and shape of tropical islands. Many of them were substantially larger than they are today; others that had been submerged coral reefs in warmer epochs, now stood high and dry as islands in their own right. Throughout the western Pacific, the entire geography was changed by the lowering of the seas. During that period many plant and animal species increased their range by island-hopping between specks of land that have now disappeared again beneath the rising sea.

The South China Sea, which separates mainland China from the Philippines and the islands of Malaysia and Indonesia, is very shallow and is littered with wrecks that have struck coral heads far from sight of land. During the most recent Ice Age, which lasted thousands of years, much of this region was dry land. What had formerly been sea-bed was covered with tropical vegetation and inhabited by a great variety of creatures which had found refuge there, while temperate regions of the world were held in a grip of permanent winter. When the great thaw eventually came, about 15 000 years ago, the melting ice-caps and glaciers released vast quantities of water. Century after century, as the global climate warmed, the oceans rose.

The process was not a steady one. Six or seven thousand years ago there was a marked surge in global temperatures which led to the final melting of the great ice-cap that had covered much of North America. Sea levels rose dramatically during that era, causing extensive flooding in many parts of the world. In Europe, the North Sea was formed and the English Channel broke through at the Straits of Dover to make Britain an island. At the low-lying eastern end of the Mediterranean, land that was the 'fertile crescent' of biblical fame was suddenly inundated by sea-water. People deserted their villages and moved to higher ground. Some may have saved their families and livelihoods by taking to boats. Like Noah, they took their favoured animals and plants on board and set off in search of dry land. This pattern must have been repeated all around the world wherever the rising sea threatened human communities. The warm era lasted almost 2500 years and for a time, the world sea level was six or seven feet higher than it is today.

With changing sea-levels and geological upheavals, islands appear
and disappear with time. This makatea islet is one of many scattered across
the lagoon of the Lau island, Fulaga.

Imagine the effects of all this on people who were living as fishermen in the coastal areas of south-east Asia. For generations they had earned a living catching fish in the shallow waters of a sprawling archipelago that would eventually be transformed into the South China Sea. Year by year the ocean continued to rise, drowning the land they had cultivated for their root-crops and forcing them to move on in search of safer places to rebuild their settlements. The Asian mainland was already heavily populated by other Asian peoples whose civilizations were well established. The coastal fishermen had only one option. They took to their boats and relied on their seagoing skills.

Rapidly, groups of these people moved through the ever-changing island world of south-east Asia, nomadically making a living wherever they could. Some built settlements and traded with the other tribes. They exchanged their fish and pottery for the wild and cultivated produce of the islands' interiors. Others sailed on eastward, in search of a homeland of their own. In the course of a few hundred years, these people developed a distinct voyaging culture as they moved from island to island, fishing the sea and gleaning the land. We will probably never know where the ancestral homeland of these seafaring people was or why they left it. The saga of those first 'Nomads of the Wind' is lost in time. They eventually emerged 4000 years ago as the *Lapita* people and became the ancestors of the Polynesians. Behind them they left a trail of pottery as they moved eastward out into the Pacific. Here they discovered islands which were not only high and fertile but uninhabited. For some of them, it was time to put down roots.

By the time the first Polynesians reached the islands of Fiji, Samoa and Tonga, perhaps 3000 years ago, the geography of that region was much the same as it is today. Since the end of the Ice Age, the sea level has risen at an average of three feet a century, but most of that rise came in a great surge. In more recent times the level has continued to change in relation to the land but at a much slower rate and often due to islands sinking rather than the sea rising. The first Polynesians lived by the sea and it is probable that many early settlements are now drowned and out of reach of archaeologists. Perhaps one day, in caves beneath the sea, divers will discover evidence that people arrived at Fiji and other islands of the western Pacific much earlier than we now believe. Five or six thousand years ago, voyaging people would have encountered a very different topography. Because the sea level was substantially lower, many islands would have been fringed by an almost vertical limestone cliff with little or no sheltering lagoon. Faced with the prospect of hazardous landings and difficult access to the interior, pioneering seafarers might well have found such islands very unattractive as a home. It is thought that many of Fiji's islands were like this as recently as 4000 years ago. The lush island of Taveuni would at that time

Vatuvara at dawn – once a low coral atoll, its hat-like profile now
rises 1000 feet from the sea.

have been a tempting place to settle, except for the formidable prospect of its
steep-sided coastline. Maybe it was fate, or their gods, that brought the
first Polynesians to these fertile islands at just the right time in their geological
and biological evolution.

Eighty miles south-east of Taveuni is a much smaller island, Vatuvara,
known to sailors as 'Hat Island' because of its extraordinary profile. It has a
flat summit and precipitous sides which plunge down a thousand feet to a scant
reef over which the waves break constantly. For countless generations of seafarers this great hat floating on the water has been a beacon for navigation;
its distinctive shape can be seen from many miles away. It is an island to be
avoided because of the tricky currents and the absence of a proper passage
through the reef.

Although Polynesians did have a settlement on Vatuvara, no-one lives there
now. Geologically it is intriguing. Its strange shape is due to the fact that it is
an ancient coral island that has been uplifted by dramatic movements in the sea-
bed. The apparently flat top of the island is in reality an indented plateau, just
like the crown of a felt hat. This was once the lagoon of a coral atoll and is now
densely covered by forest and bush. Giant coconut-crabs (*Birgus latro*) live up
there, 1000 feet above the sea, to which they return only to lay their eggs. Also
known as robber crabs, these terrestrial crustaceans have immensely strong claws
with which they can break into coconuts to gorge on the succulent flesh. Their
large claws and vegetarian diet make them good eating for people and their
survival in great numbers on Vatuvara is proof of the island's lack of appeal to

human settlers in recent times. The forest also has a healthy bird population. The dawn chorus up on the plateau is marvellous, particularly if the golden whistler (*Pachycephala pectoralis*) is in good voice. This quite large flycatcher not only brightens the morning with its melodious whistling, but the male also dazzles you with his brilliant yellow chest. It has evolved distinctly different races on various islands of Fiji, including Vatuvara.

The steep sides of the hat are limestone cliffs which were once the edge of a coral reef. In epochs long ago, this island was much like every other coral island in the tropics. As the island slowly subsided, the coral grew upwards keeping pace just beneath the surface of the sea. Dramatic geological uplifting then thrust the entire atoll a thousand feet into the sky. On the sheer limestone escarpments where sharks once hunted reef fish, peregrines now launch out from their eyries in pursuit of fruit doves. Vatuvara is a sobering reminder of the mutability of nature.

The brim of the hat is the broad plateau that encircles the central peak. Deceptively flat when seen from a distance, this was once a reef system but today is a jagged tangle of limestone fissures, hollows and ridges. Rough going for people, it is ideal for the island's more exotic wildlife inhabitants. As you precariously make your way over the broken terrain, reptilian eyes stare down from the tangle of wild hibiscus and scaevola scrub. The Fijian banded iguana (*Brachylophus fasciatus*) is a spectacular lizard, sometimes reaching more than two feet in length. Its bulky body is a mosaic of vivid greens and blues that change to match the vibrant greens of the island's vegetation on which it feeds. In the space of a few minutes it can become almost black, with only the mobile eyes catching the dappled light. When backlit by the sun, its eardrums are translucent and you can see right through the iguana's head. Its strong legs are armed with impressive claws which are used more for climbing than for aggression.

Another unlikely reptile to have reached Fiji and to have survived well on this unique island is the Pacific boa (*Candoia bibroni*). This snake can reach six feet in length and is capable of prodigious feats of constricting and swallowing its victims. Although not poisonous, it is a formidable hunter. The fruit of banyan trees attract fruit-bats as well as pigeons and doves, all of which attract boas. Coiled in the tangle of branches, they lie in wait for unwary, greedy pigeons. Jaws held wide, its tongue tasting the air, the boa uncoils and strikes with disarming speed. Even for a big boa, a fat pigeon will suffice for days.

Giant coconut-crabs (*Birgus latro*) – also called robber crabs – will climb tall palms to cut off the coconuts with their powerful claws. Deemed a delicacy by islanders, the taste of their roasted flesh is a delectable blend of crab-meat and coconut.

Above right Parrot fish (*Scarus sordidus*). *Top* Banded iguana (*Brachylophus fasciatus*).
Above Pacific boa (*Candoia bibroni*).

Where these two reptiles came from and how they crossed such vast expanses of sea is another story. Their presence on Vatuvara, along with a multitude of other creatures, is indicative of the small impact which people have had on this very unusual Fijian island. Even the perilous reef that hugs its shore is alive with bright coral and multicoloured fish. Like a Noah's Ark, the island of Vatuvara has braved the storms of time and fostered a precious cargo of species. It is now privately owned by an absentee landlord. For the sake of this unique biological life-raft, long may he and everyone else live far away.

It was this rich mix of plants and animals that was encountered by the first people to reach Fiji and the neighbouring islands of the western Pacific. Many birds, particularly the ground-dwellers such as megapodes and rails, were not only abundant but also oblivious to the potential impact of two-legged predators. Until the people could establish their crops and domestic stock, the wildlife of the islands was an essential part of their diet. Fruit-bats made good eating, and still do in islands such as Savaii where precious little native wildlife has survived the ravages of cyclones, let alone the appetites of hungry men. Whilst Vatuvara was spared because of its daunting shape and shortage of fresh-water, most other small islands in the group that now comprises Fiji were transformed by the arrival of people.

Just to the east of Vatuvara is the northern end of a chain of small islands that runs almost to the next major archipelago. Like a path of stepping-stones, the Lau Islands link the large high islands of Fiji with the low small islands of Tonga. It is a route which no doubt the first Polynesians followed as they island-hopped eastward. The main island of the Lau group is Lakeba (pronounced 'Lakemba'), which for centuries has been a seat of power. Perhaps for this reason the island has attracted much recent historical and archaeological attention. It seems that Lakeba was first settled 3000 years ago by groups of people who were essentially fishermen and hunter-gatherers. They fed mainly on the large fish and turtles that entered the lagoon, as well as on the reef-fish and shellfish that lived there permanently. They used hooks fashioned from shells and spears carved from hardwoods. Nets and traps were woven from plant fibre and fish were poisoned in the lagoon using drugs extracted from plants such as barringtonia; when ground and mixed into a paste, the hard fruit of this tree is fatal to fish but harmless to humans. Another very effective plant poison still used illicitly by Fijians is extracted from *duva* (*Derris trifoliata*). The roots of this creeper, found growing on the coast, are pounded into a fibre that is then dragged through reef pools inducing stupefied fish to float belly up to the surface.

The first inhabitants of the Lau Islands supplemented their marine diet with meat from a range of forest birds and the flying fox. Using arrows and traps, they raided the forest for wild game. Archaeological evidence shows that Lakeba was once a stronghold for a megapode and a large species of pigeon, both of which were eaten to extinction within a few hundred years of human settlement. The introduction of domestic animals also had a profound effect on much of the native wildlife. It was probably only when wild resources became scarce that restraints and prohibitions in the form of taboos were imposed by chiefs. While stocks lasted, everything was fair game.

Lakeba was once famous for its annual ritual slaughter of sharks. At the village of Nasaqalau (pronounced 'Nasanggalau'), which claims to be the oldest settlement on the island, there is a vast shallow lagoon which stretches almost a mile out to sea. Filled with silt and dotted with little mangrove-covered islets, this for centuries was the site of an extraordinary event. Each October or November, shoals of sharks would come to the lagoon in order, it is now thought, to give birth to live young in the safety of the shallow sheltered water. The men of Nasaqalau would keep watch for several weeks; a taboo was declared, signalled by planting a post to which was tied a piece of tapa-cloth. Traditionally only certain families had the power to commune with the sharks, but the village believed that its entire population was immune from these large predators. The shark was their protector, but the benevolence was not recipro-cated. As the sharks entered the outer reef on the rising tide, a priest would wade out and stand on a special coral-head at the entrance to a channel. Chanting words passed down from ancestors, he called to the sharks, inviting them to enter the lagoon. It is said that at the head of the shoal was a smaller shark, distinctly lighter than the others. Like a Judas, it led the other sharks to the priest, who drew them into shallow water where the villagers waded in for the kill; only the treacherous leading shark was allowed to escape. For weeks Nasaqalau feasted on the proceeds of their traditional slaughter.

It is more than fifty years since the villagers successfully practised their ritual, although they still claim immunity from sharks and can tell you marvellous stories to prove it. In November 1992, as part of the renaissance of their ancient traditions, they re-enacted the shark calling. Their intention was to bring back the sharks to their lagoon. For weeks they kept watch until the sharks appeared outside the reef. The chosen head-man waded to the coral-head and chanted, but the sharks moved on.

The richness of the sea that encircles the islands of Fiji, Tonga and Samoa has a deep-founded source that derives from the same geological pressures which created the 'ring of fire' on the rim of the western Pacific. Where the relentless westward movement of the bed of the Pacific comes into contact with the mighty continental plate of Asia, pressure points are released as volcanoes and islands form. The sea-bed rolls on and downwards, creating an ocean trench several miles deep. This immense underwater canyon narrows towards Tonga, from which it takes its name, the Tongan Trench. All the islands in this part of the Pacific benefit from the up-welling of nutrients that are funnelled towards them from the depths of the Tongan Trench. Off the north coast of Taveuni is an arm of this canyon, which divers know as the 'Great White Wall'. It plunges down vertically for hundreds of feet and is carpeted in white soft corals which are able to grow profusely in the currents of nutrient-rich water that surge along the marine precipice.

Bathed in mineral-laden water, the reefs around Fiji and Tonga are amongst the most prolific in the world. Although not as diverse in species as those of south-east Asia's 'Coral Sea', the reefs of Taveuni and the Lau Islands are spectacularly colourful and they teem with life. Even the lagoons that fringe the two main islands of Vitilevu and Vanualevu offer divers some of the best underwater vistas to be seen anywhere in the Pacific. Beqa lagoon (pronounced 'Mbengga'), just to the south of Vitilevu, is famed for its giant coral-heads. Created as the seas rose, they have survived as sunken gardens of living coral. Through them run a maze of tunnels and blow-holes in which shelter wildly coloured molluscs and crustaceans. Poisonous banded sea-snakes (*Laticauda* spp.) hunt through the coral-heads in search of eels and small fish. They come out of the sea to sleep and rest in rock fissures and even climb knobbly barringtonia trees on the edge of the beach. They mate and lay their eggs on land but live the rest of their lives in the rich underwater gardens just off the coast. Taveuni, the 'Garden Island' of Fiji, earns its name both above and below sea level. All these islands in the influence of the Tongan Trench have a marine wealth which is unmatched anywhere else in Polynesia.

When the first Polynesians came with their boating and fishing skills, discovering these islands must have been like finding paradise. The seas outside the reefs and the lagoons within them abounded with marine life. The forests were rich in hard timbers for building boats and houses, and the soils were not only fertile enough to support their crops but were also rich in clays from which their potters could make pots. The Fijian islands were well suited to the way of life of the people who first discovered them. In one or two villages of the Rewa Delta on Vitilevu there are still maritime clans whose men are sea-farers and whose women are potters. Most other Fijians now lead a different sort of life.

Lakeba, the provincial capital of the Lau group, now has an airport and has adopted modern ways, but a few hours sailing takes you to the neighbouring islands of Moce ('Mothay'), Kabara ('Kambara'), Ogea ('Ongea') and Fulaga ('Fulanga'), where you can discover a way of life that has probably changed little since the Polynesians came. Of course, the islanders of Lau now have iron tools and wear cotton clothes, but they hold hard to their tried and tested ways. Here you will still find the traditional crafts of wood-carving and the making of bark-cloth. Each island has developed its speciality. On Fulaga there are hereditary clans who make dugout canoes from the tall trunks of *vesi* trees (*Intsia bijuga*); on Kabara the same hard timber is carved into fine *yaqona* bowls by descendants of specialized craftsmen; the island of Moce is renowned for its distinctive *masi*, the Fijian name for bark-cloth.

The making of bark-cloth was formerly the prerogative of certain families, but now a wider range of women have acquired the skills. Every morning, except Sunday, the main village on Moce resounds to the hammering of hard wooden mallets on hard wooden anvils. The process was brought from the islands of south-east Asia and was taken with them by the first Polynesians as they migrated towards Tahiti and the eastern Pacific, where bark-cloth became known as *tapa*. In the absence of any other suitable plant fibres from which to make materials, bark-cloth became the essential material for clothes and many other functional and ornamental domestic objects. It is made from the paper-mulberry tree (*Broussonetia papyrifera*) which is a native of Asia and came to Fiji with the first seafarers. Like the bread-fruit tree, to which it is related, it is grown from suckers. The shoots seldom branch and the shrub grows tall and spindly. When ten or twelve feet tall, the *masi* stems are harvested and the fibrous inner lining of the bark is stripped with bivalve shells or simply with the teeth. This lining is soaked in water and then its outer surface scraped to remove imperfections.

Then comes the hard work, invariably undertaken by the women of the village. With a heavy four-sided baton carved from the wood of nokonoko (*Casuarina equisetifolia*), the women beat the strips of *masi* until they are wafer thin. Each side of the tool, called an *ike*, is scored with grooves of different width to allow a grading of treatment. As each strand is completed, it is laid head to tail with another and the two are beaten together to make a strip of more even thickness. Time and time again the strips are beaten and folded as more *masi* is added to the spreading sheet of bark-cloth. Sometimes a paste made from arrowroot is added, although today cassava gum is more readily available.

The sheets are dried in the sun and often printed with stencil designs traditionally cut from leaves using shells. Today the favourite stencil material is discarded X-ray film. The colours and patterns of Fijian bark-cloth are very distinctive. The vivid blacks and earth-reds come from plant roots and clays, and the designs have much in common with the bold indented patterns of *Lapita* pottery. Here on the Lau Islands, the people have remembered more of their ancestral skills than just how to plant yams and catch fish.

Women on the Lau island of Moce making bark-cloth; when soaked, the strips of *masi* are beaten with the *ike* baton.

Taveuni and the northern islands of Lau lead towards Savaii and Upolu in Samoa; beyond Fulaga and the southern end of the Lau chain is the archipelago of Tonga, which is a Polynesian word meaning 'south'. Although the sea-crossings between the three groups are quite long, even by today's sailing standards, there was evidently much contact between them in the first few centuries of their settlement. They all spoke the same language and shared the same ancestors. Their spiritual beliefs would have been identical, although little remains to tell us how they practised their religious rituals. On three islands of Samoa, archaeologists have excavated platforms with stone protrusions radiating from their bases. These so-called star-mounds contain no burial sites and there are no oral traditions to give us a clue about their ancient function.

In time, almost every island developed its own special skills and culture, largely based on the different local natural resources. Wood-carvers chose to live on islands forested with *vesi* trees, while the potters chose those with plentiful clay. As the accomplished seafarers plied the waters of the western Pacific carrying their various goods, a triangle of trade was established between the three main island groups, Fiji, Tonga and Samoa. In Samoa there were forests and deposits of superior stone; the Samoans were skilled in the use of the adze and other tools, and became renowned as the artisans of the triangle. The Tongans became the sea-traders and entrepreneurs; their chiefs introduced Samoan craftsmen to Fiji to build canoes for them. From the outset, the first people to arrive on these oceanic islands used their traditional skills to exploit the new environment.

A natural asset of the Fijian islands but scarce on Samoa and Tonga was its wealth of wildlife. One fascinating consequence of this was the trade in red feathers. On many islands of Fiji, including Taveuni and the Lau islands, lived the red-breasted musk-parrot, the *kaka*, and the collared lory, the *kula*. Neither of these parrots seems to have naturally reached Tonga or Samoa, and the people who settled those more remote islands developed an almost insatiable passion for their plumage. Some Samoans kept Fijian parrots in captivity, plucking an annual crop of red feathers to adorn their ceremonial mats and ornamental robes. Tongans used the feathers as currency. For them all, red was synonymous with wealth and paradise. It is a notion shared by many oriental people; in time, this cultural memory spread throughout all of Polynesia.

Samoan legend speaks of an ancestral underworld called Pulotu. In Tonga the same word refers to a distant land somewhere to the north-west. The

Traditional Fijian bark-cloth is stencilled with bold geometric designs; the earth-red dyes are prepared from local clays and the black is made from the soot of burnt candle-nut. This single expanse of bark-cloth is the size of a large carpet.

mythologies of both these Polynesian nations depict the ruler of Pulotu as a serpent-like ogre with a predilection for human flesh. In Fiji they still speak of a mythical place called Burotu, which, allowing for the regular change of 'r' to 'l', is the same place. The Fijians, however, visualize Burotu neither as a place of their origin nor as an abode of spirits. For them it is an island paradise inhabited only by beautiful women and where everything is red. People in the Lau group called it Burotu Kula, after the treasured feathers of that bird. All Fijian sources claim that this idyllic island is submerged somewhere east of Vitilevu and south of Taveuni. Maybe one day we shall find the 'Vanuakula', the red land of ancient Fiji. The chances are that it lies just beneath the sea near the islands of Lau, one of the earliest cradles of Polynesian culture.

For perhaps a thousand years, the first Polynesians had Fiji more or less to themselves. Some of them had discovered and settled the other islands of Tonga and Samoa to the east. They all shared the same basic physical character-istics and spoke the same language. Despite the distances between the main island groups, the various tribes traded with one another in their seagoing canoes. In time, the three groups of Fiji, Tonga and Samoa began to lose contact with each other and developed their separate ways of life. From pottery and other artefacts, we know that the Polynesians on Fiji lived mainly on the coast. Then, quite suddenly, around two and a half thousand years ago, the style of pottery changed. In place of finely decorated work, plain coarse earthenware became widespread. Archaeological evidence also shows that, at the same time, extensive areas of inland forest were felled and burned to make way for agriculture on the hills and mountainsides. It is thought that Fiji's main island of Vitilevu experienced a sudden increase of population, perhaps as a result of the arrival of people from Melanesia. The original Polynesian society on Vitilevu began to change almost beyond recognition. The descendants of the *Lapita* people had been joined by another race who had no inhibitions about leaving the coast and moving inland.

At the mouth of the great Sigatoka river which carves a route down from the mountains of Vitilevu to reach the ocean on the south coast, is a landscape of sand. Here, where the fresh-water meets the sea, was once a thriving community which made *Lapita*-style pottery. The settlement was founded perhaps 2600 years ago. Over the centuries, the prevailing winds shifted the dunes and buried the site. During the last fifty years, storms and wind have eroded the dunes and begun to expose the long history of Sigatoka. It is one of the most exciting and revealing archaeological sites in the entire Pacific. Fragments of ancient pottery have come to the surface, each layer in turn going back further in time. Here for generations, women made pots by the sea while their men traded the earthen-ware along with the fish and turtles they caught. The more recent pottery was made by the paddle-impressed technique still employed in nearby villages; but shards found deeper in the dunes bear the distinctive marks of *Lapita*. As the wind blows across the dunes, other more recent remains are revealed.

Since 1986 about seventy human skeletons have been discovered in the dunes at Sigatoka. Here was an ancient burial ground which was started almost 2000 years ago, about the time when Melanesian people came, or perhaps were brought, from Vanuatu, 500 miles to west. Almost all the corpses had been buried lying on their backs, with their legs drawn up; it was the knees of the skeletons which usually appeared first above the sand. With their heads slightly raised, they faced towards the east.

Following storms in August 1992, archaeologists from Suva Museum discovered another single skeleton that enigmatically faced towards the west. It was of a woman perhaps thirty years old. She was tall and she had perfect teeth. The jaw of her skull was of the 'rocker' form which, together with several other diagnostic features, distinguished her as directly related to the first Polynesian people. There were no others buried with her and she had apparently died of natural causes.

As the sun sets over the dunes at Sigatoka, long shadows chase over the shifting sands. The waves from the open Pacific thunder on the shore and the air is thick with salt-spray. Within sight of the ocean, the newly revealed skeleton lay for several days. Each evening the glow of the setting sun highlighted the face of this woman who died almost two thousand years ago. Her gaze looked far back in time, towards the very distant homeland of her ancestors.

CHAPTER FIVE

NOMADS of the WIND

In the first week of 1993 a cyclone hit Fiji. The deep cyclonic front, code-named Kina, was forecast on satellite pictures long before it left the Solomon Islands a thousand miles to the north-west. The people of Fiji are prepared for cyclones. They are part of the way of life of all Pacific islanders. Everyone along the exposed coast, from Sigatoka in the south-west round to Rakiraki in the north, prepared to take the full impact of the storm. Windows were boarded and ropes or chains thrown across roofs and fixed to stakes driven in the ground. At the luxury hotels overlooking the sunset, every movable object was taken inside or submerged in swimming pools. Guests were told to stay in their rooms or to join the special parties arranged to keep up their spirits.

The first victims were the Yasawa Islands. Lined at right angles to the path of the storm, these rocky outcrops provided little shelter for their inhabitants. The reef boiled with fury as the eye of the storm passed right through them without flinching from its course. When it hit the coast of Vitilevu, cyclone Kina seemed to rock the entire island. It was the worst storm for fifty years. Without mercy it whirled around the north coast and struck eastward along Bligh Water between the main island and Vanualevu. Taveuni was spared as the demon veered to the south-east and ripped through the islands of Ovalau, Gau and Moala. With a demented roar the cyclone exited Fijian waters by way of the southern islands of Lau, where Kabara, Fulaga and Vatoa were left reeling. Boats were smashed and houses flattened. Groves of coconut palms were uprooted and tossed into the air. As cyclone Kina headed south-east and spent its madness on the open ocean, Fiji picked up the pieces and counted the toll. Twenty-seven people were dead and four missing.

The south coast of Vitilevu was ruffled and on the dunes of Sigatoka parts of two more skeletons emerged from the sand. The capital, Suva, had been in the lee of the storm. The south-east corner of Vitilevu normally takes the brunt of the weather, but the winds this time had come from the west. The day after, life returned almost to normal. Birds, which, along with the human population, had held their breath, sang noisily from roof-tops and in public parks. Fruit-bats, dislodged from their roosts, flew over the town in broad daylight searching for trees which still had foliage. House-owners and hoteliers were philosophical, knowing that here in the tropics the scars would quickly heal. Within weeks new shoots would grow into lush vegetation and the red scoured earth would once again be carpeted in green.

The leaves that had been stripped from the trees had disappeared into the air, together with a miniature menagerie of small birds and bats, insects and tiny reptiles. Churned into the vortex of the storm, most of them probably perished before it died away. Some were dashed back into the sea, but others were carried for hundreds of miles toward distant specks of land. As the centre of low pressure dissipated its energy, a rain of aerial plankton fell from the sky. On the low islands of Tonga and perhaps on the Samoan Islands, new life settled on the land. Most species to arrive were not the first of their kind to have made this violent one-way trip. The colonization of remote Pacific islands would not have happened without the power of wind. Year after year, century by century, plants and animals had been carried across the sea and had settled new outposts long before the Polynesians came. With each great storm a few wild-life immigrants arrived to join the ranks of other colonists. Very occasionally an island received a new species, perhaps the seed of a plant or the egg of an insect. With luck, when they matured there would be others of their kind and a viable population would become established. In time the alien species would become a native of its adopted home. With more time, the colony would develop its own idiosyncrasies of form and behaviour, to become a distinct race or species. Such is the endemic nature of island life.

It was of course the ocean winds that carried the Polynesian people across the Pacific. Some, like the hapless wildlife caught in the storm, would have been swept out to sea in their canoes against their will. Many must have perished as victims of the elements. If they survived the storm, the privations of food and fresh-water and the effects of exposure to salt and sun would soon begin to show. It is extraordinary how resilient Pacific islanders can be in such extreme circumstances. Every few years an almost unbelievable feat of endurance makes the headlines of the Pacific press. In 1992, two fishermen from Christmas Island

Falealupo nature reserve on Savaii, repeatedly shattered by recent cyclones.

on the equator were swept from their reef by strong south-easterlies and drifted westward for forty days without sight of land. Sun-blistered, dehydrated, but alive, they eventually dragged their tiny craft onto the shore of an island in Micronesia 2000 miles from home. By ill fate, many other Polynesians must have been swept off course and by good fortune some might have survived to encounter unknown land. Such castaways may have lived out the rest of their lives on their new island refuge; others would have waited for favourable weather conditions and attempted to return. Only the most fortunate and the most tenacious came home to tell the tale.

Polynesians certainly discovered new islands in this random way, but it is very unlikely that they settled them on such a chance encounter. Fishing is mainly men's work and a boat swept accidentally to another island would have no women on board. Any hope of establishing a new colony was doomed from the start. Nor would they have the root-crops and livestock, seeds and cuttings that were essential to Polynesian life. Any colonizing voyage would have to be deliberately planned if it was to have a reasonable chance of success. Fishermen returning safely from making new discoveries would fire the minds of others. Everyone would be eager to know about the new land beyond the horizon. They would ask whether it had mountains and fresh-water streams, whether there was access to a sheltered lagoon, whether there was forest with abundant wildlife and, of course, whether any people lived there. It may not have been for decades or generations that such an island was visited again. Legend grew as the story of the first adventurous encounter with that distant island was told and retold. Details of its direction and distance were woven in patterns of sticks and cords, precious maps which one day might lead the way to a new island home.

The reasons and motives for Polynesian voyaging have puzzled and intrigued outsiders ever since the days of Captain Cook. We can only speculate on why they left one island and risked a long sea-journey in search of another. Islands by their very nature have limitations. Their resources are finite and can easily be depleted. The forests can be reduced to scrub and grassland, and even the marine wealth of the lagoon is not boundless. It was for this reason that Polynesian society imposed its own restrictions in the form of taboos. It was a proven system that contributed greatly to the people's survival.

Nature not only has limits but it is also unpredictable, particularly when at the mercy of oceans. The hurricanes and storms that spread wildlife from island to island creating new life are also forces which destroy. The islands of Samoa are characterized by a pioneering fauna and flora which seems barely to have gained a foothold on the new volcanic soils. The very forces that bring new species also threaten their survival. In recent memory, Savaii and Upolu have suffered from repeated cyclones which devastated large areas of the forest and have contributed to the near extinction of several species. It is a cycle of colonization and destruction which must have afflicted these islands ever since they rose above the sea.

Repeated natural disasters and shortage of resources would prompt people to seek a better life elsewhere. It is a natural human response. The legends of islands beyond the horizon would become rosier with time and internal strife would give added momentum to the exodus. The appeal of a new life would become greater than the fear of being lost at sea. For countless generations, the Polynesians had been a seafaring people. It was in their blood and in their spirit. They were innately adventurous and nomadic. Since their ancestors left their homeland far to the west, their restless search had brought them to the remote islands of the western Pacific. The further they voyaged from Asia, the longer became the sea routes between the groups of islands. Behind them, beyond the setting sun, lay the trail left by their forebears who had pioneered this way of life. Those who set off were true pioneers, not outcasts. They did so in the knowledge that they had the skills and stamina to find and settle that distant land which lay beyond the rising sun.

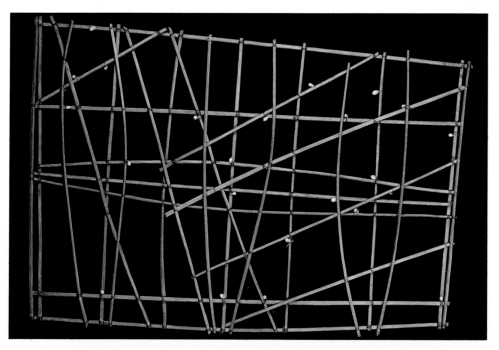

Above The only form of ocean maps carried by Polynesian voyagers were conceptual charts made from sticks and shells. Knowledge of winds and currents, together with sailing times between islands, was passed between navigators.
Overleaf Frigate birds – the nomadic aerial pirates of the Pacific.

What makes the voyaging feats of the Polynesians even more astonishing is that they travelled mainly from west to east, in total opposition to the prevailing winds and currents. For many scholars this paradox was a stumbling block when considering the origins of Pacific islanders. For most of the year, the islands of the South Seas, and also the Hawaiian Islands in the northern hemisphere, are influenced by surface winds and ocean currents that beat against their eastern shores. It is on these windward coasts that most rain falls, in contrast to the drier climate on the sheltered, leeward sides. This prevailing wind pattern in the tropical zone of the Pacific works in tandem with two ocean currents which broadly take the same path. In the south Pacific, the famed Humboldt current sweeps up the coast of South America bringing cold water from the Antarctic. Renowned to game fishermen for its wealth of big fish, it also carries giant rays, hordes of squid and great schools of whales. When it reaches Peru, still some way south of the equator, the Humboldt current veers westward and brings its cold water into the apex of the Polynesian Triangle.

It is this current which carried Thor Heyerdahl and his crew westwards on their now legendary *Kon-Tiki* expedition of 1947. For three months their raft of balsa logs was carried ever further from the coast of Peru towards the islands of eastern Polynesia. Heyerdahl had set out to show how the predictable Humboldt current might have carried South American Indians by the same route. When *Kon-Tiki* finally crash-landed on the reef of Raroia, an atoll in the Tuamotu Archipelago to the east of Tahiti, Heyerdahl had proved without doubt that such a drift voyage could indeed be made, purely by the power of the prevailing winds and currents south of the equator.

In the northern Pacific there is almost a mirror effect as a cold current of water from the Canadian north-west flows down past California to Mexico, where it also veers westward. Heyerdahl has also suggested that this current was used by seagoing North American Indians who set off from the islands in the region that is now British Columbia. Carried westward by the reliable ocean stream and by the prevailing easterlies, they could have reached the islands of Hawaii in the centre of the north Pacific.

Contrary to Thor Heyerdahl's feats of exploration and intriguing arguments, the overwhelming evidence now supports the idea that Polynesian colonization was from the other direction. It was almost certainly from the island groups of Samoa and Tonga in the western Pacific that the Polynesian people spread eastward, albeit against the main flow of winds and currents. As Heyerdahl points out, there is a world of difference between possibility and probability. It is also easy to confuse method with motive when con-

Humpback whales (*Megaptera novaeangliae*) on their southward migration.

sidering how the islands of Polynesia were first settled. The scenario that moves away from the islands of south-east Asia into the western Pacific and then on eastward fits our growing understanding of the people themselves. As more evidence comes to light about their way of life and the nature of their island world, the epic story of their dispersal through the Pacific will assume an even more logical pattern.

Unlike marine creatures under the sea, mariners on the surface are strongly influenced by wind direction. Throughout the tropical Pacific the winds predominantly blow from the east, making it difficult to sail in that direction. With modern sailing craft it is possible to tack hard against the wind, but it seems unlikely that traditional Polynesian double-hulled canoes could make much headway when the south-east trades were blowing hard. There are, however, variations in this pattern. For short periods of the year the wind direction can be reversed, particularly in the western Pacific. In some years the entire system is upset by the onset of 'El Niño', which, as well as affecting weather patterns around the world, brings a more sustained period of westerly winds to the southern tropics. This in turn can cause surface currents to reverse and flow eastward. It happened towards the end of 1982 and again ten years later.

Above On board the voyaging canoe, a small domed hut of pandanus
leaves provided the only shelter from the elements.
Right Polynesian people are tall and well-built; to survive for weeks
at sea demanded a robust constitution.

Biologists are convinced that it was the intermittent effects of El Niño which help account for the eastward spread of marine species across the Pacific. The same reversal of winds and currents could well have carried Polynesian voyagers in the same direction.

To sail eastward is a logical strategy. It made good sense from a survival point of view. Sooner or later, the trade winds would return to normal, so that even if you had failed to find land to the east, at least you could turn back. To the Polynesian, the entire world was made up of an immense ocean studded with islands. Time and time again, groups of them would have set sail toward the east following a legend or simply their instincts. They knew from generations of sailing that the further they pioneered in that direction, the greater the chance of finding islands that were uninhabited and perhaps larger and higher than their present home. Given good weather and with sufficient westerly winds, a sailing craft could cover many hundreds of miles in a few days and by methodical scanning might encounter new land. If the provisions or enthusiasm began to run out before they sighted their unknown goal, then they could turn their craft around and, with the wind at their backs, head rapidly for the safety of home. Locating a known point was far easier than combing an empty ocean in the hope of finding land.

High islands create clouds. An accumulation on the horizon offers a promise of land. As their canoe sails closer, the voyagers see more signs of life. Coconuts and pandanus fronds float towards them from the direction of the distant bank of clouds. The navigator detects changes in the swell beneath the craft. Even the colour of the sea seems different. In their wake, the sun begins to set. Above them, sea-birds wheel, curious about the newcomers. As the birds head purposefully towards the darkening east horizon, the men on board rejoice at the prospect of the dawn.

The clouds that collect over islands often reflect the colours of the land below. The lush green of a high forested interior will be mirrored in the sky. If the island is an atoll with a large lagoon, the blue under-lining of the cloud cover is a sure sign of the nature of the island. At first light, the seafarers know much about their destination before they catch sight of land. The appearance of a mountain peak confirms their hopes that the focus of their journey is indeed a new high island with its assurance of forests and streams.

Their ears tune to the roar of the reef. This is the most hazardous part of their voyage. Not every island has navigable channels through the turbulent shallow waters that surge over the fringing coral reef. When winds permit, the navigator guides the canoe around the leeward side, holding her off from the pounding reef. Keen eyes scan the white water for a channel that is deep and wide enough to enter, still under power of sail. An approach from the windward side carries the risk of being swept onto the turbulent reef. If that is their only option, then down comes the sail and the strongest men lean on the great steering oar to manoeuvre the craft into the safety of the lagoon. Everyone helps by using paddles and poles to prevent the canoe drifting towards the edge of the channel and to fend off danger from shallow coral-heads. As the canoe comes to a halt, men jump into the shallow water with jubilant shouts of gratitude to their ancestral spirits which have guided them safely to this fertile land. Tangaroa, the god of seafarers, has been benevolent. To their great satisfaction, they discover that the island is not only fertile but also uninhabited by people.

A Polynesian voyage of settlement was only successful if the large canoe
arrived intact with its precious cargo of plants.

The native wildlife of Pacific islands became established long before the coming of the Polynesians. For countless thousands of years different species of plants and animals had, by chance, arrived at every island. With the help of strong westerly winds, they had been carried in the air or by sea from other islands to the west. Their dispersal from the islands of south-east Asia had also been from west to east, but for many small creatures the winds worked in favour of their eastward spread. Near the surface of the sea the south-east trades have their greatest effect. The higher the altitude, the less pronounced the force. By 10 000 feet, which is not much more than the summits of the highest islands, the prevailing winds in the tropics are reversed from west to east.

The frequent cyclones in the western Pacific pluck small creatures and plant fragments and sweep them high into the atmosphere. Seeds, spores and small insects can be whisked along for hundreds, or maybe thousands, of miles. Some spiders are expert balloonists, deliberately spinning silken threads into a rising thermal until they are carried aloft. Even strong-flying birds change altitude to take advantage of different wind directions. Fruit pigeons (*Ducula* spp.) have spread from their original home in south-east Asia to almost every island throughout Melanesia, Micronesia and Polynesia, moving nomadically in search of the best pickings. The Pacific pigeon (*Ducula pacifica*) of western Polynesia and Melanesia is a classic example of this survival strategy. Wherever they find trees with ripe fruit, they settle and maybe breed. In times of shortage, they move on in a flock to another island.

With them travel 'hitch-hikers', plants and animals which passively make the same journey. Seeds eaten by a pigeon may take several days to pass through the bird. Deposited on another island together with a ration of fertilizer, the seeds sprout into new trees. A new generation of plants is launched on another island. Other seeds are designed to hook or stick onto feathers. The sticky fruits of pisonia trees (*Pisonia grandis*) are designed to adhere to birds and in this way have been spread right across Polynesia. In some ways pisonia has become almost too good at this task. The unripe fruits can become firmly glued to the feathers of sea-birds attempting to roost in the tree; because they are not yet ready for dispersal, the fruits refuse to break off from the twigs and the birds become fatally trapped. Another plant with tenacious seeds, *Bidens pilosa*, is a relative of the sunflower. It has fruits equipped with barbed prongs which lodge so securely in the feathers of birds that they may be carried for months. By this device, the plant has been transported widely throughout the Pacific from its native homeland of South America. It is one of the few plant or animal species to have spread from that continent, from where it has reached Tonga in the western Pacific.

The seeds of *Bidens pilosa* are equipped with barbs which grip the feathers
of long-distance fliers such as the Pacific pigeon (*Ducula pacifica*).

Even snails stick to the feathers of migrating birds or in mud on their feet.
If small enough, they remain undetected by the bird and can be carried across
great distances of ocean. It is significant that most snails on Pacific islands have
evolved from ancestors with tiny shells which were transported in this way. Once
safely on a new island refuge, the descendants of some castaways have developed
into giant species which become very successful but are unable to move again.

Other 'hitch-hikers' reach remote islands by rafting on logs and floating
vegetation. Following the impact of storms, entire trees, with their complement
of plants and animals sheltering or feeding in the foliage, can be swept out to
sea. In its bark are the grubs of insects such as wood-boring beetles and the
eggs of woodlice and spiders. If they survive the salty passage and if the tree
does not become water-logged, these creatures might end up as castaways on
a remote island.

It is thought that Fiji gained its two species of frog this way. Both of them,
the Fiji tree frog (*Platymantis vitiensis*) and the Fiji ground frog (*Platymantis
vitianus*), have no free-swimming tadpole. Their large eggs each contain
sufficient yolk for the larva to mature into a miniature adult before it hatches.
This means that the two species are no longer dependent on fresh-water for the
development of their eggs. The females lay their small clutches of enormous
eggs in the leaf axils of palm trees, where they grow into froglets without the
need of water. This may explain why these two species are the only amphibians
to have crossed the western Pacific as far as Fiji. Adult frogs would perish at sea,
but a large, yolk-filled egg could survive in the leaf axils of a pandanus tree
uprooted in a storm and swept out to sea.

Above The eggs of the Fiji tree frog (*Platymantis vitiensis*) hatch,
not as tadpoles, but as miniature adults.
Right The adult frogs, endemic to Fiji, display a great variety
of patterns and colours.

Reptiles are better sailors than frogs. The tough scaly skin of lizards and snakes resists salt water and most reptiles can go without food for weeks. Many species of skink and gecko probably rafted between islands, clinging to floating vegetation. Even the Pacific boa could survive a long time at sea before washing up on a distant shore. The hard-shelled eggs of reptiles are even better proof against exposure to sun and sea, and it is very possible that several species have been dispersed as embryos across the ocean. It is also most likely that their spread through the western Pacific happened during Ice Ages when there was much more land above sea level. Islands now lost again beneath the ocean would have acted as stepping-stones for terrestrial wildlife. With more islands and shorter distances between them, the sea in those Ice Age times presented less of a barrier to dispersal. It was only when species reached the deep water of the western Pacific that island-hopping became less likely. But even during Ice Ages, the distances between oceanic islands remained daunting. For amphibians and many other entire groups of terrestrial animals and plants, the islands of Fiji and their immediate neighbours were the final limit to eastward expansion.

One extraordinary anomaly is the Fijian banded iguana (*Brachylophus fasciatus*). This splendid reptile, found on such Fijian islands as Vatuvara, has relatives on the farthest side of the Pacific but none to the west. It seems that its ancestors came across the entire Pacific from similar coastal areas of central America, 6500 miles to the east. Although it is an expert swimmer, it is unlikely that this terrestrial lizard could survive very long in salt-water. It is also improbable that it would cling to a floating raft of vegetation and then drift all the way to Fiji, even with the help of westbound winds and currents. The most plausible explanation is that, like Fiji's frogs, it arrived as eggs which had been laid on the other side of the Pacific. The eggs of this iguana can take six months or more to hatch and, like those of all reptiles, are very resilient. Laid among the roots of a tree growing by a shore in central America, such eggs could have crossed the Pacific on board a natural raft, so that the young iguanas hatched months later on the strand-line of a Fijian island. Once there, they spread more easily from island to island, setting up home in Fiji's forests.

On one island, Yaduataba, lives a distinctly different race of iguanas with spectacular crests. This recently discovered reptile has been given its own specific name, *Brachylophus vitiensis*, and may be even more closely related to the pioneering ancestor whose eggs accidentally crossed the Pacific, perhaps several million years ago.

Fiji's spectacular Crested iguana (*Brachylophus vitiensis*).

For marine creatures, crossing an ocean presents fewer problems. They are designed for life in the sea. Turtles, perhaps the best known and best loved, of marine reptiles, spend most of their life at sea, although they must return to land to lay their eggs. One reptile has cast itself off from land completely. The yellow-bellied sea-snake (*Pelamis platurus*) lives out its entire life in the open ocean. The males and females court and copulate in mid-ocean, where they stalk and ambush small fish among the flotsam that collects where the great ocean currents meet. The secret of their independence from land lies in their method of reproduction. The females incubate their eggs internally, giving birth to live young which are able to swim from the moment they are born. As a result, these ocean nomads have become the most prolific and widespread reptile in the world.

Many ocean animals, such as sharks and other large fish, are capable of great purposeful ocean journeys. The grey reef shark (*Carcharhinus amblyrhynchos*) is found throughout the tropical Pacific. Its mobility has been the key to its success. Independent of winds and currents, it can cruise the ocean and live wherever there is a sufficient supply of prey. In an even more determined way, whales move throughout the Pacific in tandem with their food supplies. Humpback whales (*Megaptera novaeangliae*) spend the southern summer in Antarctic waters feeding on the bountiful harvest of krill. About March they move past New Zealand and through the islands of Tonga on their migration north to breed in shallow water off Polynesian islands. In September, a similar migration moves through the seas of Tahiti and some reach as far north as Hawaii. They seem to prefer migrating along routes which follow deep ocean trenches from which cold water wells up carrying rich stocks of plankton, and they are seen just off the coasts of California and Chile. Sperm whales (*Physeter catodon*) also thrive on these up-wellings but they intercept other large marine creatures that feed at much greater depths. Deep-sea squid is their favourite prey and large bull whales grapple with giant squids which can reach 100 feet in length. For whales, the entire Pacific is their world.

Other marine animals are confined to the warm waters of the tropics. Many species of fish which evolved in the 'Coral Sea' of south-east Asia have spread eastward in a broad band, and have reached Hawaii to the north and the reefs that surround the remote islands of eastern Polynesia. They were carried by currents as spawn which then hatched many hundreds of miles away. Coral is spread in the same way. On the reefs of the islands of Melanesia, you can see a multitude of species competing for space. In a riot of different colours and forms, these colonial animals have built the very fabric of coral islands. Here in the warm shallow seas in the extreme west of the Pacific Ocean is the evolutionary warehouse which has spawned so many different species.

The Grey reef shark (*Carcharhinus amblyrhynchos*) is found in tropical and
sub-tropical waters from Hawaii and Easter Island in the Pacific and as
far west as the African coast of the Indian Ocean.

To ensure successful breeding, all the coral species spawn at the same
time. This synchronization produces such a surplus of milt and eggs that the
appetite of predators is satiated, ensuring that at least some fertilized spawn is
dispersed from the reef. It is significant that on the less crowded coral reefs of
Tahiti, there is no such synchronization of spawning. In a deep ocean such as
the Pacific, corals are dependent on the existence of land just as much as
any bird or flowering plant. Only where volcanic mounts have reached the
surface is the water sufficiently shallow for corals to grow. The further east
they drift, the less are the chances of coral spawn finding a place to settle. The
remote islands of eastern Polynesia are poor in corals as well as land creatures,
for much the same reasons. In the great move eastward, many groups of
animals and plants have reached the end of the line. Only the most tenacious
went all the way.

If, by design or accident, a Polynesian voyaging expedition discovered a new island suitable for settlement, they would plant a handful of seeds before returning home. If they ever came back to their new-found territory, a harvest of useful and edible plants would be waiting for them. If they never returned, the forethought would be not be wasted; someone else would come this way again.

Choosing the right day with prevailing easterlies, the returning voyagers ease their canoe through the reef passage and out into the open sea. The wind fills the triangular sail of tightly woven pandanus matting and they turn for home. By day they use the sun and the pattern of ocean currents; by night they follow stars. Within days they come in sight of a familiar reef or island from which they can take a bearing and narrow down their route. Most Pacific island groups are strung out in chains. Finding any one of the islands is almost as good as finding home. Some returning voyagers might, by misfortune or bad weather, miss their target. Unable to beat back against a strong easterly, they are carried further west until by chance they encounter another group of islands stretched out like a safety net across their path.

There are several such groups to the north-west of Samoa, Tonga and Fiji. They lie in the eastern parts of Micronesia. This immense band of tiny islands reaches back 2000 miles towards the Philippines and Japan. Quite reasonably, many Pacific experts have in the past proposed that it was by way of this long chain that the original Polynesian people came to the base of the Triangle. They pointed out that some of the islands are inhabited by people who are distinctly Polynesian, rather than Micronesian, in their physique, language and culture. Together with other Polynesian-style islands also dotted through eastern Melanesia, these groups of islands are considered to be the 'Polynesian Outliers'.

The achievements of the Polynesians depended on their boats and boating skills, by which they harnessed the wind and fashioned a way of life in the vastness of the Pacific. For them the canoe was sacred. Whether a simple dugout or a great double-hulled sailing craft, it was their life-line and the vehicle of their culture. Today, the people of Polynesia do not voyage great distances by canoe, unless to re-enact the sailing feats of their ancestors. The art of building such ocean-going craft is seldom practised, but in some islands you still find the simple dugout canoe with its outrigger and sail. The simplest hull consisted of a single shaped and hollowed log to which was attached an outrigger system of floats and struts, usually on one side only, to give the craft stability.

Such simple canoes were ideal for island-hopping but not for ocean voyages far from the safety of land. To reach the distant islands of eastern Polynesia would have required large robust boats capable of weathering storms and sustaining a substantial crew and cargo for weeks on end. When Cook and the other European explorers arrived at Tahiti, they saw canoes that were 100 feet long. Constructed of two enormous hulls, between which was strapped a massive deck, these vessels were probably of the traditional design used long ago by Polynesians for making their pioneering voyages of settlement. The stable double-hulled canoes needed no additional outriggers and their decks were several feet above the water-line. One or more deckhouses were built to shelter crew and livestock, and the hollow hulls also acted as stowage compartments. The carrying capacity of these catamaran-style canoes was impressive. When they set off to settle new lands, the first explorers of Polynesia carried with them all the essential resources to establish a new life.

For weeks the islanders had prepared for this event. The great canoe had long been ready. More than a year before, two giant trees had been felled with due ceremony. The craftsmen selected a site at which they would put into practice their ancestral skills. A fattened pig was ritually killed and prepared for the earth-oven. Tufts of its hair were plucked as a first offering to Tane, the great god of forests and of artisans; its tail would be set aside as the final offering of the feast. At dawn the following day, the craftsmen awakened their stone adzes by dipping them in the sea. Then began the labour with stone and shell tools to carve the hulls and fashion the planking. For months the village resounded to the rhythm of their work.

No women were allowed near the huge open-sided building that housed the massive canoe and its creators. Their task was to plait the fine matting for the sails and to keep the labouring men supplied with food. Others prepared provisions for the voyage. Fermented bread-fruit pulp was parcelled in leaves of the *ti* plant. When baked, this dried food would keep for months. Bananas and other fruits were also dried in the sun and sugar-cane was cut as a ready source of energy. Gourds and large bamboo canes were fashioned into containers to carry fresh-water and other provisions, and also to help protect and nourish the living plant material which would form the basis of their future crops. Seeds and rhizomes, cuttings and saplings had been carefully harvested from the forest or cultivated in gardens. Many essential plant tubers such as yams and taro would perish at sea unless carefully packed in soil to preserve their vitality. Roots of the paper-mulberry tree were cut and preserved so that one day on the distant land bark-cloth could be made. Even coconuts would require expert handling if they were to survive the long voyage.

The best breeding stock was selected from the domestic animals. Pigs would be essential and so would the tamed jungle fowl that provided Polynesians with much of their meat diet. Dogs went too, not just as companions for the forest hunt, but many of them as food; these dogs for eating were bred as vegetarians

The Polynesian rat (*Rattus exulans*) travelled through the Pacific
on board Polynesian voyaging canoes – probably as essential domestic
stock – not just as uninvited stowaways.

so that they could be fed plant remains and human waste while at sea. If the
voyagers caught insufficient fish, they would relish the sweet-tasting flesh of
these canine herbivores which apparently had the added appeal of being unable
to bark. Native Polynesian rats, which thrived on fruits and seeds of plants such
as pandanus, were also taken on board in cages woven from stout plant fibres.
They made good eating for Polynesian people, and would have been intentionally taken to help stock the new island. Other animals came uninvited. Hiding
in the hollow hulls might be skinks, lizards and other stowaway creatures which,
if they survived the voyage, would spread their species.

Everything was ready. The people who would form the nucleus of the new
island had been preparing themselves physically and spiritually for the voyage.
To conserve food and water supplies, they had learned the art of self-restraint.
Those with ample reserves of body fat would be able to survive for weeks on
modest rations and would suffer less from the extremes of salt and sun, and the
chill of the ocean winds. Strong young men would be vital to sail the canoe and
to build the new life. Healthy young women would be needed to procreate
their line. Older men and women possessed the ancient wisdom of their
ancestors and understood the ways of the ocean. With their eyes firmly on the
eastern horizon, they all waited for the westerly wind.

CHAPTER SIX

BURNING
their BOATS

The moon, in its first quarter, cast a ghostly light on the ocean. Riding in gentle waters some thirty miles east of the active volcanic island of Tofua in the western Pacific, a vessel about ninety feet long had just made its way through the chain of islands that we know as Tonga. Ahead lay hundreds of miles of open ocean. On board were forty-four experienced seafarers and a valuable cargo of plants. There were no women and the ship was sailing westward towards Asia. This was clearly not a voyage of settlement, but one of trade. The prized cargo stowed in the hull and on the deck was destined for tropical islands in another sea. The men had come to Polynesia from quite a different world and this night they would make history.

It had been three weeks since HMS *Bounty* set sail from Tahiti. With the full benefit of the prevailing easterlies behind her, she had already covered one and a half thousand miles. By eighteenth-century European standards, she was a small ship but the purpose of her voyage was the most extraordinary commission ever given to a naval crew. Under the command of Lieutenant William Bligh, who had previously sailed the Pacific with Captain Cook, the *Bounty* had left England in December 1787. The purpose of her long voyage to Tahiti was to collect saplings of the prolific Polynesian bread-fruit tree and transport them to the West Indies where they would be cultivated to provide cheap food for slaves.

So far the mission had been a great success. On Tahiti, 774 saplings had been collected and carefully placed in pots. The natives had been very helpful and accommodating. Anyone who was a friend of Captain Cook was welcome in Tahiti. Bligh had remained on board for most of the five-month visit, but his second in command, Fletcher Christian, together with the crew, had enjoyed

Tahitian hospitality. Even Bligh was reluctant to leave. 'I left these happy islanders in much distress,' he later wrote, 'for the utmost affection, regard and good fellowship was among us during our stay.'

Now, three weeks into a voyage that would again take them halfway round the world, everyone was missing the paradise they had left behind. At dawn on April 28th, 1789, Bligh woke to find himself victim of what he would later describe as 'one of the most atrocious acts of piracy ever committed'. Since that now legendary event, countless writers and film-makers have speculated on the reasons for the mutiny. It is what happened afterwards that helps illuminate this natural history of Polynesia.

By noon that day Bligh and eighteen others were cast adrift on the ocean in a twenty-six-foot open boat. With a ship's sextant and some elementary charts, Bligh and his hapless companions were committed to continue their westward voyage at the mercy of the prevailing winds and currents. By that evening they had managed to reach Tofua, where a young seaman fell to his death searching for water and the eggs of sea-birds. Forty days later, after sailing more than 3500 miles through some of the most treacherous water in the world, Bligh and his loyal companions landed at the island of Timor, the nearest European settlement in the East Indies. It was a remarkable feat of seamanship.

Fletcher Christian and the mutineers had turned their sophisticated sailing vessel round into the wind, and headed east on a voyage which would take almost three months to complete. On January 15th, 1790, the mutineers arrived at their final destination. Here, far from the mainstream of the Pacific, they hoped to fashion a new life without fear of retribution from a vengeful Royal Navy. In a reckless act that destroyed their only means of escape, they set fire to the *Bounty*. By burning their boat, they had committed themselves to total isolation.

When they parted company, William Bligh and Fletcher Christian had followed opposite courses. While Bligh and his castaways were swept ever westward by the prevailing ocean winds and currents, the mutineers in possession of the *Bounty* were able to tack against the wind and to travel eastward in search of their ideal island. Bligh's passive journey parallels that of many wildlife species which were plucked from the safety of their island homes and dispersed haphazardly by the power of the elements. The fate of Polynesian fishermen caught in storms and swept out to sea was much the same. With luck such accidental journeys end when the victims become castaways on another island. The *Bounty*'s voyage, on the other hand, mirrors those made by the great whales, large ocean-going fish and sea-birds. Such ocean creatures also embark on deliberate, purposeful migrations in search of places which offer better supplies of food or shelter from adverse weather. Polynesian voyagers were motivated by the same concerns, but unlike the *Bounty*'s mutineers, they kept their options open.

It is now thought likely that most Polynesian islands were first discovered and settled by a sequence of multiple voyages which established a network of communication between the parent island and the infant communities on their island outposts. Goods were traded and ideas exchanged over great distances. Such communication did not require individuals repeatedly to make long voyages; the commodities and information could be relayed across the ocean by a process of island-hopping. In time, as populations developed their separate societies in different quarters of the ocean, these long-distance links were broken. Instead the people established and maintained more local trading and cultural contacts; but seldom did the Polynesian islanders become complete castaways. If for some reason, ecological or social, the new life lost its appeal, they could at least retrace their steps.

In contrast, the natural process of island colonization by wildlife is often accompanied by a commitment to isolation which becomes irreversible. Unlike the cosmopolitan Pacific pigeon, the tooth-billed specialist that became so successful on Savaii was at a great disadvantage when conditions changed. With the coming of people and other predators, it almost went the way of the dodo, but by retaining its power of flight, this endemic pigeon had not completely 'burnt its boats' and was saved from extinction. Repeatedly this biological dilemma has destined the natural history of Pacific islands.

When the Polynesian societies on Samoa and Tonga started exploring further east, they did so in the expectation of finding many new islands. To them the entire world was composed of islands linked by an ocean which was there to be crossed. Although the distances are great, it seems likely that, having established communities in the western Pacific, Polynesian seafarers would soon have explored further east. Perhaps as long ago as 3000 years, they built large canoes and ventured across the vast expanse of ocean between 'the cradle of Polynesia' and the faraway islands of Tahiti and beyond. The Society Islands lie 1500 miles to the east of the islands of Samoa and Tonga, perhaps too far for direct contact. Halfway is a chain of islands that runs north to south for almost a thousand miles. Any voyager who was travelling eastward from either Tonga or Samoa would have a good chance of encountering at least one of them.

Today this strung-out archipelago is known as the Cook Islands. Their inhabitants are very Polynesian and speak a language which has similarities with

Overleaf The centre of Rarotonga, the largest of the Cook Islands, is rugged and virtually untouched. The population of 10 000 lives on the fertile coastal plain and alongside the lagoon.

both Tahitian and New Zealand Maori. Indeed, today's Cook Islanders have great cultural affinities in both those directions. It is uncertain when the first Polynesian communities were established there. Legends trace their ancestry back only 600 years but artefacts suggest that a permanent population has been there twice that long. What is likely is that the Cook Islands, although in the direct line of eastward Polynesian expansion, were initially stepping-stones for the first great migrations.

Although now one nation, the Cook Islands form two distinct groups with quite different geological and biological characters. The southern group are mainly young volcanic islands or else older atolls that have been raised high out of the sea, whereas the northern group are low coral atolls. They were all formed at several volcanic hot-spots on the bed of the ocean and have moved north-west over geological time. The highest island, Rarotonga, in the south is also the youngest, whereas all but one of the much more ancient atolls of the north take on the classic Pacific form of a ring of coral islands around a central lagoon. Although attractive to escapist holiday-makers, such atolls are not ideal for settlement. They are so low in the water that cyclones will sweep waves right across the islands, carrying everything in their path. Fish may be abundant in the lagoon but atoll soil is only marginally fertile and finding sweet fresh-water is always a problem. Compared to high islands, life on atolls is hard.

Manahiki in the northern Cooks is reputed to be one of the most beautiful atolls in the entire Pacific. Nearly forty coral islands, some no more than tiny islets, encircle a lagoon that at its widest point is only six miles across, but being totally enclosed there is no access for boats. Together with neighbouring Rakahanga and the most westerly atoll, Pukapuka, it has a scant human population which today is renowned for the beauty of the women, a reputation which has enticed sailors to risk landing ever since the islands were discovered by the Spanish explorer Alvaro Mendana in 1595. Legends on Pukapuka recall a great tidal wave that swept the island four generations before the coming of the Spanish. Only two women and fifteen men survived to begin rebuilding the community.

Not only are people constantly at risk on low coral islands but so is the terrestrial wildlife. Very few species have become established, and those that live there retain a strong ability to survive the ravages of the sea. Coconut palms and barringtonia trees can be easily uprooted and swept away by storms, but their fruits are ideally suited to being carried by the sea and hurled onto another coral strand. Successful dispersal by ocean currents demands buoyancy and protection

The coconut palm – nomadic plant of tropical islands – takes root wherever
it is swept by the wind and by the ocean's currents.

from salt, aided by a long germination and ample built-in reserves. The coconut is perfectly designed for life on the ocean wave. Its thick husk keeps it afloat; its shape and internal structure ensure that the developing embryo is protected from sea-water. An entire nut complete with husk can survive more than a hundred days at sea, by which time a favourable current can have carried it 3000 miles. Germination often takes much longer, thereby ensuring that a new palm will sprout if the coconut is eventually cast ashore on a tropical island. Thankfully for the Polynesian voyagers, the humble coconut has never lost its seagoing qualities; for them it has been the saving grace of life on coral atolls.

The islets of the northern Cooks are favourite roosting and breeding places for sea-birds. Essentially creatures of the open sea, species such as frigate birds, boobies, noddies and terns establish breeding colonies in the vegetation or simply on the open ground of the more remote islets. Before the first people came, the birds had the entire atolls to themselves. Their expert power of flight has enabled them to shift and adapt in response to the natural and man-made calamities inflicted on them. They have evolved cycles of breeding behaviour that match the weather patterns in different regions of the ocean, but if a cyclone wipes out their eggs and chicks, they can take to the air and start again. The sooty tern (*Sterna fuscata*) is so successful at colonizing islands that it has become the most widespread and abundant bird in the Pacific.

The male Greater frigate bird (*Fregata minor*) inflates its extravagant throat pouch as part of its sexual display.

Caroline Island, between Tahiti and the equator, has a strand where a colony of more than a million sooty terns congregate to breed. This coral atoll is at the southern end of a chain, called the Line Islands, that straddles the equator for 1000 miles. The largest island is Christmas Island, almost on the equator itself. Seventeen million sea-birds regularly nested there, until in 1982, an El Niño year, the sea was starved of fish. The breeding season was a catastrophe and the birds dispersed to distant islands. Slowly they are now returning to this giant atoll in the centre of the Pacific. Caroline Island, just to the north of the equator, is much smaller. It is the coral-fringed remnant of an ancient volcano that was once a high island like those of Fiji to the east and Tahiti to the south. Perhaps sixty million years ago, Caroline was a substantial fertile island with a tall forest nourished by rich volcanic soil and sustained by moist trade winds. It became a haven for countless species of plants and animals that arrived there from Asia, and maybe also from the American continents. Here they evolved into a unique community. In time, many of the island's endemic species were lost to the process of erosion, a natural cycle that is at work on every high island in the Pacific. The only species to survive the final demise of the high island would have been those which had retained some seagoing competence or the capacity to be dispersed through the air.

One ancient mariner survives to help us tell the tale. Green turtles are great ocean travellers, covering huge distances during their long lives. Like all reptiles, they are primordially creatures of the land and must return to the shore to mate and lay their eggs. As a solo wanderer, each turtle spends most of the year on its own, gleaning the harvests of the open sea. Islands such as Caroline serve as a focal point for the turtles' infrequent social gatherings. For millions of years a handful of beaches have been the meeting and breeding places for the species. When this pattern first evolved, Caroline was a high island cloaked in tropical forest; now it is a coral atoll that can barely keep its head above the sea. Year by year, the turtles keep faith with Caroline and come back to lay their eggs in the white coral sand of its beaches. Their duty done, they disappear one by one into the vastness of the ocean.

Caroline must have once been like Rarotonga, the largest and youngest of the southern Cooks. This kidney-shaped island is the apex of a submarine volcanic island that emerged above the surface of the sea about two million years ago. It rose almost a mile into the air, since when the mountainous centre collapsed to form a massive caldera surrounded by jagged peaks. Later the northern rim slipped into the sea and more volcanic activity changed its profile again. Today Rarotonga is one of the most striking high islands of the Pacific. Like Borabora to the east, it combines the visual appeal of a partially weathered high island cloaked in green forest with the beauty of a coastal lagoon and reef.

It is the only island in this part of the Pacific with mountains high enough to attract clouds. Almost 2000 feet above sea level, the dramatic peaks are graced by lush cloud forest which is home to several plant species unique to Rarotonga. The two most spectacular endemic species are the large Te Manga Cyrtandra (*Cyrtandra lillianae*) with its glorious lily-like flowers, and the Rarotonga sclerotheca (*Sclerotheca viridiflora*), which as its name suggests has predominantly green flowers. The forests of Rarotonga also boast some eighty-eight species of fern, four of which are found nowhere else in the world.

On the animal count, the island has collected an impressive number of snails. From fossil and other evidence, it seems that there were forty-two species of land snail in pre-European times, twenty-four of which have never been discovered anywhere else. One, called the Te Ko'u snail (*Tekoulina pricei*), is the only species known to hatch its eggs and nourish its young within its body. When it gives birth, the adult snail produces hundreds of minute but fully formed offspring. If there were other high islands nearby, this and the other endemic species of snail would surely be carried to them on the feet or the feathers of birds. Perhaps by the time Rarotonga eventually goes the way of Caroline and sinks into the sea, another new volcanic island will have burst from the ocean floor and become clothed in forest reaching to the clouds. Those species of snail which remain small enough would be transported by birds and become natives of the new land. So would the ferns and other plants with spores or seeds that can be carried through the air. The only evolutionary victims would be species that had become landlubbers.

The forests of Rarotonga have already evolved an endemic plant which has lost the ability to escape the confines of the island. The *neinei* (*Fitchia speciosa*) is a Polynesian sunflower which has its ancestral origins in South America. Today it has close relatives on Raiatea and other islands of French Polynesia, each of which boasts its own unique species. It is no mystery how it crossed the ocean. The seeds of this genus of daisies are designed for flying. Equipped with barbs which hook into the feathers of birds, they can be carried for hundreds of miles across the ocean. Tropic birds (*Phaeton* spp.) rear their young among the high forested ridges of Raiatea where fitchia daisies grow. Clinging to birds, the plant's seeds were carried westwards as far as the southern Cooks. On Rarotonga, however, the endemic *Fitchia* species has dramatically changed its form. To hold its own in the lush tall forests of this high island, it has become a tree. The *neinei* has a tall trunk supported by a network of stilt-like roots which help it reach up to the canopy of the forest. Here it produces large, brilliant-orange flowers with an abundance of nectar that attracts insects and

The Green turtle (*Chelonia mydas*) – an ancient mariner.

small birds which in turn ensure pollination. The *neinei* has become a very successful member of the Rarotongan forest but there has been a price to pay. To boost its offspring into the upper sunlit layers of the canopy, the tree-like *neinei* produces seeds of enormous proportions. More than three inches long, they are the largest daisy seeds in the world, far too large to be carried by birds, let alone by the wind. The *neinei* has 'burnt its boats' and, unless by human intervention, will be forever marooned on Rarotonga.

Of all the islands in Polynesia on which people might choose to be marooned, Rarotonga must rank high. It is extravagantly beautiful. The jagged mountain interior is lush and green but too steep for settlement. This has kept it wild. In contrast, the flat coastal plain is ideal for human habitation and horticulture. Everywhere, plantations of palms and fruit trees give an air of arcadia. In the valleys, terraced taro gardens are irrigated by a sophisticated system that diverts the mountain streams. Around the entire island is an almost continuous white beach bounded by clear shallow water and an outer reef that holds back the rumbling ocean. Today as you drive round the island's circular road lined with neat gardens brimming with flowers, you have the feeling that at dawn someone sweeps the entire island clean. After sunset, in the bars of the island's cosy capital, Avarua, drummers beat out the complex rhythms of their heritage, while in the hotels traditional Cook Island dancers gyrate beneath the gaze of Tangaroa, their well-endowed god of the sea. For centuries, Rarotonga has been central, geographically and spiritually, to the Polynesian world.

Surprisingly it was one of the last major islands to be encountered by Europeans. The most likely first arrival was the *Bounty* on its way back from the infamous mutiny in Tongan waters. Rarotonga is on the direct route from there to Tubuai in the Austral group, to which Fletcher Christian and his crew were heading. Their encounter with Rarotonga was entirely accidental as the island did not exist on Bligh's charts. From the safety of their ship the mutineers traded with the islanders. They left pumpkins and oranges, which became important crops for this island of gardeners. But Rarotonga was not the secure haven for which they were searching. To find true isolation they would have to voyage, like the ancient Polynesians, much further towards the rising sun.

Most of the mutineers had planned to head straight for Tahiti. They made no secret of their passion for the island where they had spent five glorious months. Fletcher Christian knew that word would soon get back to England about the loss of the *Bounty* and a search party would be sent to Tahiti. It

The *neinei* (*Fitchia speciosa*) – a tree-sized sunflower which has successfully 'burnt its boats' on the island of Rarotonga.

was just a matter of time before there would be a price on all their heads. The island of Tubuai, 500 miles to the south of Tahiti, seemed an ideal hide-out. When they arrived, they began to build a fort. The crew unwisely antagonized the natives in their bartering for the island's meagre stocks of food. They stole pigs and they took girls by force; many islanders were killed in angry confrontations. Fletcher Christian took the *Bounty* back to Tahiti to fetch supplies and the women they had left behind. By deceit, they persuaded the ever-generous Tahitians to stock their stolen ship with 460 pigs, 50 goats and countless chickens, dogs and cats, together with the precious bull that Cook had presented to them on his last visit. Eleven young women were invited aboard and thirteen Tahitian men stowed away until the *Bounty* was well on its way back to Tubuai. The mutineers' renewed attempts to settle this hostile island failed. The islanders continued their resistance and the crew once again became restless for Tahiti. Christian took them back and, in spite of the threat of capture, sixteen chose to stay. One night, under cover of darkness, Fletcher Christian and eight hard-line mutineers, together with a dozen or so Tahitian men, women and children, left for an unknown destination.

For two more months the *Bounty* sailed aimlessly through the South Seas, stopping to check out islands and take on supplies, until by chance, Fletcher Christian found a reference to Pitcairn. After a long sail east, they encountered this small rugged island standing on its own in the eastern Pacific, halfway between New Zealand and South America. Even the naval reference proved to be three degrees out of true. There were no established sea-routes within hundreds of miles. Here the mutineers had a chance of permanent retreat.

Lonely Pitcairn Island – last refuge for the *Bounty* mutineers.

They sailed the *Bounty* several times around the rocky outcrop searching for a safe landing. Pitcairn has no fringing coral reef and the sea swells have eroded the margins of the island into forbidding cliffs. Christian and a small party of men went ashore in the ship's cutter and landed with difficulty at a little indentation in the cliffs which would later become known as Bounty Bay. On shore his hopes were confirmed. Although Pitcairn was indeed deserted, there were signs of ancient occupation. Mature coconut palms and bread-fruit trees had been planted wherever there was space on the rugged terrain. Although stony, the soil seemed fertile and luxuriant evergreen vegetation grew over most of the island. Christian and his companions toiled to the top of the island which rises to a thousand feet. From here they looked out over a vast empty ocean. A soft warm breeze fanned the palm trees. Pitcairn was perfect.

On a peak that overlooked the *Bounty* being held offshore, they discovered the remains of a stone temple. Rocks had been carefully arranged to form a quadrangular platform and at each corner stood a human effigy carved in stone. Each had its back to the sea, its weathered features facing inland. Fearful of reprisals from these pagan spirits, the mutineers toppled the statues from their temple and rolled them over the cliff-top into the sea. Beneath the temple floor they found a human skeleton that had been interred with its head cradled on a pillow fashioned from a giant clam shell. Elsewhere, as they began to dig the foundations of their new homes, they unearthed other skeletons, together with stone adzes and shell tools. Shallow pits lined with stones confirmed where the previous occupants had built their earth-ovens. On the nearby cliffs were petroglyphs of birds and men, together with strange geometrical shapes made up of circles and stars. Whoever had once lived on this isolated outpost of Polynesia had obviously long since gone. The mutineers were now the sole inhabitants of Pitcairn.

Riding on the ocean swell, the *Bounty* stood out boldly against the sea. On an island with no bays there was nowhere to hide her. Fletcher Christian ordered everything on board to be brought ashore. The vessel was stripped of all usable pieces of timber and metal until little remained except the hull. On 23 January 1790, one of the mutineers sealed their fate. In a fit of drunkenness, Matthew Quintal set fire to the hold. The motley crew of sailors and Tahitians helplessly watched from the shore, as the *Bounty*, their lifeline to the outside world, was engulfed in flames and swallowed by the waves.

Today's Pitcairners commemorate the 23rd of January by towing a model of the *Bounty* across their 'bay' and setting it alight. It is a long time since that event and they care little for the way in which it has fired the imagination of the rest of the world. They are proud of their ancestry but indifferent to the saga that has been built around the mutiny. They are realistic about the way their tiny,

isolated community was founded and how it fared. When they settled Pitcairn, Fletcher Christian and the other eight men were not inspired by any ideals of freedom or equality. By all accounts, they treated their Tahitian companions as inferiors. Ironically, the community experienced its own bloody mutinies in which most of the mutineers, including Fletcher Christian, were killed. By 1800 only one of them was still alive. Stricken with remorse, Alexander Smith changed his name to John Adams and vowed to bring up the surviving children and their Tahitian mothers to be God-fearing Christians. He succeeded so well that by the time their secret hideaway was discovered in 1808, the fugitives had become a happy and pious people. John Adams was pardoned and allowed to fulfil his paternal role until he died in 1829.

Since being discovered by the outside world, Pitcairn has spread its population. Most of the descendants of the *Bounty* now live on Norfolk, another

Above 'Great Ears', the fishermen's god of
the Cook Islands shares the basic features common
to all *tiki* carvings of Polynesia.
Left A romantic depiction of John Adams, the repentant
Bounty mutineer, surrounded by his Polynesian
women and children on Pitcairn.

remote island nearly 4000 miles to the west. Today only about sixty men, women and children remain on Pitcairn. They are sixth-, seventh- and eighth-generation descendants of the mutineers and Christian is still an island family name. The community runs on a fragile island economy, largely subsidized by the British government and by a flourishing trade in pretty postage stamps bearing the head of the Queen. The Pitcairn language has the sound of rustic English combined with the fluency and speed of the Tahitian tongue, giving it a warm lilting texture. Pitcairn conversation is full of banter and good humour, and is renowned for its swearing, although nowadays most islanders are devout Seventh Day Adventists. Pitcairners all have strong family values and, as in any small community living cheek by jowl, there can be deep-seated animosities and rivalry. Their disarming manner easily diffuses tension and they have created their own form of social regulation.

Since the opening of the Panama canal, Pitcairn has been on the sea route to New Zealand, from where this British island is now administered. The islanders supplement their modest incomes by making carvings from *miro* and other native timber. Polished wooden fish and dolphins are popular with visiting yachts, and so are hand-carved models of the *Bounty*. In some months as many as thirty ships will halt briefly off Pitcairn; in others there are none at all. Cut off from the mainstream of life, the gentle people of Pitcairn are surprisingly worldly. On their tiny island, they lead a life which, in its own way, keeps faith with the rest of Polynesia. Christianity has replaced spiritualism and ancestor-worship. In place of chiefs and taboos, there is the Pitcairn Island Council.

The islanders collectively own two forty-foot aluminium long-boats. Called *Tin* and *Tub*, they are their life-lines launched to greet passing freighters and tourist boats. They go out with fresh fruit and vegetables, bags of mail and the carvings completed since the last ship called. They return with cash from the tourists and with domestic goods ordered months before by post.

Only occasionally do the islanders venture from the safety of Pitcairn, usually to one of the three other islands belonging to the Pitcairn group. The beautiful low atoll of Oeno, with its tranquil lagoon and white sand beaches, is seen as a perfect holiday destination by the Pitcairners. For them it is a place to get away from the bustle of life on 'mainland' Pitcairn. Ducie, the other coral atoll in the group, is further away and seldom visited. It is a temporary retreat strictly for the sea-birds that tramp this part of the Pacific. The fourth island, the largest of the group, is called by the very un-Polynesian name of Henderson. It too is composed of coral but is raised high above sea level. It was initially created some thirteen million years ago by a volcano which built up successive lava flows from the ocean floor almost two miles below. In time, Henderson's volcano became extinct and coral reefs formed on top of the sinking mountain of volcanic rock. Henderson then became a classic coral atoll. When Pitcairn erupted from the ocean bed a million or two years ago, its weight depressed the earth's crust and initiated a see-saw flexing which lifted Henderson clear of the sea, a process which is still continuing very slowly year by year.

Henderson Island is so young that perfectly preserved coral-heads stand alongside the trunks of trees that make up its forest. Almost the whole of the plateau is covered in dense vegetation. It is from here that, every year or so, the Pitcairners come to harvest *miro* wood for making their carved souvenirs. Near the southern end of the island the trees peter out and erosion has carved the stranded coral into a weird, fretted terrain of honeycombed limestone which retains neither water nor soil. At the southern extremity the combined action of rain and micro-organisms has eaten into the exposed rock like tooth decay.

Left high and dry, the ancient coral-heads of Henderson Island's former
lagoon, have been weathered into limestone sculptures.

Here tropic birds nest beneath the limestone towers and in the creeping carpet
of fleshy-leaved plants sheltering from the salt-laden wind. A recent scientific
expedition recorded seventy-two different species of flowering plants on the
island. Most of these plants arrived as seeds, either in the stomach or on the
feathers and feet of sea-birds.

In spite of its isolation, Henderson is regularly visited by migrant birds
from shores thousands of miles away. The bristle-thighed curlew (*Numenius
tahitiensis*) breeds in Siberia and Alaska and then heads south for 12 000 miles
over the most open part of the Pacific to arrive at islands such as Henderson.
Here it avoids the northern winter and finds a varied diet of fruit, insects and
crustaceans as it forages along the shoreline and on the plateau. By the time it
leaves, the curlew has put on enough weight to have reserves for the marathon
journey north to its breeding grounds. How the curlew homes in on this speck
of land is an extraordinary feat of navigation. Like the ancient Polynesian
navigators, it uses star patterns, but also has the benefit of looking down on
the ocean from an altitude of several thousand feet and spotting islands far
beyond the normal horizon.

Above Sally lightfoot crab (*Grapsus* sp.) one of the terrestrial crustaceans
that thrive on Henderson Island.
Right The Henderson warbler (*Acrocephalus taiti*) – another successful castaway.

Other ocean-going birds use Henderson as a refuge on which to raise their young. Fairy terns, petrels, tropic birds, noddies and boobies take advantage of its isolated position and the protection afforded by its height above sea level. Despite the menace of piratical frigate birds, there is little danger of freak storms and tidal waves devastating their nests. The forest on Henderson does, however, harbour predatory animals. Marauding land-crabs prowl the plateau, ever watchful for unguarded eggs and fallen nestlings. There are also rats, albeit of the less aggressive Polynesian kind. This species was established on Henderson at the time of occupation by Polynesian people over a thousand years ago. Although in some seasons the island offers plenty of native fruits and seeds, the normally vegetarian rats relish the chance of extra protein provided by sea-bird eggs and chicks. They particularly victimize the gentle petrels on Henderson, where hardly a single chick survives to adulthood.

Four species of land-bird have made this isolated island a place of international significance. Together they represent a cross-section of the avian life of Polynesia. The little Henderson fruit dove (*Ptilinopus insularis*) has developed a mutually beneficial relationship with various fruit trees on the island, just as the tooth-billed pigeon has done on Savaii in Samoa. It is a poor flyer, preferring to clamber or walk whenever possible. On a windy island such as Henderson, taking to the air could prove fatal. Natural selection favours individuals which stay in the shelter of the forest canopy. The Henderson lorikeet (*Vini stepheni*) is the island's only parrot. It uses its brush-like tongue to sup nectar from blossoms of low bushes which sprawl over the higher parts of the island. Henderson's insects support the Henderson warbler (*Acrocephalus taiti*). An estimated 15 000 breed on this relatively small island, often co-operating in the incubation and feeding of young. With this extra guarantee for survival, the species has maintained a viable population ever since its ancestral parents were cast away on this speck of land.

Of all Henderson's natural history enigmas, the species which Pitcairners call the 'chicken-bird' is the most notable. There was a time when almost every Pacific island was home to rails of one kind or another. What is so intriguing is

Above The flightless Henderson rail (*Nesophylax ater*) – marooned
but thriving in its isolation.
Left Henderson's own fruit dove (*Ptilinopus insularis*).

that most were flightless. The Henderson rail (*Nesophylax ater*) is no exception. Its ancestors must have arrived here by air and only subsequently lost the use of their wings, which are now worthless feathered stumps. In the absence of effective predators, the rail dispensed with the energy-consuming business of flying in favour of staying firmly on the ground. The Henderson rail has metaphorically 'burnt its boats' but, so far, the strategy has paid off. In the absence of any people, the breeding population of 10000 rails seems secure. Henderson Island has the distinction, along with New Zealand, of being the last refuge in this vast expanse of Polynesia where flightless birds have survived to the present day. Elsewhere, sadly, they have all gone the way of the dodo.

For what it's worth, remote, uninhabited Henderson Island has been internationally recognized as a World Heritage Site. If it is left entirely alone, its unique community of Pacific plants and animals has a chance of surviving in splendid isolation.

CHAPTER SEVEN

The LAND of MAN

After five or six weeks at sea, a landmark called the Bay of Virgins seems as good a place as any to stop and stretch the legs. From January to September a steady stream of yachts makes the 4000-mile voyage from the Panama Canal to the Marquesas Islands in the eastern Pacific. Lying just ten degrees south of the equator, this little known archipelago is on the sea route to Tahiti and the other exotic islands of the South Seas. Fatu Hiva, the most southerly of the group, is a convenient port of call. The village of Hanavave tucked in the Bay of Virgins offers yacht travellers their first hot shower and fresh food since setting out on their transpacific journey. For those heading for New Zealand, this island is just about halfway.

Unless they had made a detour to visit the Cocos or the Galapagos Islands, Fatu Hiva is their first land-fall. The spectacle of the sculptured pinnacles that tower a thousand feet above the bay might never be surpassed throughout the rest of Polynesia. Being in the direct path of the south-east trades, Fatu Hiva is the wettest of the Marquesan islands and consequently also the one with the most luxuriant vegetation. It consists of remains of two concentric volcanoes which have split and partially slipped into the sea. The surviving landscape is dramatic to the eye. From the peaks which rise more than 3000 feet, the mountainous interior plunges down towards the ocean in a series of razor-backed ridges clothed in dark green. At the island's edge, they drop sheer for hundreds of feet to a foaming cauldron of deep blue sea. Despite being so close to the equator, the Marquesas archipelago has no fringing reefs. Cold currents from the east restrict coral growth to a few sheltered north-west facing bays. The full force of winds and currents beats against the exposed cliffs, making landing

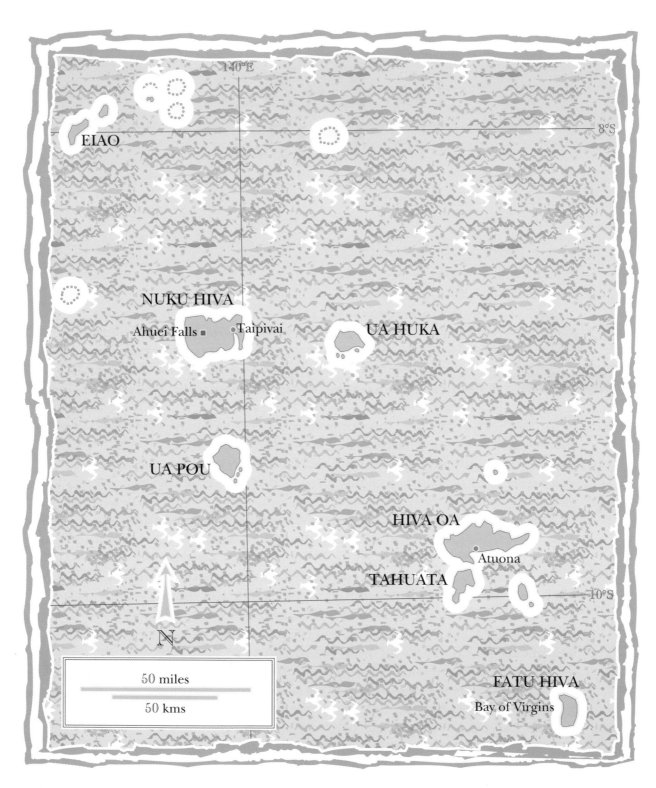

EIAO

140°E

8°S

NUKU HIVA

Ahuei Falls ■   Taipivai

UA HUKA

UA POU

HIVA OA

Atuona

TAHUATA

10°S

N

FATU HIVA

Bay of Virgins

50 miles

50 kms

dangerous. At times, the swell is too great for yachts to anchor and after sending ashore for water and provisions, the modern mariners move on.

Fatu Hiva was the first island to be sighted by Alvaro Mendana, the Spanish explorer who came here from Peru in 1595. This gives it the great distinction of being one of the first islands in Polynesia to be encountered by Europeans. Mendana at first thought that Fatu Hiva was uninhabited, but then dozens of outrigger canoes appeared, paddled by about 400 robust, fair-skinned islanders. Filled with innocent curiosity, they swarmed aboard Mendana's vessel, but ended up fleeing from gunfire. The Spanish stayed on the nearby island of Tahuata for fifteen days, during which brief time Mendana and his crew succeeded in massacring 200 natives. Before they left, they erected three large crosses and carved on a tree the date of this historic first encounter. It was Mendana who gave the islands their present name in honour of the Marquis of Mendosa, the viceroy of Peru who had sanctioned the expedition, which was heading for the Solomon Islands.

The Bay of Virgins, splendid respite for transpacific yachts.

For historians, Mendana and his Portuguese pilot, de Quiros, partly redeemed the tarnished reputation of the expedition by giving a first-hand account of their fifteen-day visit. An interesting part of what we know about pre-European life on the Marquesas is based on that brief encounter. They described the settlements with their 'well-paved avenues' and their canoes which were 'handsomely wrought out of one piece of wood with a kind of keel'. The women of the Marquesas had 'most beautiful faces, delicate hands, a good shape and slender waist; many of them far exceeding a most accomplished woman of Lima'. The islanders were considered 'white, but not ruddy' and the women were 'clad from the waist down with a sort of tunick, curiously woven of a delicate fine palm-tree leaves'. According to the Spaniards, the islanders ate 'hogs and fowls like those in Spain, sugar-canes, very fine plantains, cocoa-nuts, the bread-fruit, a fruit like chestnuts . . . many of them roasted and boiled'.

Nearly two centuries passed before there was any further mention of these remote islands. By the time that the courteous Captain Cook called at the same islands of the southern Marquesas, on his second Pacific voyage in 1774, not all the wounds of that first confrontation had healed. The islanders gave him a wary reception. Cook and his colleagues tried to make it clear that they were not in pursuit of gold or souls but were in search of scientific knowledge. Cook later wrote: '. . . but what ruined our market the most was one of them giving for a pig a very large quantity of red feathers he had got in Amsterdam, which these people much value and which the other did not know, nor did I at this time that red feathers was what they wanted'. Cook and his crew stayed only five days before sailing for the more welcoming shores of Tahiti, without ever encountering the other islands of the group, just to the north.

Some of the artefacts they collected and brought back from the Marquesas are still prized exhibits in museums around the world. In his journal, Cook estimated that the population of the southern Marquesas Islands totalled between 50000 and 100000 people, which was probably an overestimate. Today only six of the ten main islands of the entire group are inhabited and the total number of residents has fallen to 7500. The story of these wild and beautiful islands is both extraordinary and sad. To see them today, often without a person in sight, it is difficult to imagine that this isolated archipelago was once one of the most populated and successful centres of Polynesian culture.

Few of the yachting folk who call at Fatu Hiva see more than the Bay of Virgins. To reach the main village of Omoa is a strenuous but exhilarating hike with breathtaking views. From there, once a week, a speedboat takes three hours to reach the island of Hiva Oa where there is a modest airport with links to Tahiti and the outside world. The Marquesas Islands seem to be on the route to nowhere, and yet in their glorious past they were at the very hub of

Polynesia. To the north, just over 2000 miles away, lie the islands of Hawaii. Sixteen hundred miles to the south-east is lonely Easter Island, beyond which lies the coast of South America. Their nearest neighbours, the islands Pukapuka and Napuka, are part of the Tuamotu Archipelago, 300 miles due south. To the south-west, nearly 800 miles away, is Tahiti, the capital of French Polynesia to which all the Marquesas Islands were integrated in 1880.

It is to cosmopolitan Tahiti and the other Society Islands that most yachts head. Their next stop is the Cook Islands where, according to the season, they may decide to turn south-west to reach New Zealand or continue due west to Tonga, Samoa and Fiji. Unwittingly, these modern seafarers are retracing the routes of ancient Polynesian voyagers who, 2000 years ago, embarked on a series of epic migrations that in time would result in the discovery and settlement of the entire Polynesian world. For hundreds of years, the rugged islands of the Marquesas gave impetus to that voyaging culture, serving as the springboard from which it reached every corner of the vast Triangle.

It seems certain that the first inhabitants of the Marquesas Islands came from western Polynesia, most probably from Samoa, more than 2000 miles across the ocean. Unlikely though it seems, their route was against the prevailing winds and currents. Even more astonishing is the probability that this happened 2000 years ago. At the time when legions of Roman soldiers were marching through Iron Age Europe, great wooden canoes carved with Stone Age tools were forging across the world's largest ocean. To voyage from west to east, the Polynesians tacked against the prevailing winds and currents. Marquesan legends refer to their ancestors as having come from 'below' and 'up' the wind. To other sailors this meant that they had sailed from the west.

From islands such as those of Samoa, the Marquesas would have been a natural target. If the westerlies blew for a few days, they could have sailed their canoes due east; when the prevailing south-east trades resumed, they would have begun to tack against the wind. Their course not only took them eastward but gradually further north as well. It was almost inevitable that the high islands of the Marquesas, rather than those of the Society Islands, became their final destination. During their 2000-mile voyage, they would have sighted and probably landed on islands such as the northern Cooks and the southern Line Islands. Being low atolls, none of these landmarks offered more than just temporary stopovers. Ahead lay nine high islands that stretched in a chain for 200 miles at right angles to their path. Once they had found any one of the Marquesas Islands, they could easily find the others.

Although, to us, the idea of repeated voyages over such vast distances might seem improbable, they were very possible. The pioneering Polynesians who ventured from Samoa and the neighbouring islands came from a society which was founded on ocean sailing and which had fostered the concept of colonizing faraway uninhabited islands. For people living on well-populated islands in the cyclone region of the western Pacific, the prospect of another life far to the east was compelling. To them, the ocean was not an obstacle; on the contrary, it was the vehicle that carried them to their new home.

The twenty or so islands that form the Marquesas group are all of volcanic origin. Their foundations are on the ocean floor 13000 feet below. Like the Line Islands to the west and the Hawaiian chain to the north, the most recently formed islands are in the south of the group. Fatu Hiva is little more than a million years old, whereas Ei'ao in the north has existed for perhaps seven million years. All the islands are young by geological standards, which accounts for their height and ruggedness. Wind and rain have sculpted the peaks and ridges into fantastic forms. Like medieval battlements, they tower into brooding clouds, their sides painted in myriad shades of grey and green that come from the lichens and other primordial plants clinging to the rocks.

Streams cascading down from high plateaus often combine to tumble as a single waterfall. The Ahuei fall on the island of Nuku Hiva is one of the highest in the world. It spouts from the basalt rock as a single jet of water, gouging an ever deeper channel in the rim of the precipice. Before it reaches the basin over a thousand feet below, the water vaporizes into a fine mist and rain, covering the vertical walls of the canyon with a permanent gloss. Every crevice is filled with dwarf ferns that luxuriate in the fine warm fresh-water spray. Each canyon points towards the sea. Along the rock-strewn valley floors, the water weaves its downward route and seeps into the rocks and eventually out to the ocean. These valley bottoms are consequently very fertile and vegetation grows in profusion.

The leeward sides of all these high islands receive far less rain and are often barren, almost desert-like. The green forest with its hot and humid atmosphere is replaced by open slopes covered in coarse grass and scrub, where the sun can be blisteringly cruel. Like people, most of the wildlife on the Marquesas thrives in the valleys; only a few insects and lizards brave the parched north-western terrain, together with occasional flocks of opportunist pigeons.

Off the coast, the sea floor drops away almost vertically. Unrestrained by any fringing reef, the full force of the Pacific swell crashes at the base of precipitous cliffs. The redeeming features of the islands' coast are the bays. Often fiord-like, they reach like arms to meet valleys and canyons that in turn link back to the mountains. For wildlife and people these radial highways have not only provided natural access to the rugged islands but have also been the focus of life.

The Ahuei fall, in the centre of the island of Nuku Hiva, cascades
1200 feet as a single jet of water.

Admired for its elegant courtship flight, the Red-tailed tropic bird
(*Phaeton rubricauda*) is portrayed in traditional Marquesan dance.

From the mountain track that winds down to the village of Taipivai on Nuku
Hiva, you can look down on one of today's most prolific Marquesan valleys.
Well-tended plantations of coconut and banana climb in lines up the distant
slope. Along the valley bottom are homesteads with colourful gardens. In every
available space are bread-fruit and other tropical shrubs and trees. Fruit doves
(*Ptilinopus dupetithouarsii*) share in the bounty of the land and Marquesan
long-billed warblers (*Acrocephalus caffer*) sing their fluty melodies from the wild
bush that encroaches on this successful cultivation. High above the valley floor,
white-tailed tropic birds (*Phaeton lepturus*) speed from the coast carrying in
their crops the bounty of the sea. With their long tail-plumes streaming behind
them, these beautiful white birds streak towards the head of the valley, where
they rear their young. Part sea-birds, part creatures of the land, the tropic birds
are, for Marquesans, a symbol of their way of life which has focused on the
islands' fiord-bays and great canyons. Each valley and bay has developed its
own character. For people, they have special significance. When you meet a
Marquesan today, he will ask you about the valley from which you came.

As would be expected, the fauna and flora of the Marquesas has been
restricted by the extreme isolation of these young islands. Unlike Savaii, for

example, there are very few representatives of mainland Asian creatures. Only lizards, geckos and numerous insects have managed to cross so much open Pacific. There are no bats and very few birds. It has probably always been that way. As in Samoa, those species that have made land-fall have become unique to the islands. Over 100 endemic plants have been recorded on the Marquesas and even the marine life of the islands is characterized by a high degree of endemism. Many of the fish, crustaceans and molluscs that abound in the cool rich waters have evolved into novel species and because of their adaptation to these waters have made them their exclusive home.

The islands were once protected by fringing reefs. Paradoxically, it seems that, when much of the world was in the grip of the Ice Ages, this region of the Pacific enjoyed warmer water than today. Coral reefs grew around the shoreline and no doubt attracted many other tropical creatures. Some of these have survived and evolved into the endemic marine life now found in Marquesan waters. When sea levels rapidly rose about 12 000 years ago, the coral growth could not keep pace, and as the reef receded into darkness, the corals died. Today, about 300 feet down, the drowned reef is home to deep-water fish that seek shelter from surface storms and swell. Here tuna, bonito and wahoo are plentiful, together with sharks of many kinds. The waters around the Marquesas are renowned for their big and often spectacular fish. Massive manta rays cruise into the deep bays, feeding on plankton, and in the more shallow water, sting rays and spined lion-fish lurk amongst the sparse green-grey coral that has become established in a few sheltered bays. Occasionally, turtles can be seen just beneath the surface, and schools of dolphins frequently come into the bays to rest and play.

This was the natural scene that awaited the first Polynesians. When they came is hard to tell; the evidence is very slight. The oldest relic is a fireplace in a rock shelter on the island of Ua Pou. Carbon dating of the embers suggests that the fire was first lit in 150 BC, plus or minus about a hundred years. This site was on the coast but very well protected from the sea. Access must have been difficult for the inhabitants, and it is thought that it was used as a base for fishing rather than as a permanent settlement. If this evidence is supported by other similar finds, it suggests that there have been people on the Marquesas for at least 2000 years.

The very structure of these islands, together with their climate, favours the preservation and discovery of ancient sites. Compared to Tahiti and other islands with wide coastal plains, the Marquesan coastlines of 2000 years ago are rarely underwater. On Tahiti and the other Society Islands, the oldest finds date back only as far as AD 700. It is possible, however, that earlier sites could have been destroyed by storm action or erosion, or might simply still be awaiting

discovery. On the evidence available to them, many experts believe that the Marquesas had the oldest settlements in eastern Polynesia and that people came there from the west more than two millennia ago. Before they were so discourteously trespassed by the outside world, they had perhaps eighty generations in which to develop their own extraordinary island culture.

When they first arrived, the people settled near the coast. As there were no lagoons, they must have adapted their traditional fishing skills to capitalize on the marine wealth of the bays and the open sea. It is significant that, as time went on, Marquesan people became less dependent on the resources of the ocean and more committed to their crops and livestock on the land. Very few of the native plant species would have sustained them; with such precipitous coastlines, it is doubtful whether even the hardy coconut would have gained much of a natural foothold on the islands. The first people to settle the Marquesas brought their landscapes with them. It was the plants and animals aboard the Polynesian voyaging canoes that provided the essential food and raw materials to foster the infant communities.

Much of what we know about those early days has been discovered from an archaeological site on the north-east coast of Nuku Hiva. In the now deserted and very beautiful valley of Ha'atuatua, a tidal wave exposed an ancient burial area around which were traces of buildings and broken tools, some of which seem to have been brought from western Polynesia. The settlers had built low, thatched houses near the mouth of a stream. Some way inland was a small temple consisting of an oblong paved enclosure. Two basalt uprights formed an *ahu* where gods were invoked to descend and enter the stones. Around this central altar were the burial places of the first settlers. There were clear signs of cannibalism, probably of a ceremonial nature. Male skulls were specially preserved, suggesting the practice of ancestor worship. Everything about this little colony is reminiscent of post-*Lapita* settlements in Fiji and Samoa.

As they moved up the valleys, the first Marquesans fashioned new lives in unfamiliar surroundings. In front of their houses there was usually an open area, sometimes paved, where most of the day-to-day activities took place. The settlers probably continued to use pottery during the early years of settlement. Some fragments found in the oldest sites had been made in Fiji. Although the Marquesas have deposits of clay, the art of making pottery there seems to have died out, possibly because the islanders could not find suitable mineral tempers to harden their earthenware permanently. An alternative, intriguing reason is that potters may not have joined the long voyages of settlement. In time, on the

Top left Manta ray (*Birostris*).
Left Lionfish (*Pterois*).

islands of the Marquesas, like everywhere else in Polynesia, the ancestral skill of the potter was forgotten. In place of the pottery, large hollow bamboos made ideal water-containers and could be plugged to make airtight vessels for storing dried food and precious feathers.

For cooking, the traditional earth-oven continued to be the principal way of baking food. Great middens of discarded shells suggest that all kinds of shellfish were an important part of the Marquesan diet. Other artefacts of bone and beautifully fashioned mother-of-pearl were employed in fishing. Many of the fishing hooks, together with the stone adzes found from that early settlement period, suggest links with Samoa and Tonga. In the sands of Ha'atuatua, shell discs have been found which are almost identical to those incorporated in the handsome turtle-shell headdresses called *kapkap* which were also fashionable in Fiji and Melanesia more than 2000 years ago. Whether the first inhabitants of the Marquesas sailed directly from the western Pacific or migrated by an island-hopping sequence is the puzzle now facing the experts.

Marquesan society continued to develop over the next thousand years on very much the same traditional lines. People clung to the coasts and adjacent valleys, although, with increasing populations, some were forced to settle on less hospitable islands or in valleys with more difficult access. They discovered that the bread-fruit tree grew extremely well on the Marquesas. Eventually these celebrated trees, brought intentionally to the islands by the first voyagers, became the staple diet of the islanders. In no other part of Polynesia have people become so dependent on one fruit. Even today, every Marquesan family has at least one tree and in the forest there are many stands of tall bread-fruit trees which, by common assent, are regularly harvested.

The appeal of this copious fruit is that it can be prepared and stored to offset the effects of famine. The Marquesas Islands are renowned for their extremes of climate. For several years in a row, the rains can fail, bringing devastation to crops; in other years, the rains never seem to stop. The bread-fruit is ideal for conserving the good harvests of more normal years. When ripe, the football-sized fruits often weigh as much as ten pounds. Using a long forked pole with a small woven basket on the end, people picked the fruits with a simple twisting movement and lowered them to the ground to prevent bruising.

The cores were removed using sharpened bamboo tubes and the holes filled with crushed vine-leaves or salt-water to help the fruit ferment. After a day or two, the yellow outer peel was removed by scraping with peelers fashioned from cowrie shells. Bamboo blades were used to slice the softened fruit which was trampled to a pulp in a special wooden vessel lined with leaves of the *ti* plant. This was a task for the most eligible young man of the community. The bread-fruit, they believed, would store for longer if he was still a virgin.

Traditionally, only young men who are circumcised but still virgins
may tread the fermented bread-fruit in the *opua ma tauna*, the funnel-shaped
enclosure lined with banana leaves.

The final product, *ma*, was stored underground in pits known as *ua ma*. These were often faced with large flat stones and lined with plaited leaves. Protected by a covering of more stones and green leaves, the fermented *ma* would keep for months, even years.

As with the harvesting of bread-fruit trees, consumption of *ma* in times of famine was a matter of strict taboo and chiefly control. Whilst some influential families benefited from their status, many commoners died from starvation. The rigours of the Marquesan climate persist and have certainly contributed to the depopulation over the last two centuries. There must have been many other periods in the more distant past when famine forced Marquesans to leave their islands and migrate to kinder climates. It may well have been such environmental pressures that prompted successive waves of long-distance voyaging to escape the islands and spawn new communities in other parts of the Pacific.

Life on the Marquesas seems to have been relatively peaceful for more than a thousand years. Its people had learned how best to adapt their Polynesian ways to the unpredictable pattern of life on these remote islands. They had lost contact with their homelands to the west. Their ancestors were buried here on the islands which they perceived as being at the centre of their ocean world. In the north of the archipelago they called their islands 'Te Henua Enata' and in the south, 'Te Fenua Enana', which broadly translated both mean 'The Land of Man'.

At a time when European countries were locked in medieval battles, warfare broke out on the Marquesas Islands. Population pressure reached bursting-point, especially on the fertile east coasts and valleys of the larger islands. Defeated groups sought refuge in tiny, inaccessible valleys or on the arid west coasts. The smaller northern islands were colonized and Marquesan émigrés migrated south where they reached the eastern Tuamotu and Gambier Islands. There the high island of Mangareva became an important Marquesan outpost. Contacts were re-established with the Society Islands and there was probably considerable exchange of goods and ideas. The Marquesans were expanding and their well-developed culture was being carried to other parts of eastern Polynesia. What Cook and the other European explorers encountered on Tahiti was part of a civilization that most likely had roots in the wild and rugged islands of the Marquesas.

What is extraordinary about the Marquesas is the way that such apparently hostile islands generated a human society with time and energy to indulge in art and religion. During the four centuries prior to the time of Captain Cook, a culture flourished which in many ways epitomizes the social and spiritual values of all Polynesians. Experts refer to this period in Marquesan annals as the 'classic' phase. In all the principal valleys, great paved public areas were built, often with considerable collective effort. Called *tohua*, these community centres were used for ceremonial gatherings and attracted vast numbers of people. Akin to the plazas of Europe, they combined religion and entertainment and served as a focal point for the pride of the entire community. In times of war, they were used to rally local fervour and to parade victims. To capture and desecrate an enemy's *tohua* was the greatest insult that could be inflicted.

It seems that tribal competition between adjacent valleys found expression in the construction of monumental edifices which glorified the local people and their gods. Large tikis were carved in wood and stone, and a stylized human form evolved. The Marquesan tiki were characterized by bodies which were divided into three almost equal parts. The head was disproportionately large because it incarnated the power and *mana* of the god with which it was associated. The eyes were almond-shaped and greatly exaggerated, as was the stretched frog-like mouth with its protruding tongue, a symbol of provocation. The body was correspondingly short and squat, the hands clasped over a well-rounded abdomen. Below that, the bent legs gave an impression of a demon about to spring at its victim. To encounter one of these stony faces in the overgrown ruins of a Marquesan *tohua* is a sobering reminder of the power of matter over mind.

For the Marquesan craftsman, the making of any new object was an act of creation. It was a link with the past. All objects had a functional purpose, whether they were wooden bowls or warriors' clubs. Each was fashioned by talent dictated by tradition and inherited from ancestors. There was a great homogeneity of design for objects that had a common purpose. The famous war-clubs of the Marquesas that now adorn collections around the world all have the same complexity of decoration. The master craftsmen that made them were motivated and guided by the same spirits. For the same reasons, houses were constructed with great care and ceremony. The rear posts were often decorated with a geometric design and the front posts carved with human forms. The innumerable joints of the timber frame were lashed with decorative bindings made of coconut-fibre sennit. Often dyed black or yellow, these elaborate braidings are reminiscent of the *magimagi* decorations found today in Fijian houses and public buildings.

Like the Fijians, the Marquesans thought highly of the root of the *kava* plant (*Piper methysticum*). Beautifully engraved wooden bowls were used to mix the sacred drink of their ancestors. *Tapa* was also manufactured with great respect and embellished with refinements. It was often perfumed with ground sandalwood and other sweet-smelling plants, and dyed in various shades of red and yellow. Unlike Fijian bark-cloth, geometric designs were not part of

Above left Marquesan clubs, *u'u*, carved from ironwood
(*Casuarina equisetifolia*); its Marquesan name, *to'a*, means 'warrior'.
Above right The art of tattooing is enjoying a renaissance in the
islands of Eastern Polynesia; some young men proudly choose to
be inflicted with the more painful traditional techniques.
Right A scene at Nuku Hiva in the late 18th century: a woman is being
tattooed on her right hand – the boar's head is her reward.

the Marquesan tradition, possibly because this would distract from the great artistic expression of Marquesan culture, the tattoo.

Our name for this body decoration comes from the Tahitian word *tatau* and has been incorporated into most European languages. The practice was first recorded in 1769 by Captain Cook, who observed it while on Tahiti and described it in his journals with great precision. All Polynesian societies excelled in this highly decorative art. It was probably the fair skin of Polynesians, compared to Melanesians, that made their tattoos so distinctive and the practice so popular. Other people who have developed body tattooing to such an art-form include the Japanese and some people of island south-east Asia, such as the Dayaks of Sarawak. On the other side of the Pacific, some Amerindian tribes, particularly in Amazonia, were accomplished practitioners of the art. In Polynesia, it was in the Marquesas Islands and New Zealand that the skills and designs reached their artistic zenith and where the tattoo had its greatest social significance.

Generally women were less tattooed than men, but for both sexes it was expected that thighs, hands and feet should be adorned. In the Marquesas, geometrical designs were the most popular, but stylized representations of fish, birds and plants reflected their respect for nature. Intentionally, these works of art are taken by their owners to their graves. The canvas is perishable and seldom preserved. What we know about early designs has been recorded in the form of petroglyphs on rocks and cliff-faces. More recent designs were described in detail by the first European explorers. They all agree that tattooing was one of the most extraordinary aspects of Marquesan life.

Tattoos were not confined to certain ranks or classes of society, although only the most wealthy could afford the best. The tattoo artist was the *ta'ua patu tiki*, which roughly means 'expert in hammering images'. He and his entourage of helpers, the *ou'a*, had to be fed and housed as well as receiving final payment in the form of pigs, bark-cloth and valued objects such as war-clubs. Although all adults aspired to have at least some tattoos, for women it was often more of an obligation than a mark of distinction. Their right hands had to be adorned before they reached the age of twelve, so that they could be allowed to prepare *popoi* from bread-fruit and to anoint dead bodies with coconut oil. For their own part, no self-respecting woman would contemplate marrying a man who was not tattooed. The greater his decorative coverage, the greater his wealth, style and endurance of pain. From the birth of his first boy, a father would save for the day when his son would become an *opou*, a patient of the tattoo artist. In the islands today, you will hear such people referred to as 'victims', so painful and dangerous was the traditional process.

Before the appointed day, the father of the *opou* would build a special house where the tattooing would be performed. A taboo was declared and the father was required to refrain from sexual relationships. His duty was to prepare the powder from which the dark pigment would be made. In this task he could be aided by a virgin woman. Shells of the candle-nut tree (*Aleurites moluccana*), called *ama* in the Marquesas and *tutui* in Tahiti, were heated to open them up. The kernels were then placed over a fire set in specially arranged boulders over which a large smooth stone was placed in the main path of the smoke. On its underside, a thick deposit of soot built up, often to a depth of an inch or more. Scraped onto a banana leaf, it was left to dry in the sun. To make the dye, the father mixed the black powder with a little water in a polished coconut shell.

Interestingly, it is the same candle-nut kernel and the same process of soot-collecting that is used today on the Lau Islands of Fiji to make the black dye for their traditional bark-cloth designs. The geometrical shapes of Marquesan tattoos echo those of ancient Fijian art and even the intricate patterns of *Lapita* earthenware. Over a time-span of several thousand years and over a distance of several thousand miles, this perception of beauty had been carried in the collective mind of the Polynesian culture. In the Marquesas, the art-form was transferred from clothing and pottery onto the human body itself.

The *ta'ua* arrived with four or five of his disciples and the boy was laid on the ground, an assistant on each arm and leg. After outlining his designs on the body using charcoal, the artist selected his instruments from their bamboo case. He would use a selection of toothed hammers and a baton made of ironwood. The comb-like teeth of the main tools were carved from tortoise-shell or from human bones, fish-bones or the leg-bones of sea-birds such as the booby. Sometimes the *ta'ua* would employ sharks' or boars' teeth. Held in his left hand, the tattooing comb was repeatedly tapped with the baton in his right hand, in which he also held a piece of *tapa*-cloth with which he deftly wiped away the blood. The comb made a series of punctures in the skin, into which the dark pigment was encouraged to penetrate. The assistants rubbed the dye into the wounds and would often be responsible for filling in the outlined designs.

It was a very painful process but the *opou* would try to contain his agony as a sign of bravery. As the tattoo progressed, the artist chanted in rhythm to his tapping. To help soothe the pain, his assistants also chanted and played the nose flute. The more comprehensive the coverage of the body, the more assured the son would be of attracting admiration. Men would respect his bravery and women would be aroused by the beauty of his body. It would be worth the pain.

It was usual to spread the initial work over three or four months, and then to add further designs later in adulthood. After each application, the patient would experience several days of inflammation of the skin, then swelling and fever, which was sometimes fatal. Juice extracted from banana stems made an ointment called *paku* which hastened healing, and the application of hibiscus leaves relieved the inflammation. The most effective healing agent was a medicine made from the nono tree (*Morinda citrifolia*), called *noni* in the Marquesas. Related to the coffee plant, the fruit of this tree was so potent that, after the tattoo operation, it was offered to the gods at the local *me'ae*, the Marquesan equivalent to the sacred *marae* of Tahiti.

The tattooing over, the *ta'ua* was paid, the *tapu* lifted and the special house burnt. Those who had been helping to service the event were allowed to wash their bodies and apply fragrant ointments. An elaborate celebration was arranged at which all the young men and women who had been decorated with tattoos would be viewed. Friends and relatives gathered to admire the new works of art. Drums were beaten and people danced. Feasting and fornication lasted through the night. Women who had endured the ordeal of being tattooed were allowed the very special privilege of eating the flesh of hogs.

For the Marquesans, their passion for tattoos was not just an adornment of the flesh, it was an expression of their entire cultural well-being. Despite the privations of these wild and remote islands with their unpredictable climate and paucity of natural resources, they had built an astonishingly self-sufficient system. It was based on a high productivity of domestic crops and stock and an efficient organization of their society. This sound ecological and political framework supported a large population. During its 'classic' period, the economy of that handful of small, rugged islands probably sustained in excess of 50 000 people.

This density, relatively greater than many other parts of Polynesia at any time, was achieved by intelligent use of the land for agriculture in the traditional Polynesian way. Large groves of bread-fruit trees were complemented by extensive systems of terraced taro fields irrigated by water channelled from mountain streams. Surplus crops were stored and distributed by chiefly supervision. The wealth of these ruling classes was used to patronize community projects such as the building of new religious *me'ae* and vast *tohua* for communal enjoyment. The wealthy became patrons of the arts and craftsmen flourished. Monumental works of art were built in every major valley and chiefs competed with each other in their sponsorship of decorative wood-carving, the making of bark-cloth and the adornment of their bodies with elaborate tattoos. The social competition and the pressure on land led inevitably to conflict and to war. Fortifications were built at the passes into valleys and raids were launched against neighbouring tribes. Although cannibalism in the Marquesas was no doubt far less prevalent than we have been led to believe, the taking of captives must have helped preserve this symbolic victory ceremony.

It was this flamboyant society that Europeans encountered when they came to the Marquesan Islands in the late eighteenth century. Many were horrified by the apparent depravity. Here, more than anywhere else in the South Pacific, they saw a suitable case for their missionary treatment. The Reverend Robert Thomson, who spent several years on the islands, spoke for them all when he wrote of the Marquesans and their islands: 'The lights and shadows of natural scenery, with the abundant supply of produce which Providence has so bountifully bestowed upon these children of nature, are subjects of more pleasing contemplation than the field of moral degradation which now opens before us. The depraved Marquesan now stands before us, a fearful example of what man becomes when left to the sad results of his own depravity.'

In the wake of the missionaries came loggers to fell the forests of sandal-wood. With them they brought firearms and diseases that spread amongst the innocent community. Venereal diseases did not kill most people, but measles, typhus and whooping cough contaminated entire communities. Then, from North America, came whalers to raid the fertile seas around the islands. To protect their new commercial interest in the Pacific, American warships came to the Marquesas in 1813 and established a base on Nuku Hiva. They stayed for more than a year, putting great strain on the Marquesan economy which, three years earlier, had been weakened by a severe famine. When the American navy left, more Yankee whalers came, armed with alcohol and cheap trinkets to buy up the pigs and chickens that were the basis of the native economy. By the time the French annexed the ailing islands in 1842, the population had already fallen to 80000. At the end of the century, an official French report prophesied that the Marquesan race would be extinct in thirty years. A head count in 1927 revealed that the entire population of the archipelago totalled 2700 people.

Without the influence of others, the internal strife of the Marquesas would have given way to sounder political sense. It was just a matter of time. For almost 2000 years, in relative isolation, these Polynesian people had been fashioning their particular form of island ecology and social organization. Once discovered and pervaded by the outside world, this endemic system was doomed to failure and almost certain extinction. Against all odds, part of Marquesan society has adapted and survived. If you have a chance to go there, you will discover that the ancient Marquesan spirit lives in every one of the 7500 people for whom these wildly beautiful islands are home. They have a passionate pride in their long distinctively Marquesan past. In the now deserted valleys, stone tikis overgrown with vegetation speak silently of an ancient heritage. Today's Marquesan craftsmen have inherited the skills of their ancestors and the belief that to create beautiful objects is an expression of the human spirit. For all Marquesan people, these dramatic islands are still 'The Land of Man'.

A maiden from remote island Ua Pou, dressed in white tapa-cloth and with
red tail feathers adorning her hair, gracefully performs her island's traditional
dance in celebration of the tropic bird – creature of land and sea.

CHAPTER EIGHT

OUTPOST of the RISING SUN

'One has only to climb to the summit of Maunga Terevaka, the north-west volcano and the island's highest point, and scan the sea equidistant in every direction to understand why this is truly an island at the centre of the world.'

FATHER SEBASTIAN ENGLERT, Easter Island, 1965.

The flight from Tahiti to Easter Island belies its remoteness. For more than five hours, the jet speeds through darkness while its passengers sleep. If it was daytime, there would still be nothing to see except the endless ocean. For the pilot, there are no radio beacons along the way, no familiar landmarks to punctuate his course. By computer he aims for a speck of land that has the distinction of being the most solitary inhabited island in the world.

Between Tahiti, which is at the heart of Polynesia, and the coast of the South American continent lie almost 5000 miles of the Pacific Ocean. After a brief stop at Easter Island to change crews and passengers, the Lan Chile flight continues eastward for another five hours with no sight of land. Its final destination is Santiago, the capital of Chile to which Isla de Pascua now belongs. In one long day, the aircraft spans two worlds. Easter Island is conveniently halfway. From the cockpit of the Boeing 747, the triangular outline of the island, faintly visible in the pre-dawn light, seems devoid of all life. As the blood-red glow of sunrise leaks over the edge of the far horizon, electric blue runway lights suddenly beam into the sky. Like beacons in outer space, they blaze a path that points east towards the dawn.

After the tropical atmosphere of Tahiti, the cool morning air of the airport at Mataveri is refreshingly different. Gone are the swaying palms and the lush green foliage; in their place is a rolling landscape of grass. For first-time visitors there is a feeling of expectancy as they line up to have their passports stamped 'Isla de Pascua'. In place of French, the common language is now Spanish. Returning islanders, weary from their night-flight, are met by exuberant relatives chattering in the Polynesian language they call Rapa Nui. For everyone who knows the island by birth or by repute, there is a unique spirit of homecoming.

Considering its size, just fourteen miles by seven, it is extraordinary how much world attention has been attracted by this mote of land. Although we may not be quite sure in which ocean Easter Island lies, its giant stone statues are images that we immediately recognize. Intriguing, mysterious, enigmatic, they fire the imagination. Who built them and why? From where did their creators come to this lonely island, and why did they disappear? What motivated the rise of their unique culture and how did it come to such a cataclysmic end? No-one who has gone there, or simply dipped into the volumes written about it, can fail to be enthralled. The island's secrets have become public property. Like global detectives, we turn over old ground in search of new clues. The fascination does not fade with each discovery; like a giant expanding jigsaw, the riddle of Easter Island has now become part of the puzzle of our entire planet.

Above The triangular outline of Easter Island seen from the space-shuttle
as it passes high over the Pacific; the huge crater of Rano Kau
is clearly visible.
Right The mile-wide crater of Rano Kau with its fresh-water lake; the
south cliff of the caldera drops 1000 feet to the ocean.

Three volcanic cones have combined to create the island as it is today. To climb any one of them is an impressive lesson in geology. To look down from the rim of Terevaka is indeed an eye-opener; only then can you really feel the isolation. The three volcanoes, which rise 10 000 feet from the ocean floor, were created at a 'hot-spot' just to the east of the Albatross Cordillera, the great mid-oceanic ridge that runs north to south down the Pacific basin. Easter Island is moving very slowly towards South America. In this geological respect, it is the only Polynesian island to have an eastward affinity.

Terevaka is not only the highest but also the youngest cone. It first erupted about a quarter of a million years ago and it is 12 000 years since the last major volcanic activity. The lava quite clearly poured out from it in a very fast and fluid way, creating a landscape of gentle gradients as, on its southern side, the molten rock flowed towards the other two older peaks, forming the triangular shape of the entire island. From the now silent rim of Terevaka, you can look south across to the cone of Rano Kau, which is about a million years old, and due east to Poike, which has probably existed for three million years. Beyond each of them is the vastness of the ocean. Not a single feature interrupts the view to the encircling horizon. Above you is a great celestial dome which seems to be uniquely fashioned to embrace this atom of land.

In 1722, the Dutch explorer, Jacob Roggeveen, sighted the island on Easter Day and gave it that name. Had he climbed its summit, he might have been more inspired. Today's Polynesian name for the island, Rapa Nui, dates from the nineteenth century. Tahitian sailors likened it to the island of Rapa, 2400 miles to the west. The islanders still use this name, a reflection of their spiritual affinities with the rest of distant Polynesia. However, the name that most appropriately encapsulates the individuality and remoteness of this place is its more ancient title 'Te Pito o Te Henua', which came to mean 'the centre of the world'. Whoever they were, the true discoverers of this island conceived their adopted home as the physical and spiritual epicentre around which the entire universe revolved. From the top of Terevaka, this ancient name befits the island.

Amongst the many legends that abound on Easter Island, two have been consistently repeated ever since Europeans began to take interest in them. One describes the creation of the island; the other concerns the origin of its first people. A potent god called Uoke, who came from a place called Hiva, roamed the Pacific. Armed with a gigantic lever, he malevolently prised up islands and tossed them into the depths. When he attempted to do the same to Te Pito o Te Henua, he snapped his monstrous lever and fled. The fragments he left behind survive today. Similar stories are heard throughout the Pacific; they all reflect the fearful natural forces that have shaped and re-shaped the islands.

Mythology ascribes the discovery of the island to a chief named Hotu Matua who was forced to flee a 'large, warm, verdant island to the west', known by the name of Marae Renga. It seems that this was a remnant of Hiva left intact after Uoke had done his mischief there. Some versions tell of a cataclysmic tidal wave that drowned the homeland; others suggest that ecological or political pressures prompted the exodus. These ingredients, reinforced by the name 'Hiva', suggest the Marquesas as a possible point of departure, but the islands of Pitcairn and Mangareva to the west are geographically closer. To sail so far east and encounter such a tiny speck of land, would have required great tenacity and seafaring skills. To have rafted or sailed from the coast of South America, as Thor Heyerdahl maintains, would have had the benefit of winds and currents on the outward voyage but also the constant fear of being unable to return. Sailing from the west would have been against prevailing winds, but was accompanied by the reassurance of being able to turn back. Either way, the chances of discovering Easter Island seem very remote, but once discovered by accident, it is marginally easier to find again. If the original people of Easter Island are essentially Polynesian, then the logical conclusion is that they came from the west. Following the rising sun in search of new islands, Easter Island became their final outpost. The next stop would have been the coast of South America.

Legend holds that before Hotu Matua came to Easter Island, a reconnaissance voyage was made from Hiva. Six young men were sent to explore an island that had been seen in a dream. Unimpressed by what they found, the party prepared to return to Hiva, but discovered that Hotu Matua had arrived in his double canoe with his wife and a large party of colonists. This part of the legend neatly avoids the need for a return voyage, but probably accurately reflects the accidental circumstances of first settlement. Hotu Matua and his people disembarked on the beach at Anakena on the north coast, the only really safe anchorage. Here his master builder, Nuku Kehu, built the first of the distinctive Easter Island houses, called *hare paenga*. The wife of Nuku Kehu had been left on Hiva and every evening he was saddened by the setting of the sun as it disappeared in the direction of his homeland.

If they had come from the Marquesas, settling this new island would have presented quite a challenge. Tradition says that as soon as they set foot on land, they began to plant the crops brought with them on their canoe. Easter Island lies just south of the Tropic of Capricorn and, compared to the Marquesan Islands, has a more temperate climate. Temperatures are moderated by the cool Humboldt current and it is often very windy. Drizzles and mists are common and heavy dew forms overnight. Rains are possible all year round, but the porous volcanic rock soon absorbs the downpours. As a result, there are no permanently flowing streams. Most water disappears underground to emerge around the rim of the island, which is probably why nearly all the ancient settlements were near the coast. In spite of its exposed position, Easter Island is potentially quite fertile.

Today's bare landscape is man-made; but at the time it was settled, the island was covered in woodland which, because of its remoteness, had a very limited range of trees. Palms had certainly arrived naturally; complete trunks have been preserved in lava from eruptions that took place many thousands of years ago. It seems, however, that this was a species that would have been completely unknown to Polynesians from the west. The lake sediments of Rano Raraku contain huge quantities of pollen from an extinct palm related to the Chilean wine palm (*Jubaea chilensis*). As its name suggests, this is a native of South America, where it grows as far south as Valparaiso in Chile, making it the world's most southerly palm tree. It has a smooth trunk with a diameter that often reaches three feet or more and it can tower more than seventy feet, where a crown of large feather-like leaves contains clusters of its fruits. Like the coconut, each of these fruits has an outer fibrous layer which protects the hard-shelled nut. The native Chileans regard this, their only palm tree, as a great source of food. The trunk produces a sap that can be concentrated to make a delicious palm honey and sugar, which can be fermented into wine while the oily kernel of the nut is prized as a delicacy. Almost identical nuts have been recently discovered fossilized in a lava cave on the Poike peninsula of Easter Island. It seems likely that the cluster of thirty-five fossil nuts was a cache stored in the cave as food. Most of them bear the marks of teeth, others are pierced by neat holes in the shell. It appears that they had been gnawed by rats.

The mystery palm tree became extinct on Easter Island six or seven hundred years ago. When the first settlers arrived it was the most conspicuous and useful tree; not only did it provide oils and sugars, but its timber must have been invaluable for fuel and for building houses and boats. Very few of the tree species imported by the settlers had a chance of surviving in this climate. It proved too cold for bread-fruit, a traditional staple food; even coconut grows poorly this far south. Other important plants such as the paper-mulberry, used for making bark-cloth, might not have taken in this cold, windy place. Bananas, however, do well and today the islanders cultivate several varieties. Forty varieties of yam and fourteen different taro roots were also known to the islanders in earlier times, and sugar-cane and the sweet-tasting *ti* plant probably fared reasonably well.

Thick beds of totora bulrush (*Scirpus riparius*), blown in as seeds from South America, have been growing for at least 35 000 years in the fresh-water lakes of the main craters. One South American plant whose presence defies convincing explanation is the sweet potato (*Ipomoea batatas*). Its origins lie in the High Andes but it was growing in several parts of Polynesia long before the Europeans could have introduced it. It became an important root-crop on islands where the climate did not favour bread-fruit, places such as Hawaii, New Zealand and Easter Island. The people of Easter Island adopted it as their staple root-crop and developed twenty-five varieties.

How it came to be anywhere in pre-European Polynesia is a mystery. The general Polynesian name for the plant is *kumara*; some Indian tribes of Peru call it *kumar*. Thor Heyerdahl reasonably argues that it came with the first people who sailed out from the coast of South America; others are equally adamant that it must have been brought back by Polynesians who accidentally voyaged to the eastern limit of the Pacific and returned with the root-crop as a valuable trophy. Whichever is right, it seems an oversight that the ancient travellers to or from South America did not pick up seeds of other equally useful South American plants. The diet of most North and South American Indians is based on maize, beans and squashes. It seems extraordinary that none of these found their way to Polynesia along with the sweet potato.

All products of the soil which can be eaten are known on Easter Island as *inaki*. They serve as accompaniments to meat. In legends there is no mention of pigs or dogs; if they were brought to the island by the first settlers, they seem not to have survived for long. A traditional island tale describes how Hotu Matua longed for his native Hiva which he remembered as 'a land of much food and greasy lips'. Anyone coming from the Marquesas without their pigs would feel that way. No pig or dog bones have been found in the ancient middens on which the islanders discarded their refuse. Chicken bones are common, as are the bones of wild birds such as rails and pigeons, long since eaten to extinction. Surprisingly, the most conspicuous bones in all these ancient refuse-tips are those of rats. The little Polynesian rat, called *kio'e* on Easter Island, must have come with the first settlers. Intentionally released into the bush, it would have bred like all rodents do and, in the absence of natural predators, would soon have overrun the entire island. Land-birds, such as rails, became victims of these new invaders and many sea-birds would have been forced to breed on the tiny offshore islands.

In time, as the native birds became extinct or inaccessible, the islanders relied increasingly on their domestic fowl, which they called *moa*, and on the resources of the sea. Unlike the Marquesas, where with time the islanders invested more effort in cultivation than in fishing, here on Easter Island deep-sea fishing became vital to support the growing population. Large tuna, called *kahi* by the islanders, patrol the offshore waters, together with bonito and many other ocean fish attracted by the food-laden currents that well up around the island. As with the Marquesas and Pitcairn, there is no protecting coral reef. Fishing was a treacherous business which must have lost many Easter Island men to the open ocean.

Because of the absence of large hardwood trees, their canoes were built of small planks adzed to a perfect fit and sewn together with hibiscus fibre. Perhaps because coconut palms did not grow well, the traditional Polynesian sennit made from husk fibres was not used on Easter Island. As fishing became more and more essential to support the community, the chiefs imposed strict taboos on tuna and other game fish between May and September. Some Easter Islanders still believe that they will be afflicted with *mare*, a kind of asthma, if they break this ancient rule. Catching smaller fish with nets was possible in the shallower water off the south coast but the great number of different fish-hooks found at old settlements suggests that shore fishing with lines was the most usual and probably the safest way of harvesting the sea.

With no pigs and dogs, human bones were sharpened and re-curved to make fish-hooks; other popular materials used to fashion hooks included basalt stone, which was tough and fine-grained and could be beautifully ground and polished. Obsidian, a volcanic glass rarely found on Pacific islands, was abundant in the Maunga Orito quarry. Its sharp edge was perfect for cutting, scraping, drilling and filing these handsome but very practical fishing tools. Obsidian was also used for carving wood, for fashioning eyed-needles from human and bird bones and for making the *uhi tatu* with which the islanders practised the traditional art of tattooing their bodies. Although many of these artefacts were devised in response to the special requirements and mineral resources of Easter Island, there are conspicuous links with the designs and techniques of the Marquesas. A distinctive harpoon-head found very recently near the beach at Anakena is identical in design with a form known from the Marquesas.

The early settlements consisted of a number of low elliptical dwellings, the more elaborate of which had sturdy foundations of large, precisely fitting basalt blocks. Their top surfaces were drilled with holes, several inches in diameter, into which were inserted stout wooden poles, bent and lashed together to form the curved roof-ridge, which was then thatched. These houses, the *hare paenga*, were entered by crawling through a small tunnel. To give added protection from the wind, there were no windows. The whole structure looked rather like an upturned canoe.

There were circular and rectangular houses too, and they were usually all clustered in lines around small plazas. Most daytime activities took place out-side, including the cooking of food in the stone-lined earth-ovens, the *umu pae*. Hundreds have been found across the island. Chicken and fish would have been baked in just the same way as people have done for thousands of years across Polynesia and the western Pacific. Although Easter Island has a good source of workable clay, the islanders have never made pottery. Unlike the contemporary native peoples of South America, they had no knowledge of the skill.

The first Easter Islanders brought neither pigs nor pottery, but they came with an obsession for building monuments to honour their ancestral spirits and gods. Their new home was geologically blessed with volcanic rock which could be cut by hand and fashioned into building blocks and sculptured forms. Whereas other island cultures had mainly carved in wood, the craftsmen of Easter Island developed their special skills in stone. Their monumental works of art are awe-inspiring. To explore Easter Island is like visiting a vast open-air museum; every corner of the island has an ancient archaeological site which enthrals the eye and stimulates the mind. It is a place to conclude a trip through Polynesia; it is not a starting point. To have seen some of the other islands with their own particular cultures and archaeological remains gives an insight into the extraordinary achievements of the people on this most remote of islands. They clearly came with preconceived ideas and with traditional skills. They brought with them their ancestral religion and their mythology, their language and their artistic values. They came with tools and the knowledge of how to use them. On Easter Island, they developed their ideas and skills in complete

Top and above Petroglyph rocks at Orongo; the images of the ancient
god *Makemake* and of 'birdmen' date from the time when each spring,
the island celebrated the arrival of the migratory Sooty tern by a daring
competition between young men to scale the cliffs, swim to the furthest
offshore islet and bring back the first elusive egg. The sponsor of the
winner became the island's powerful and sacred birdman for that year.

isolation. In time, these people created their own extravagant works of art which were expressions of their special place at the very centre of the world.

Evidence from carbon-dating and a few other clues about the island's culture have placed the first settlement at some time between AD 400 and 500, but very little is known in detail about their way of life at that early time. Archaeological excavations at Anakena have shown that there was indeed an ancient settlement there, just as legend relates. The bulk of the discoveries refer to more recent times, but expert interpretation has produced a scenario which traces the development of the island's culture during the thirteen centuries between first settlement and the arrival of Europeans. Because the islanders had no written language that we can understand, this long and eventful period in the extraordinary saga of Easter Island is referred to as its 'pre-history'. No other place in the world is less deserving of such an inappropriate term to describe its illustrious past.

It must have taken several generations for the first inhabitants of Easter Island to adjust to their new world. The cool wet winters and the hot dry summers put unfamiliar strains on the people and their crops. There were undoubtably many failed harvests and lean times. Traditional techniques of cultivation had to be adapted to suit the new environment. The scarcity of free-flowing water limited their ambitions; the shortage of hard timber taxed their ingenuity. Colonizing a new land was not easy; on Easter Island the process probably took centuries.

The sheltered, sandy beach at Anakena where Hotu Matua, the first king of Easter Island, is believed to have landed. The 25-ton *moai* was restored to its platform by Thor Heyerdahl's 1955 celebrated archaeological expedition.

In time, with a faster growing population and a practical division of labour between its various groups, a structured society was established. As well as the chiefly groups, there were now various other acknowledged social orders. Those people who were primarily devoted to the cultivation of the land were known as *Tangata heuheu henua* whereas those men, and their families, who fished in boats were called *Tangata terevaka*. There were priests and tattooists, master craftsmen to build canoes and construct houses, stonemasons to sculpt rock, toolmakers and carvers, musicians and orators. All these artisans and artists needed to be fed. It was the task of the chiefs to motivate and regulate society to ensure that it worked to the common good. Just as in the Marquesas and elsewhere in Polynesia, it was this powerful chiefdom which capitalized on surplus production and channelled time and labour into community projects. Here on Easter Island the chiefs became patrons of one of the greatest building projects ever known in the world.

It seems that by AD 1000, at about the time of the Norman Conquest, the characteristic monumental stonework of Easter Island was well under way. There were already several types of temples, each of which had a particular significance in the religious life of the island. Some were for the performing of religious ceremonies and the communing with gods, spirits and ancestors. Others were for ritual sacrifices or for the burial and cremation of deceased people. The basic type of temple was the *ahu* which to all intents and purposes was the same as the *marae* of Tahiti and the Marquesas. They were individually built and owned by the different kin-groups which had set up small communities where there were good sources of water and safe landing places. About 300 of them formed a line around the island; very few were built inland. Some were rebuilt on the rubble of a previous creation. Over the centuries, styles changed; fashion no doubt played an important part in their construction.

As Easter Island society became more affluent, the more successful kin-groups and communities expressed their wealth in stone. The most spectacular innovation was the *ahu moai*. These temples had platforms on which were placed the *moai*, the statues for which Easter Island became so famous. Each temple was different but they all had a basic common structure. The most constant feature was a narrow flat-topped platform. Some were 600 feet long, up to 15 feet wide and as much as 25 feet high. The walls were usually constructed of closely fitting stones or specially cut blocks which were sometimes engineered with amazing accuracy. At one end of some platforms, were placed enormous flat slabs of rock which acted as the pedestals for the statues themselves.

The *moai* are believed to have represented revered ancestors and deceased chiefs. Like the carved tiki elsewhere in Polynesia, they were not intended to

The seven statues of *Ahu Akivi*, one of the few inland platforms, were re-erected
in 1960 by archaeologist William Mulloy with the help of islanders.

resemble specific people, but were perceived as 'mediums' in which the spirits
could reside. On other islands such as the Marquesas, Raivavae in the Australs
and on Pitcairn, there were once stone statues with conspicuous human forms.
Those on Easter Island were not only much larger but were carved in a unique
style. Although each statue is subtly different, they all have the same distinctive
features which make them peculiar to this island. They are all legless figures
which stand on a flat base at about the level of their hips. Their long arms hang
stiffly at their sides, and their elongated hands with slender fingers are stretched
towards each other across an extended abdomen on which the navel is
accentuated. It was in the belly that much ancestral knowledge was believed to
be carried. Although the general physique of the *moai* is masculine, the nipples
of the breasts are usually clearly defined. On their backs are carved geometric
designs reminiscent of tattoos. The head is disproportionately large and
elongated, with a very prominent manly chin. The mouth is pursed and tight-
lipped. The ears have elongated lobes and the prominent nose has flared nostrils.
The eyes are deep-set beneath heavy brows.

Only when the statues had been erected on platforms were the faces carved with eye-sockets. It seems that many, if not all, of these were then fitted with eyes fashioned from white coral, with an iris of red scoria rock or black obsidian. With these staring eyes in place, the statues took on a very different appearance. Instead of being lifeless, brooding forms, they became powerful figures. It is thought that they gazed slightly up towards the sky. Most of them faced inland, overseeing the settlements that had created them. In all, a thousand *moai* have survived in varying stages of construction or demolition, including 150 that remain unfinished in the island's sacred quarry, Rano Raraku. There the largest of them, sixty-five feet long, still lies where it was carved; weighing 270 tons it was probably too heavy to be moved.

To walk up the escarpment of the Rano Raraku crater is the highlight of a visit to Easter Island. It is here that for centuries the stonemasons laboured to create their works of art. All around you stand silent reminders of that ancient industry. On the southern outside slope of the crater dozens of finished statues face out over the island. When completed, each *moai* was stood erect in a specially prepared hole, ready to be transported to its final destination. On the upper parts of the slope are other statues in different stages of production. Some are barely started, just outlines in the rock; others are ready to be severed from the quarry and lowered down the slope.

The yellow-brown volcanic rock of Rano Raraku is composed of compressed ash and small fragments of lava. When exposed to the weather its surface becomes iron-hard, but when freshly worked, it is not much tougher than chalk. The figures were carved on their backs, with their bases usually pointing downhill. As each torso was sculpted, a spine of rock was retained along its back, securely attached to the bedrock. The last blows of the pick freed the figure from the side of the volcano.

Various suggestions have been made about the methods employed to transport the statues from the quarry. It is probable that the islanders used a well-proven system of ropes and posts to haul and lever them over the rocky terrain. Trunks of the native palm tree would have made perfect rollers; other statues may have been hauled overland on timber sledges. The key to success was a plentiful and experienced work-force and an endless supply of timber and rope. The only plant that was suitable for making cordage on the island was the shrub that the islanders called *hau*, a form of hibiscus with a fibrous inner bark. Another source of material from which they made rope were the leafy crowns of the now extinct wine palm. The supply of rock was as large as the volcano itself. The enterprise was limited only by the energies of the craftsmen and the renewable natural resources needed to motivate them and their creations.

Above A fallen statue at Hotu-iti bay; in the distance is the volcanic crater
of Rano Raraku, the quarry where the statues were carved.
Right In March 1774, Captain Cook came to Easter Island. Expedition artist,
William Hodges, produced this painting of a row of statues, some still
complete with red scoria topknots. The fallen masonry and human bones
and skull are evidence that Easter Island society was already in decline.

Isolated, windswept Easter Island became a productive, wealthy land. By
AD 1600, with most of the major monuments in place, the island must have
looked spectacular. On almost every promontory and at the head of every
beach was a row of magnificently carved *moai* standing at the focal point of
their *ahu*. These stone gods, skilfully and lovingly fashioned from the very
fabric of the island, watched over the lives of the people who had created
them. Each kin-group, and each small settlement of this close-knit island
community, was proud of its local accomplishment. Although peace reigned
across the island, there was healthy rivalry between neighbours. Such
competition is part of human nature. Chiefs wished to be seen to be wealthy;
they enjoyed the mantle of public acclaim. The greater and more lavish their
patronage, the greater became their personal prestige.

More and more statues were commissioned from the quarry, each one
bigger and better than those already delivered. Embellishments were devised in
the form of more elaborate carved designs on the backs of the *moai* and in the
placing of topknots on their heads. These *pukao* were the crowning glories of
the more recently carved statues. Hewn from the soft red scoria rock of the
quarry at Puna Pau, the cylindrical blocks are thought to have represented hats

or even the red hair of some chiefly clans. Feathered headdresses were worn by warriors and, as in the rest of Polynesia and beyond, red was a treasured colour, identified with the spiritual power of the gods. Some of these massive blocks weighed more than ten tons. Lifting them into place on the heads of the *moai* was a feat of engineering which still defies explanation. Only the most wealthy and extrovert leader could afford this ultimate adornment. On Easter Island, human society had become decadent.

At the peak of the statue-building era, the island's population had reached 10 000, perhaps even twice that figure. The coastal areas were overcrowded and settlements had sprung up further inland. Most of the woodland had been felled and burned to make way for crops; as the trees disappeared, the irregular rains leached out minerals from the volcanic soil and the incessant winds blew away the valuable loam. Competition for food and natural resources led to in-fighting as each small community defended its land and the *ahu* which symbolized its identity. Trees that could act as poles and rollers for transporting the sacred *moai* became precious possessions; only on Easter Island does the Polynesian word *rakau* mean both 'tree' and 'wealth'. Even the humble *hau*, for centuries their source of rope, became like gold. With no timber for house-frames, most people built shelters of stone or simply lived in caves. As meat became a luxury, chickens were protected from thieves by confining them to stone-walled pens.

For a time the island's collective allegiance to its self-centred cult held it back from outright warfare. Then came revolution. Starved of patronage, the stonemasons laid down their tools. Tradition tells of a bloody battle at Poike between the *hanau eepe* and the *hanau momoko*, translated as the 'long-ears' and the 'short-ears'. This legend has formed the basis of much archaeological debate and has been embellished in numerous articles and books. Hollywood has descended on Easter Island to perpetuate the myth on film. There were many violent clashes between rival clans all over the island, but there is no clear evidence of a battle at Poike ditch. The traditional name for this ditch, which is undoubtably part natural feature, part man-made, is *Ko te Umu o te Hanau Eepe*, which means 'the earth-oven of the Hanau Eepe'. The legend states that this is where the island's ruling class met their well-deserved end, burnt alive in the flaming ditch. Heyerdahl found conclusive evidence of extensive fires which he maintains validates the myth. Others claim that the traditional name of the ditch means just what it says; it was simply a convenient place to prepare food for the armies of stonemasons working in the nearby Rano Raraku quarry.

There were certainly two distinct classes of islanders, the chiefs and the commoners. The ruling people, the *hanau eepe* were the well-built, well-heeled, well-fed, upper class; the word *eepe* in fact means 'heavy set', not 'long-eared'. Slightly built and no doubt stunted by a poor diet, and bowed from generations of servility, the working-class majority were disparagingly known as the *hanau momoko*. This word did not refer to the size of their ears but derived from the Polynesian name for the lizard. Each of the island's clans would have consisted of a privileged chiefly minority and a greater mass of hard-working commoners. When times became hard on Easter Island and food supplies ran short, it is feasible that the long-suffering *momoko* rose up collectively against oppressive masters.

Whatever the motivation, the *hanau eepe* were overthrown; so were their statues. The master stone-carvers whose ancestors had for centuries sculpted religious monuments now made weapons of war. The *mata'a* was a large spearhead made of obsidian. Attached to a short handle, it became a dagger for close, hand-to-hand combat; on a longer shaft, it served as a lethal spear. Tens of thousands are scattered across this tiny island. Other men favoured the use of wooden clubs called *pa'oa*. These were short, flattened weapons with tapered edges, much like the medieval cutlass and equally effective in splitting skulls.

Anarchy reigned as *matatoa* warriors terrorized the island.

In all this ferment, there must have been many who wished to escape. Even an island at the centre of the world has a horizon beyond which there is hope. The conflicts raged on for almost a hundred years. During that time many attempts must have been launched to find another life. Following the true Polynesian way, people's eyes turned again towards the rising sun. This time the strategy failed. In the orgy of decadence, they had cut their traditional lifeline. When their ancestors had come to this island, more than a thousand years before, it had been cloaked in forest. Now, with the island's economy in ruins, there was no means of escape. They no longer had timber from which to construct seagoing canoes to carry them away. Whether to transport a sacred *moai*, to make weapons of war or simply to fuel their domestic fires, the final tree had been felled. Whoever executed that irrevocable act had committed the island to its fate. Their isolation was final. No other island society had so effectively 'burnt its boats'.

By the time it was discovered by the outside world, this vibrant, creative culture was almost extinct. When Captain Cook visited the island in 1774, the violent breakdown of its society had taken a heavy toll. Most of the statues had been toppled and the people lived in fear of their lives. Anarchical power was in the hands of fearsome warriors known as *matatoa*, who around AD 1600 had taken over the island and instituted their own cult of the 'Birdman'. They had terrorized the population and subjected them to horrifying treatment. The

defeated clans cowered in caves where the marauding victors fell on them like piratical birds of prey. There are clear signs of cannibalism. At the site of Tongariki, archaeologists have uncovered an earth-oven with the cut and charred bones of a child. Cook and his crew stayed only four days before sailing towards the welcoming shores of Tahiti.

Today, Easter Island has an extraordinary beauty. If you have a chance to visit this island at the 'centre of the world', climb to the rim of Rano Raraku, 500 feet above the plain, and look down into the extinct crater. From there, the sad fate of Easter Island is startlingly apparent. All along the inside slope of the southern wall are statues in different stages of construction. Those that are upright face the tranquil crater lake; others lie staring at the sky. Every one of those stone giants was destined to be hauled for several miles across the island. Hundreds had gone before them; nearly 400 still stand in the silent quarry, waiting to be moved. To pause for a moment on the highest point of the crater rim, with the ocean behind you and this spectacle laid at your feet, is a sobering lesson in the fragility of man.

The prevailing winds blow hard against the sacred crater of Rano Raraku. A solitary frigate bird, caught in the updraught from the ocean, rises to the rim. Hovering motionless, it looks down into the silent quarry where, for centuries, countless men toiled for the glory of their gods. Then, tipping its wings against the wind, this free spirit sets off across the restless sea.

CHAPTER NINE

The THEFT of PARADISE

Straddling the Tropic of Cancer in the immense expanse of the North Pacific, the Hawaiian chain of islands is the most isolated archipelago in the world. The coast of North America lies almost 2500 miles to the east, while Japan, on the other rim of the Pacific, is about 3500 miles away. Due south, almost on the equator, is Christmas Island, beyond which lie the many archipelagos of the South Pacific. It is from such places that curlews and other migratory birds fly north each year. For some, the Hawaiian islands are a convenient pit-stop at which to rest and refuel before continuing their marathon flight to breeding grounds in Alaska. For a few days they mingle with other creatures that have also discovered these oases of land in the vast desert of sea. For many of these species, this archipelago has been a permanent home for millions of years.

In all, there are 132 Hawaiian islands; most are small outcrops or sandy keys and reefs. The eight principal islands at the eastern end of the archipelago make up ninety-nine per cent of the land. The others are strung out in a chain that extends westward for 1600 miles. Together they form a classic geological sequence. Their creation began tens of millions of years ago; no-one can be sure how old the oldest underwater peaks might be. From a 'hot-spot' on the ocean floor, molten magma poured from the earth's crust and created a massive mountain range. By the time the peaks broke the surface of the sea, they had already risen more than 15000 feet from the bottom of the ocean; many went on rising, as more lava flowed from their volcanic cones. Today, the two largest peaks, Mauna Kea and Mauna Loa, are both more than 30000 feet from the ocean floor. This gives them the distinction of being higher above their base than Mount Everest is above its own continental foundation.

NIIHAU

KAUAI

Kauai Channel

OAHU

Honolulu

Kaiwi

MIDWAY

PEARL AND
HERMES REEF

HAWAIIAN

NORTH PACIFIC
OCEAN

LISIANSKI   LAYSAN

MARO REEF

GARDNER PINNACLES

ISLANDS

FRENCH FRIGATE SHOALS

NECKER

NIHOA

KAUAI

NIIHAU

OAHU

MOLOKAI

LANAI   MAUI

HAWAII

Channel

MOLOKAI

MAUI

LANAI

Haleakala

▲

Alenuihaha Channel

KAHOOLAWE

HAWAII

Mauna Kea ▲

Hilo ●

KONA COAST

▲ *Mauna Loa*

N

50 miles

50 kms

The largest Hawaiian island is also the youngest; appropriately known as Big Island, it is the one from which the entire chain takes its name. Poised almost directly above the geological 'hot-spot', this massive mountain is growing daily with new lava. Two of its volcanoes, the giant Mauna Loa and the smaller Kilauea, are linked directly to the source of the magma, which frequently erupts to the surface or beneath the sea just off the south-east coast. These are two of the most active volcanoes in the world. Sometimes magma forces a way through lateral vents in the mountain, spewing molten lava, hot gases and cinders into the forest, from where the lava stream flows swiftly towards the sea. On leaving their fissures the red-hot streams pick up speed and pour over the surface of the ground. The outer layers cool, solidify and come to a halt; but inside the hardened crust, a fluid core of lava continues to flow downhill. Even after the eruption has ended, this molten core may continue to drain away, leaving an empty tunnel through the solid volcanic rock. If they reach the coast, the hot-headed tongues of molten lava hiss and spit at their meeting with the sea. Strange contorted shapes and underwater vaults are fashioned as the volcano's fiery fervour is doused by the ocean. There are few places in the world where the earth's crucible so dramatically performs its alchemy for us all to see.

The ocean floor beneath Hawaii is slowly moving to the west. Every year each island in the chain is carried two or three inches further from the deep-seated source of the magma. In time the volcanoes die and become victims of the natural process of erosion. Beneath the surface, their immense bulk collapses to the ocean floor; above, the forces of wind and waves, sun and rain combine to steal away the land. As with other chains of tropical islands, all that eventually remains is a coral atoll. In time, that too is reclaimed by the ocean. From Big Island, which is still growing, to the most distant atoll in the chain, represents a time span of perhaps forty million years. Beyond that most westerly point, there are underwater mountains which, in much earlier epochs, were the high volcanic peaks of the first Hawaii.

It is this ancient lineage combined with their extreme isolation that gives these islands their unique character. As one island is reclaimed by the sea, another erupts from the ocean floor. Like an endless geological conveyor belt, a procession of land-forms from high mountains to flat atolls has been moving steadily through time. Throughout its long natural history this fleet of islands has offered plants and animals an uninterrupted array of rich tropical habitats. This ecological continuity has made the Hawaiian archipelago one of the world's great living museums of evolution.

It seems certain that these oceanic islands were never connected with the continents on either side, and that no vanished lands can help account for the presence of wildlife on them. Every species of animal and plant must have arrived across the vastness of the ocean, either in the air or across the waves. The remoteness of Hawaii has restricted its native flora and fauna to those species which could be naturally dispersed over very long distances. There are no native land-reptiles and no amphibians. The tiny mouse-sized Hoary bat (*Lasiurus cinereus*) is the only land-mammal that has made the crossing on its own. From North America, it was swept to Hawaii on its delicate twelve-inch wing span, and it flourished on the multitude of insects for which these islands are renowned. There it evolved in isolation and is now very different from any other bat in the world.

Today, most plants, insects, molluscs and birds that naturally occur on the Hawaiian islands are endemic. The statistical chance of arriving at the islands was very small; but having successfully become established, each new species thrived because there was so little competition. Each colonizing species diversified to take advantage of the great variety of ecological opportunities offered by the chain of islands. In time, a single species evolved into a wide range of related, but subtly different, variations. There are now more than 10 000 distinct species of insects on the islands, all of which are reckoned to have evolved from no more than 250 original pioneer species. With a few exceptions, such as crickets and grasshoppers, today's Hawaiian insects are all diminutive. This suggests that their ancestors were tiny wind-blown adult immigrants; larger insects are more likely to have arrived as eggs stuck on the feet or feathers of birds. Hawaii's 1061 endemic species of snails and other molluscs evolved from ancestors which crossed the ocean in the same way. Like the insects, they all evolved from miniature ancestors.

Hawaii's flora tells a similar story. Its 1394 endemic species of seed-plants and 119 endemic species of ferns nearly all have seeds or spores which are light enough to be carried entirely by the wind; others may have originally been brought by birds. Not surprisingly, it was also birds which became the most conspicuous inhabitants of these remote islands. Forty-six species of bird now live on Hawaii that are found nowhere else in the world. These endemic species all evolved from ancestors which, incredibly, flew to the islands long ago and began an extraordinary process of evolutionary adaptation and radiation.

If Charles Darwin had visited these islands before he went to the Galapagos, he would surely have been inspired by their remarkable natural history. On the Galapagos Islands, he used the great variety of finches to help illustrate the basic principles of biological evolution. On Hawaii he would have certainly chosen the Hawaiian honeycreepers. This family of birds (*Drepanididae*) is unique to Hawaii and is assumed to have evolved there from a single ancestral founding species. More than forty species and subspecies have been identified as direct descendants of the original honeycreepers that blew in to these islands. Experts

do not agree about the direction of their origin. It was at first assumed that they came from North America, but Asia now looks more likely. Whichever way they came, only a single pair need have made land-fall. The different species evolved in response to the great diversity of habitats and food available to them. It is their bills which show the most marked range of adaptation. Some are short and thick for crushing seeds; others are long and delicate for sipping nectar. Various honeycreepers prospered on all the main islands, where they expanded to take advantage of every suitable ecological niche.

The same story can be told of all the other groups of plants and animals that became natives of these islands. Its insects and spiders, rainforest trees and alpine plants are nearly all unique to Hawaii. With the coming of people to the islands, this astonishing evolutionary extravaganza was destined to end.

The islands offered a similar richness and diversity to the first human migrants who eventually discovered them and took up residence on this isolated paradise. They also adapted to the special character of the remote archipelago and developed their own distinctive way of life. In time, the Hawaiian islands became the most populated corner of Polynesia. Inevitably, much of Hawaii's natural diversity was changed to suit the needs of the people. It was not an intentional act of annihilation, but one that was a consequence of the traditional Polynesian lifestyle. Some species continued to flourish, others succumbed to the effects of the end of isolation. Thirteen centuries later, Hawaii with its native community of people and wildlife would be assailed by a new wave of human migrants. From the distant shores of the Pacific would come an invasion that would transform these islands into someone else's paradise.

The story of man's interest in Hawaii probably began in the Marquesas Islands, lying south of the equator, 2200 miles away. The Polynesians who discovered that archipelago had come from the islands of the western Pacific. They had gradually adapted to the new conditions and modified the landscape to fulfil their needs. In time, political and ecological pressure, or perhaps just the Polynesian spirit of voyaging, prompted some to seek new island homes. Some sailed south and settled many of the coral islands of the Tuamotu Archipelago. Others sailed on a little further to the west and encountered the high volcanic islands of Tahiti and her neighbours. More adventurous voyaging against the south-easterly winds took some canoes to Pitcairn and, no doubt, to Easter Island.

The *i'iwi* (*Vestiaria coccinea*) – one of the Hawaiian honeycreepers, a family of birds unique to the islands. There are 40 or so species, all evolved from the same founding ancestors. The curved beak of the *i'iwi* enables it to feed on the nectar and tiny fruit flies in the lobelioid, *Clermontia arborescens*.

This flow-chart shows how the Polynesian people might have spread through the Pacific. Every year, new information and understanding emerges about these epic voyages of settlement.

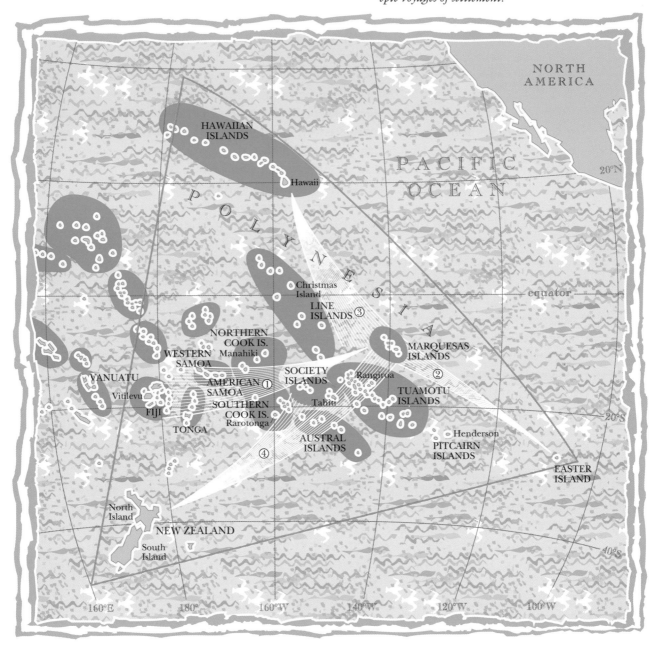

1. *Having established Polynesian communities on the islands of the western Pacific – Fiji, Tonga, Samoa – pioneering groups set sail towards the east. Perhaps by way of the Cook Islands, but possibly voyaging 2000 miles across open ocean, some successfully reached the 'high islands' of Eastern Polynesia where they established communities on Tahiti and the other Society Islands, and on the Marquesas. This probably happened around AD 150.*
2. *The Marquesas Islands are thought to have been an important centre of dispersal from which, over several centuries, successive voyages of exploration discovered and*

To sail north is possible but not easy. The south-east trade winds soon lose their impetus and in the equatorial doldrums there are counter-currents which can confuse the best of navigators. In the North Pacific, the prevailing trade winds blow from the north-east. For a canoe to reach Hawaii from the Marquesas it must sail across the wind. This fits the logical strategy of Polynesian voyaging, since the seafarers could return south if they discovered no new suitable islands; indeed the chances of encountering the Hawaiian chain are realistically high, as several modern sailing expeditions have proved. What is different now is that we know that the Hawaiian islands are there in the middle of the North Pacific; for the first Polynesian voyagers, it was an extraordinary act of faith.

To see the Hawaiian islands from the air is the nearest we can come to sharing the Polynesian experience of first encounter. Arriving from the east, your first impressions are of the Big Island with its massive, cloud-wreathed cones, smouldering with latent power. If you visit in winter, the same peaks are capped with snow. The southern coastline is fringed with black sand and in places the ocean boils as molten rock spills from the land. If you arrive at night, the lava glows sunset-orange. For the Polynesian voyager, such apparitions would have been awesome. At the heart of Hawaii's rich mythology is Pele, the goddess of fire, who dwells in the fire-pit of the Kilauea crater on the slopes of Mauna Loa. The southern coastline of Big Island would have been a daunting place to settle.

The west coast is more hospitable. From the air, you can see the long white beaches of the district called Kona, a Hawaiian word meaning 'leeward'. The coral sands are formed from the young reefs which fringe this side of the island. Being in the lee of the mountains, this coast is also the driest, making it popular with tourists. More fascinating to visitors captivated by the island's natural history is the east coast of Big Island. Some say this is the wettest place on earth, which accounts for the extraordinary lushness of the rainforest on the slopes

then settled other island groups. Easter Island was probably encountered by Marquesans who, by accident or design, voyaged far to the east of their homeland. They probably established this Polynesian 'outpost' by AD 400.

3. The Hawaiian Islands were most likely discovered during this same adventurous era of Polynesian voyaging from the Marquesas. Later voyages of settlement came from Tahiti, bringing different cultural influences to this isolated northern archipelago.

4. The islands that are now called New Zealand became the final corner of the Polynesian Triangle. Perhaps quite by chance, this cooler southern land was encountered and settled by a handful of Polynesians who arrived there from the southern Cook Islands or from islands even further east; there are many cultural and physical similarities between the Maori of New Zealand and the people of the Marquesas. New evidence suggests that this final migration took place as recently as the thirteenth century.

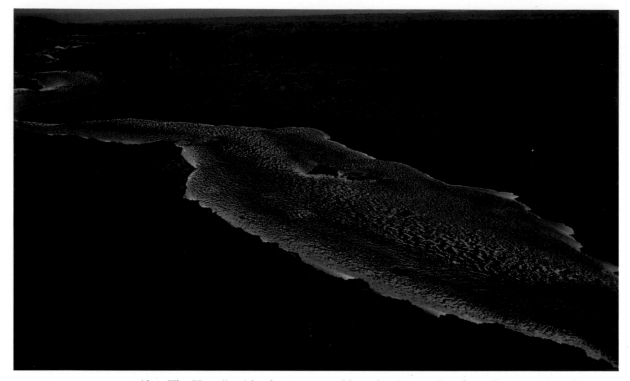

Above The Hawaiian islands were created by volcanic eruptions from the
ocean floor; the process still continues. On Big Island, rivers of molten
magma flow from the Kilauea Crater, reaching speeds of 20 miles per hour
as they surge towards the sea.
Right The mountainous interior of Maui, the second largest Hawaiian island,
rises to 10 000 feet. Much of the island is now a US National Park, with
a network or trails across ancient forest.

above Hilo. This little town, sandwiched between Pele's angry mountain and
the full force of the Pacific, boasts 'the largest rain-drops in the world'.

As the aircraft begins its descent towards Honolulu international airport on
the island of Oahu, you can see the twin peaks of Maui and the two smaller
islands of Kahoolawe and Lanai which have fragmented from it. The valleys
which once joined them create sheltered bays, ideal for Polynesian voyagers in
search of a safe haven. Looking down on this scene, it is not difficult to visualize
a lone double-hulled canoe riding the swell. It is, however, almost inconceivable
how it made its way from those faraway islands to the south.

The coastline of the main Hawaiian islands totals almost three-quarters of
a million miles. Much of it is towering cliff and the high, young islands have very
little protecting reef. The older islands to the west of the chain have well-
developed coral reefs that surround sheltered lagoons. In selecting a permanent

home, the first settlers had to make a compromise between the advantages offered by a high island and the protection afforded by a fringing reef. It is significant that archaeological evidence indicates that the island of Oahu attracted early Polynesian settlers. It is large but has no active volcanoes. Its summit rises to a respectable 4000 feet, high enough to attract plentiful rain but not so lofty that forests cannot clothe its summits. Blessed with numerous permanently flowing streams and a rich volcanic soil, the island was ideal for cultivation of Polynesian crops. Kane'ohe Bay on the east coast once had the most developed coral reefs in the entire archipelago, making it ideal for Polynesian fishermen.

For the first Hawaiians, the resources of the sea were vital to help them sustain their traditional way of life on these otherwise unfamiliar islands. Much of the marine life of Hawaii would have been known to them from the tropical South Pacific, for, in contrast to its land species, far fewer species of fish and shellfish are endemic to Hawaii. The islands' waters are home to about 450 reef and shore fishes, 150 different crabs and other crustaceans, and about 1000 molluscs, including large octopus. Various turtles visited the islands to graze on sea vegetation, and once a year would haul up on beaches to mate and lay eggs. In those pristine days, monk seals played in the shallow waters of the islands' bays and basked on its beaches. On the cliffs and strands nested thousands of sea-birds; almost every species known to Polynesians found a breeding refuge here. They feasted on the rich shoals of fish that fed in the nutrient-laden waters around the islands. For the same reason, the archipelago was a focus for large carnivorous ocean fish such as the mahimahi (*Coryphaena hippurus*) and bonito (*Euthynnus yaito*) for which the Hawaiian fishermen trolled with hooks and lures, beautifully made of bone and shell. Understandably, they built their first settlements on Oahu right by the sea.

During the winter of 1967, human bones appeared on an exposed face of a sand dune at the Bellows United States Air Force Base. Archaeologists from the Bishop Museum in Honolulu excavated an ancient burial ground and extensive habitations that dated back to the fourth century AD. The site was fifty yards from the present shoreline and just inland was an area of low-lying marshy ground which would have been ideal for traditional Polynesian taro cultivation. Just offshore, the Mokulua islets are still an important sea-bird sanctuary and would have provided the settlers with extra protein during the nesting season.

Above right The Ghost shrimp (*Stenopus pyrsonotus*) against the brilliant
scarlet of a sponge that encrusts the rocks of Hawaii's reefs.
Right Octopus, such as this species, *Octopus cyanea*, flourish in the rocky reefs of
Hawaii; to catch them, Hawaiian fishermen devised cunning lures.

The archaeologists discovered that the settlement consisted of clusters of pole-and-thatch dwellings which had small open hearths and areas paved with pebbles. Beneath one of these they unearthed the skeleton of an elderly woman. It seems that, as in many other Polynesian societies, it was usual to bury deceased relatives under the floor of their homes. The Bellows site was occupied for almost 700 years. Later burials included a young child who had been interred wearing an anklet of pig tusks and an ornate necklace. The sand around her skeleton was stained red, possibly from the red dye of the bark-cloth in which she had been carefully wrapped. It seems that this young person was of chiefly descent.

Other notable finds included fish-hooks fashioned from mother-of-pearl shell, very reminiscent of the style known from ancient sites in the Marquesas and in the Society Islands. The inhabitants also used specially shaped cone-shells to grate the flesh of coconuts. Pendants made from porpoise teeth and carved from oyster shell suggest that this hamlet had time to practise its artistic talents as well as its skills of survival.

From this scant but revealing archaeological evidence emerges a portrait of early Hawaiian life. The settlement on the banks of the Waimanalo stream flourished over several centuries into a successful community. The Polynesians cultivated root crops in the nearby fertile valley, and raised pigs, dogs and chickens. They also ate the ubiquitous Polynesian rats. Reef-fish and shellfish were other important parts of the ancient Hawaiian diet and they hunted sea-birds and collected their eggs. To exploit the varied resources of the sea, they invented the distinctly Hawaiian two-piece fish-hooks which they carved from wood or bone. These proved particularly effective for catching fish that fed on the sea-bed just offshore.

The habitat most favoured for settlement during the first few centuries of occupation was the dry forest of the valleys and lower mountain slopes. It was probably more of an open parkland type of forest cover, rather than an enclosed canopy. The endemic Hawaiian trees included *wiliwili* (*Erythrina*), the light timber of which was used for canoe outriggers, fishing-net floats and surf-boards. The *naio* (*Myoporum*) and the sandalwood *iliahi* (*Santalum*) were trees which were also familiar to people from South Pacific islands.

The open lowland forests were home to a great variety of endemic land-birds. There were several species of rail, a flightless ibis and various species of flightless geese. Archaeological records prove that the now famous Hawaiian goose, the *nene* (*Nesochen sandwicensis*), was widespread on several of the

Male and female *nene* (*Nesochen sandvicensis*) – the Hawaiian goose which survived the first Hawaiians, but is now rare.

main islands when Polynesians first arrived. It was one of the few large birds to survive to European times, no doubt because it had retained its ability to fly; the rest were eaten to extinction. Many other less edible species became extinct because of the regime of burning. The fires helped clear the ground for cultivated crops and also encouraged the growth of *pili* grass (*Andropogon contortus*) with which the people thatched their houses.

To make baskets and fish-traps they used *ie'ie* vines (*Freycinetia arborea*), a climbing form of pandanus palm which grew abundantly on higher slopes. Here the dominant tree was, and still is, the impressive *koa* (*Acacia koa*). Growing to a great height of 100 feet or more, these trees are sometimes called the Hawaiian mahogany on account of their red wavy-grained timber which was used for making canoes. Their nearest relatives are the wattle trees of Australia.

Many other trees and shrubs grew beneath the *koa* canopy, providing food and shelter for a range of insects and other invertebrate creatures as well as birds. Many have gone, but one tenacious survivor is the *elepaio*, a wren-like bird with a strident song. It was considered to be the guardian spirit of canoe-makers who felled timber in this upper forest. The fearless bird would come down to inspect their activities. If it began to peck at the cut tree, the craftsmen considered that they had been given a sign that their chosen timber was unsound. Other trees would be felled until the pecking ceased. Today this bold and curious bird follows hikers through the surviving *koa* forest, scolding them with its chattering alarm-call.

The high mountain habitats of Hawaii have survived relatively intact to the present day. Out of everyday reach of the early Polynesian settlers as well as the islands' modern occupants, the rainforests and bogs of the upper elevations still retain some of their primordial splendour. The *ohi'a lehua* tree (*Metrosideros polymorpha*) is the dominant species, but an impressive range of other trees and shrubs, including palms and tree-ferns, jostle for space on the rain-sodden windward slopes. It is here that you can discover the marvellous lobelias of Hawaii. Gardeners familiar with these small and colourful plants are amazed by the seemingly infinite variety of shapes, sizes and colours that have evolved from a handful of pioneer immigrants. Lobelias and their relatives have small seeds, which accounts for their presence here so far from their mainland origins. Some of Hawaii's lobelioid species grew extremely tall and palm-like. Many have become rare or extinct, but the species *Cyanea leptostegia* that survives on the island of Kauai is truly fantastic. Like its close relatives, its

The giant *koa* tree (*Acacia koa*) once dominated the higher
slopes of the main Hawaiian islands; providing shelter for many
other native plants and animals, and timber for canoes.

narrow stem seldom branches but rapidly shoots up to the forest canopy where it produces a topknot of leaves and long pink flowers. The extraordinary range of lobelia-type plants is one of the botanical wonders of the Hawaiian islands.

After driving from the tropical coastline of Big Island, up through the steamy rainforest, it comes as a great surprise to emerge eventually into an alpine landscape. Free-roaming sheep and goats introduced in recent times have grazed the flora to a mere shadow of its former splendour, but the famous silverswords (*Argyroxiphium*) still grow in the cinder deserts at these elevations. Related to the ancient tarweeds of California, the ancestors of these impressive plants probably came from the desert areas of North America and flourished on the volcanic cones of Hawaii because of their inherent resistance to extremes of temperature and the low humidity at this altitude. Hot during the summer day but freezing at night, these summits often have heavy snowfalls in winter. Even in summer, the chilled air is a reminder of the height of these islands, which are merely the tips of giant mountains rising five and a half miles from the

Above The flowers of *Metrosideros* trees produce tiny seeds that have been carried by the wind or by birds to almost all the high islands of the Pacific. On Hawaii, the plant evolved into the *ohi'a lehua* tree (*Metrosideros polymorpha*), a successful colonizer of cinder fields and lava flows.
Right In the dry open landscapes of Kauai island grows the bizarre *iliau* plant (*Wilkesia gymnoxiphium*). Related to the tarweeds, its pole-like stem bears a massive cone of resinous flower heads.

ocean floor. The first Polynesians who came to Hawaii had no inkling of the depth of the ocean or the age of the islands, but they knew that they were now a long way from their ancestral homeland. Here, at the most northerly point of Polynesian settlement, they began to tame this unfamiliar land of ice and fire.

The indigenous flora of Hawaii has no plants that contain sufficient carbohydrate and proteins to make them suitable as a staple diet for people. The settlers would not have starved, but they would never have prospered without their imported crops. Of the thirty or so plants that the first Polynesians introduced to the Pacific islands, only six did not arrive in Hawaii. The first settlers also brought with them certain native plants which they had found useful as food or medicine on the Marquesas or the other islands from which they came. They also carried tubers of the sweet potato, a valuable root-crop which they had somehow acquired from South America. Equipped with this genetic larder of varied crops and a menagerie of pigs, dogs, chickens and rats, they set foot on the windward shore of Oahu where the high rainfall would favour their traditional plant and animal husbandry.

Hawaiians became Polynesia's foremost cultivators of the land. At the time of European contact in the eighteenth century, their agricultural and horticultural production was impressive. Captain Cook, in a classic under-statement, remarked on their achievements. 'What we saw of their agriculture furnishes sufficient proofs that they are not novices in that art.' Over the centuries of occupation they had not only built on their traditional knowledge and skills, but had devised sophisticated forms of engineering to counter the physical features and climate of these islands. With only the simplest of tools, Hawaiians modified natural streams and exploited the slope of the terrain to carry water into their fields by an efficient network of aqueducts. Although these *auwai* were primarily for irrigation, they also served to supply water to houses. As water belonged to the gods, the precious resource was shared for the benefit of all.

The extensive system of terraces greatly enhanced the area available for cultivation, particularly for the taro crops, called *kalo* in Hawaiian. To grow effectively, wetland taro must be constantly flooded with water and a single *auwai* served several families as it wound down the terraced hillside. The Hawaiian planter had a sophisticated knowledge of his crops. Several hundred varieties of taro and sweet potato were developed, each with its individual name. He also grew sugar-cane in extensive special grounds and on other plantations there were stands of bread-fruit, banana and coconut palms. Yams and arrow-root were planted in cooler places where they needed little tending. The paper-mulberry, usually known in Hawaii as *wauke*, was planted as the raw material from which to make *kapa*, their bark-cloth. As in all the other Pacific islands, pandanus leaves were used for matting, for canoe sails and for a multitude of essential day-to-day objects. The Polynesian *ti* plant was grown for its leaves, in which food was wrapped for cooking, and for its sugary roots, which could be eaten when other more appetizing crops failed. Hawaiians cultivated the bottle gourd (*Lagenaria siceraria*), from which they made various containers for the house and musical instruments for their pleasure.

For the Hawaiian islanders, their collective system of agriculture, along with a well-developed web of social, political and religious relationships, tied people to the land, to their chiefs and to their gods. The fertility of the soil was the essence of their lives. Each year they celebrated the harvest of the land at the *makahiki* festival. From mid-October to the end of January was the season when they honoured Lono, the god who controlled their agricultural endeavours. This benign deity brought peace and prosperity to the islands.

Taro, called *kalo* in Hawaii, was usually grown in terraces, watered by a sophisticated system of aqueducts, called *auwai*.

The other three principal Hawaiian gods, Ku, Kane and Kanaloa, were equivalent to Tu, Tane and Tangaroa of ancient Tahiti and the other islands of eastern Polynesia. Ku was the patron deity of all manly activities, including men's crafts, fishing, politics, sexual prowess and warfare. He was the only god to which human sacrifice was made. His fearsome image was often portrayed as a mask adorned with brilliant red feathers of the *i'iwi* honeycreeper, with eyes carved from mother-of-pearl and with a jagged mouth of dogs' teeth. In contrast to Ku, who revelled in human sacrifice, Kane was god of sunlight, fresh-water and forests. Hawaiians respected him as the procreator and as the ancestor of all chiefs and commoners. Kanaloa was lord of the oceans and the winds, and was often embodied in the form of the octopus or squid. Together with his companion Kane, he moved about the islands opening up new sources of fresh-water for the benefit of man.

With increasing prosperity, the population of Hawaii expanded. Small settlements were established wherever ecological conditions were favourable; even the more arid and marginal lands were pressed into agricultural production with the help of irrigation or dry field systems. Elaborate fishing tackle was devised to exploit the marine resources around the islands. Dogs and pigs were reared in greater numbers to provide meat for craftsmen and other male commoners as well as for chiefs. Hawaii not only became an affluent society but also very populous. The first voyaging canoes that beached on Hawaiian shores, during the centuries when Christianity was first spreading across the other side of the world, carried only a handful of founding families. By the time of the Norman Conquest, the population of Hawaii may have only reached 20000. During the next six or seven centuries, while Europe battled through its Middle Ages, Hawaiian society flourished and expanded throughout all the main high islands. In time, the population numbered several hundred thousand.

The impact of people on the islands was inevitable. The Polynesian traditional system of *tapu*, which became *kapu* in Hawaii, did much to conserve resources. The islanders' skills in land management seem to have been more efficient than anywhere else in Polynesia. In their noble efforts to modify their island home and build a fruitful life, the human inhabitants gradually but irreversibly changed the nature of Hawaii. After millions of years evolving in total isolation, the islands had developed an exuberant life of their own, one in which the native species had achieved some kind of natural equilibrium. With the coming of the Polynesians, this barrier of isolation was broken and the vulnerable paradise began to change.

Not only did the people modify the landscape, they also selectively altered the balance of species within it. The effect on Hawaiian birdlife was particularly dramatic. Before people came, there were at least forty other endemic species of bird. As well as the flightless birds, this list includes owls, ravens, a hawk, an eagle and many songbirds, all of which were casualties of the changes brought by the newcomers. In the centuries between the arrival of the Polynesians and the arrival of the first Europeans, more than half of the endemic species of Hawaii's land-birds became extinct.

On January 19th, 1778, during his third and final expedition to the Pacific, Captain Cook found the islands of Hawaii. It was an exciting encounter for both worlds. For the Europeans, the islands were the last archipelago to be discovered in the Pacific; for the islanders, it was the end of isolation. Like the endemic wildlife of Hawaii, their world would never be the same again. Despite Cook's attempts to limit the inevitable impact of the intrusion, the seeds of destruction were sown. In his wake came an armada from the new worlds that now lay beyond every horizon. In the years that followed, alien diseases took a rapid toll of the human population; in the seas there was bloody slaughter as whales and other marine life fell victim to foreign exploitation; on land, the unfettered introduction of opportunist mainland species of plants and animals overwhelmed the endemic flora and fauna. In the brief space of time since the European encounter with Hawaii, half of all the islands' species, which had survived more than a millennium of Polynesian occupation, have been wiped off the planet.

Hawaii today is still a vibrant, productive place. The lowland valleys and hillsides which were cleared by the Polynesians to create terraces for taro are now planted with pineapples from Brazil picked by workers from the Philippines. The native forests, which were savaged by foreign loggers for sandalwood and other precious timber, are now alive with foreign wildlife. More than 2000 alien insects and spiders have taken over the canopy and forest floor. These creatures now provide food for some of the fifty alien species of bird that have become established on the islands. These, in turn, are pursued by eighteen imported mammals, such as the predatory mongoose which has played havoc with much of the islands' endemic animal life. Hawaii's natural vegetation has been swamped by more than 900 species of alien plants, a total equal in number to the entire indigenous flora.

The fate of the native wildlife of Hawaii has been matched by the fate of its native people. Since the annexation of the islands by the United States of America in 1898, Hawaii's destiny has been manifest. No longer a Polynesian kingdom in the middle of the Pacific, the fiftieth State of America is now part of a wider world. Hawaii has become someone else's paradise.

The first Hawaiians named this mile-and-a-half strip of beachside land, *Waikiki*,
meaning 'spouting water' because of the springs that kept the swampland wet
for taro and waterfowl. Today, on that now world-famous beach, the replica canoes
are the only reminders of Hawaii's link with Polynesia.

Captain Cook was killed on Hawaii by angry islanders. After exploring further
north, he had returned there in mid-January, at the height of the *makahiki*
celebrations. Cook's two ships were escorted into Kealakekua Bay by a great
fleet of canoes. It was a very sacred place to Hawaiians. Cook was accorded great
respect and he and his senior officers were given lavish hospitality. After two
weeks, amid joyous acclamation, he and his two crews left the islands at the end
of Lono's peaceful season of *makahiki*. It was a fitting departure for a man of
such conspicuous power.

Off the north coast of Big Island, the ships ran into a fierce winter storm
and were forced to turn back to make repairs. By the time they unexpectedly
returned later in February, the spirit of *makahiki* had come to an end; the
islanders were once more under the influence of Ku, their vengeful god of
war. No longer was Cook given privileged status; he was perceived as a mortal

Above The death of Captain Cook marked a turning point for the people of the Pacific. In the wake of European exploration came an era of exploitation. (The artist of this engraving was John Cleveley, whose twin brother James had been ship's carpenter on the *Resolution*, on Cook's third and final voyage.)

who made mistakes. At the climax of a tragic series of misunderstandings, for which Cook and his officers were equally to blame, he and four of his crew were clubbed and stabbed to death. To the horror of those on board, a delegation of Hawaiians returned his mutilated body wrapped respectfully in fine *kapa* and shrouded in a cloak made of rare black and white feathers. So great was this man's *mana* that most of his bones and hair had been dispersed amongst the chiefs. The British crew retaliated by setting fire to temples and killing many natives, before sailing home without their much loved and respected captain, whose remains they buried at sea.

This was the last great voyage of discovery to the Pacific; the next ships to sail across this ocean would be in pursuit of wealth and power. For Polynesians and for the outside world, the death of Captain Cook marked the end of an age of innocence.

CHAPTER TEN

LAND of the LONG WHITE CLOUD

Before the Europeans pierced the far horizon of their island world, the people of Polynesia had no concept of the written word. It was one of the few cultural achievements that they did not master on their own. Instead, they developed one of the richest oral literatures the world has ever known. In myth and legend, story-telling, poetry and song, they have recorded not only their epic history but also their perception of the physical and spiritual universe of which they and their ancestors are a vital part. The stories that have been carefully handed on from generation to generation have no doubt evolved with time; each has been embellished or modified to suit the Polynesians' changing perception of themselves.

There are many legends about the first Polynesian encounter with the islands that we now call New Zealand. Two of them are particularly notable for their consistency of detail; one tells of an accidental voyage of discovery, while the other chronicles the first settlement. The hero of the first legend was a brilliant fisherman and navigator called Kupe. His home is believed to have been the sacred island of Raiatea, near Tahiti. From there he set off during the lunar month of November with a handful of other fishermen in pursuit of a giant octopus that had repeatedly stolen their bait. Far beyond the setting sun, they encountered a 'great southern land with high hills covered with mist, uninhabited except by birds'. Kupe and his companions returned to tell the tale. By counting generations, folklore traces his discovery of Aotearoa, 'The Land of the Long White Cloud', to the tenth century.

According to the other major legend, a flotilla of canoes set off from eastern Polynesia some time in the fourteenth century with the purpose of colonizing

Kupe's distant land. Each had left the homeland of 'Hawaiki' because of tribal feuding; when they arrived at Aotearoa, they settled different parts of the coast and flourished into the various Maori tribes, continuing their rivalry in this new and spacious country. It is only in recent years, with the resurgence of passion over the issue of Maori land claims in New Zealand, that this legend has been played down. Understandably, those tribes that are not specifically featured in the account of the founding event feel poorly represented in their country's oral history. Nor did this legend place the discovery and settlement of New Zealand sufficiently far back in time to match the existing archaeological evidence; carbon-dating seemed to indicate that Polynesians had established this south-west corner of their Triangle by the eighth century AD. However, anthropologists, including at least one notable New Zealand scholar, have recently re-analysed ash and pollen samples from the earliest known Maori settlements. It now looks possible that the islands remained uninhabited until the thirteenth century, a date which more closely matches the arrival of that legendary founding flotilla.

As with the discovery of Hawaii to the north, it is probable that belief in the existence of a southern land was based on observation of the migrations of birds. At the beginning of the southern summer, huge flocks of petrels and shearwaters migrate from the north Pacific to breed in New Zealand. Day and night for weeks at a time, they stream south across the tropics. Polynesians living on tropical islands across the Pacific could not have failed to deduce that, somewhere beyond their southern horizon, lay a large land that was the home of these long-distance travellers.

To reach New Zealand by sailing boat from anywhere in eastern Polynesia is a challenge, even if you know for sure that the islands are there. It is a complex voyage that takes you across the prevailing south-east trade winds into a more southerly belt of unpredictable winds and then eventually into latitudes where the westerlies prevail. Even for today's sailors with modern navigational aids, it is daunting. As with the migrating birds, the ideal time to set off is in October and November when the winds are still set firmly on the tail and when there is little fear of cyclones. At that time of year, Venus is clearly visible in the south-west for the first three or four hours after sunset, giving a reference point among the changing constellations of the southern sky. Although there is no 'pole star', the Southern Cross, clearly visible during that season, not only helps the navigator to keep on course but also helps to tell him how far south he has sailed, as would the temperature of the water.

Unlike the relatively small oceanic islands from which the voyagers had come, the islands of New Zealand, which extend over 800 miles from north to south, presented a substantial target. If the first settlers had come from

Rarotonga and the other islands that are now the southern Cooks, the voyage would have been nearly 2000 miles; from the Austral Islands or Tahiti it would have been that much further. For three or four weeks the voyaging canoes had tracked westwards across open ocean; now, ahead of them, the sun sank for the first time behind a misty shape on the horizon. As they sailed closer, the clouds that gathered over Aotearoa stretched left and right as far as the eye could see. These were not only the largest islands that the Polynesians had ever encountered, they were the last ones left to discover. This was the final uninhabited corner of the Pacific; in fact, New Zealand was the last substantial tract of land to be settled by people anywhere in the world.

For eighty million years, these large islands had existed in isolation. Once part of the vast super-continent of Gondwanaland, the ancient bedrock of New Zealand has been repeatedly thrust up by geological forces, worn down by erosion and inundated by the sea. It is a land of glaciers and volcanoes which have moulded and remoulded the contours of the land. There are very few countries in the world of similar size that have such a diversity of landscapes and natural environments. The interior climbs from dry desert-like plains to snow-capped alpine peaks, and the long coastline embraces subtropical islands and deep fiords fed by permanent glaciers. To explore New Zealand today is an exhilarating experience; for the South Sea islanders who first discovered this land of contrasts, it was a whole new world.

The Tasman Glacier forges the great valley to the west of Mount Cook.

At the time they came, Aotearoa was essentially a forested land. From offshore, the lush vegetation appears to tumble into the sea. If the voyagers had arrived at the east coast in December, the most propitious time of year, they would have seen pohutukawa trees (*Metrosideros excelsa*), the 'Christmas trees' of New Zealand, in a blaze of red blossom. Thinking that this new land abounded with red-feathered birds, the first Polynesians rejoiced at their good fortune. Symbolically, they cast their ancestral feathered heirlooms into the sea before realizing that their celebration was a little premature. They were soon to be reassured. Not only did the new land have its own red-feathered birds, but the forests and grasslands were alive with other avian species which would provide them with ample supplies of plumage and meat.

Numerous species of flightless birds grazed in forest clearings. They were impressive creatures with massive thighs and long necks. To the Polynesian eye, they resembled scaled-up versions of their domestic fowl, so they called them *moa*, their name for 'chicken'. Many were the size of small turkeys, but some were ten feet tall. The leg bones of these avian giants stood taller than a man. The presence of *moa* bones in the charred remains of the fireplaces of the first settlers, shows how important these birds were to their survival. There are no

bones of their traditional domestic fowl, nor of their pigs. It would appear that they set off without them. The new land offered new sources of meat. As well as eleven species of *moa*, there were numerous other birds, many of which were flightless and easy to catch.

In the bush, the small flightless kiwi (*Apteryx* spp.) scuffled through the undergrowth at night. It is possible that this extraordinary bird was given its Maori name because it reminded the first settlers of the bird they knew as *ivi*; the bristle-thighed curlew has a similar compact body with down-curving bill and long legs. Its migrations seldom reach New Zealand and the first Maori might well have transferred its name to a locally common feathered creature. Found only in New Zealand, the kiwi is, in reality, unlike any other bird. Its wings, which end in a claw, are very small and it has no tail feathers. Its plumage is more like shaggy hair than true feathers. In place of flight muscles, it has developed powerful legs which make up a third of its body weight. Although its eyes are small, its face and the tip of its long, curved bill carry sensitive bristles to help it find its way by touch; its senses of hearing and smell are equally keen. It is the only bird in the world with nostrils at the tip of its bill. At night it probes the leaf-litter, smelling for its supper of earthworms, woodlice, insects,

Above The male of the North Island brown kiwi (*Apteryx australis mantelli*), in breeding burrow.
Above right Re-creation of the extinct giant moa (*Euryapteryx geranoides*). Towering ten feet high, these powerful but flightless birds once roamed the grasslands that are now the Canterbury Plains.
Left Ancient rainforest along the Milford Track, South Island.

spiders and snails. Though shy and retiring, the *kiwi* had long been a very successful native of New Zealand. Its fortunes began to change with the arrival of people.

As on all the other Pacific islands, indeed islands anywhere, the power of flight is only valuable for escaping from predators and for moving across the sea. On New Zealand there were no ground-living predators. The only large carnivorous creature was the giant eagle, *Harpagornis*, but this was a daytime predator, swooping on large *moa* as they fed on open ground. A small nocturnal bird like the kiwi was safe in the vast forests of Aotearoa. So were the rails and the parrots, the pigeons and numerous other smaller fruit-eating birds. This was a land of birds. The only three species of mammal were both insectivorous bats and the only reptiles were insect-eating skinks and geckos and the tuatara (*Sphenodon punctatus*), a survivor from the age of the dinosaurs. Together with several primitive species of frog, this ancient reptile was cast adrift from the rest of the world when New Zealand became a separate group of islands.

The tuatara (*Sphenodon punctatus*) – New Zealand's reptilian survivor from the age of dinosaurs, now mostly confined to offshore islands.

When the first Polynesians arrived, they found a country largely covered in evergreen forests. In the south these were dominated by southern beeches (*Nothofagus*) which produced a dense canopy from which emerged tall podocarp trees, especially *rimu* (*Dacrydium cupressinium*). Other typical New Zealand podocarps included the *kahikatea* (*Dacrycarpus dacrydioides*) and *totara* (*Podocarpus totara*), trees that were widespread in many other temperate regions of the world before the era of Ice Ages. The floor of these forests was carpeted with ferns and a rich mix of mosses and liverworts. In the north of New Zealand, the beech was replaced by the famous *kauri* (*Agathis australis*). These majestic trees had trunks which frequently reached 100 feet into the air and were often twenty-five feet in circumference. For people coming from oceanic islands poor in timber, these giants must have been an awe-inspiring spectacle.

No less impressive were the coastal regions. Great rivers surged down from the high peaks and spread out across vast coastal plains. Eels moved up from the sea on their spawning migrations and were so plentiful that in time the Maori came to give the two native species 150 different names, reflecting their great range of size, shape, colour, taste and behaviour. In later centuries, eels became an important part of the Maori diet and were accorded great respect. They were honoured for their mythological origins and for their phallic symbolism. Easy to capture, they were taken by spear, net and pot or simply by hand. In early autumn on a dark night, a good migratory run might bring two or three thousand large eels into a single net stretched across a specially prepared channel. In more recent times, the eel became so central to Maori life that it is now a focus for contemporary grievances over the conservation and exploitation of New Zealand's natural resources.

The sea around New Zealand was also full of life. It had a very different richness to that of the tropical islands from which the first settlers had come. Here in the southern Pacific, the ocean is considerably cooler, but that does not make it less productive. The currents and up-wellings, particularly off the east coast, bring nutrient-rich water in which a multitude of marine creatures thrive in large numbers. The rocky reefs are home to numerous fish species, many of which are just as colourful and certainly as substantial as those found on coral reefs. In the waters around North Island, Maori fishermen caught snapper (*Chrysophrys auratus*), kahawai (*Arripis trutta*), trevally (*Caranx georgianus*) and mackerel (*Trachurus* spp.); while the cooler water of the south abounded with barracouta (*Thyrsites atun*), red cod (*Pseudophycis bacchus*), ling (*Genypterus blacodes*) and blue cod (*Parapercis colias*).

Throughout New Zealand waters, there are also abundant groper (*Polyprion oxygeneios*) and various wrasse (*Pseudolabrus* spp.), which would have looked familiar to people from the tropical Pacific, as would have been the whales and dolphins that regularly visit New Zealand waters. Large colonies of seals and sea-lions lived on the rocky edges of the land. Feeding on the wealth of coastal sealife, these mammals provided a new and novel source of food. At low tide, there was a natural harvest of edible shellfish, notably cockles (*Chione stutchburyi*) and pipi (*Amphidesma australe*) which became indispensable to the Maori as the easier catches of moa and seals declined. The famous New Zealand abalone, the *pau'a* (*Haliotis iris*), clung to the rocks within reach of the surface, where there were also large spiny urchins and some of the largest crayfish and crabs anywhere in the Pacific.

All around the immense coastline of both main islands, as well as on the many smaller rocky outcrops, were the land-based haunts of countless sea-birds. For millions of years, New Zealand had been the sea-bird centre of the south-western Pacific. Almost every species known to Polynesians from their tropical homelands lived in even greater abundance on the munificence of these southern waters. Aotearoa may have been a cooler place for those first New Zealanders, but it was a very large and bountiful land.

Above Female Southern fur seal (*Arctocephalus forsteri*) with nursing pup.
Top right Detail of the *pau'a* shell (*Haliotis* sp.) – the exquisite abalone of New Zealand.
Right Yaldwyn's triplefin (*Notoclinops yaldwyni*), one of the
colourful temperate water species of New Zealand, on a colony
of tunicate sea-squirts.

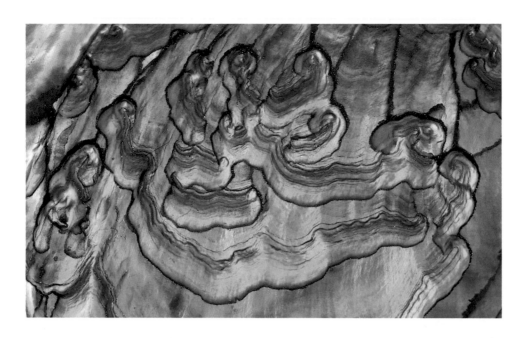

If the Polynesians first came to New Zealand, say, 1000 years ago, they arrived at an ideal time in the recent history of the world's climate. The so-called 'Little Climatic Optimum' affected temperatures around the world, raising them perhaps one degree centigrade above those we know today. This global warming started about 1200 years ago and lasted until well into the fourteenth century. One degree warmer does not seem significant, but in Europe it not only changed the distribution of many species of plants and animals but was changing human history.

All through the 'Dark Ages', northern Europe had experienced severe winters in which wildlife had perished, forcing species further south. By the end of the Saxon invasions of England, the climate was distinctly improving; by the end of the millennium, northern Europe had become almost 'Mediterranean'. The Norman Conquest not only brought people from France, it brought grape vines which flourished in the newly improved English climate. At about the same time, the Vikings were setting off across the Atlantic. Erik the Red discovered Greenland in AD 982 and, at that time, it really deserved the name he gave to that great northern land. Much of its coastal plain was covered in verdant vegetation, unlike the icy waste it is today. If Erik or his Viking compatriots did in reality sail on further and discover America, long before Columbus, then they did so when the world's climate favoured such enterprising ocean voyages.

It is surely no coincidence that the migrations of the Polynesians from their long-established homelands in the eastern Pacific took place very broadly at the same time. The warmer global temperatures may have contributed to the severity of famines in such places as the Marquesas. It is from there that the first migrations north to Hawaii are thought to have set out. Easter Island may have been successfully discovered and settled for the same reasons. However, it is the westward dispersal of Polynesians to the Cook Islands and south of the tropics to New Zealand that would have gained most impetus from the effects of this Little Climatic Optimum. With clear skies, few storms and persistent, predictable trade winds, a voyage of settlement to Kupe's distant land would not have been such a daunting prospect.

The much respected Maori historian and anthropologist, Te Rangi Hiroa, also known as Sir Peter Buck, described his Polynesian ancestors as 'Vikings of the Sunrise'. Setting off from islands of the western Pacific, they had voyaged eastward across the Pacific in search of new lands. From Samoa they had discovered the Marquesas and from there they had dispersed through the numerous tropical islands of the eastern Pacific, even reaching the distant outpost of Easter Island. To discover New Zealand, their last great migration, they had changed course and headed back towards the setting sun.

Once discovered, the new land was rapidly explored. The first settlers used their canoes and seafaring skills to travel up and down the long and varied coastline. Temporary camps and then permanent settlements were soon established on both coasts of North and South Islands. Archaeologists investigating some of the earliest sites have been astounded to unearth stone implements that were fashioned from rocks found in many different, widespread regions of the country. It seems that within a century or two, or even a matter of a few decades, the Maori people were travelling the entire 800-mile north to south sweep of the two large islands. They favoured the less rugged, more sheltered and warmer east coasts of both islands. Even so, they would have found conditions quite different to those of their original Polynesian homelands.

As well as lower air and sea temperatures, this southern land had very different seasons. Tropical islands essentially have a cool, dry season and a hot, wet season. The pattern of summer and winter, with its intermediary seasons of spring and autumn, was unknown to the newcomers. If they arrived in high summer, much of North Island would have felt and looked very much like home. The Bay of Islands, for example, has clear, warm, blue water and beaches of white sand fringed with palm trees and giant tropical ferns. Dolphins play in the shallows and even the red-tailed tropic bird drifts this far south. By winter, the scene dramatically changes. North Island avoids the worst weather, but in parts of South Island it can freeze for weeks and rain for months. Adapting to these extremes was a challenge, even for hardy Polynesians.

The greatest test of survival was faced by the cultivated plants that they had brought with them in the hope of establishing their traditional crops for food and raw materials. Like their ancestors before them, these Polynesians had arrived with carefully conserved tubers and runners, cuttings and seeds of all the plants on which, for centuries, their island lifestyle had been based. The success of all their previous colonizations had been dependent on the wholesale transportation of domestic plants and livestock from island to island. For generations, as they dispersed through the Pacific, they had fashioned each new environment into one that would suit their way of life. Wherever they had voyaged and settled new lands, the Polynesians had taken their familiar landscapes with them.

Here in temperate New Zealand their traditional survival strategy began to fail. The coconut palms and pandanus, the bread-fruit and banana trees, the sugar-cane and arrowroot, all died. The winters were simply too cold. Even the plants that did take root were at the extreme limit of their climatic tolerance. All their many varieties of yam struggled to grow. Taro and the paper-mulberry tree only did well in the very north where frosts were rare. Even the tubers of the sweet potato, the *kumara* adopted somehow from South America, was slow to sprout and reproduce. Instead of remaining a major part of their staple diet, this tuber became a luxury. Seldom growing much larger than an inch in thickness, the tubers were carefully stored underground in specially constructed *kumara* pits, to protect them from winter frosts. Some of these subterranean structures were elaborately lined with stones and entered by way of a tunnel. In some parts of ancient New Zealand, it was only on special occasions that this root store was opened, and its precious contents eaten as part of a celebratory feast.

The new season of spring became known as the time to plant *kumara*, and their cultivation became a major endeavour. Hillocks of earth were prepared, two or three feet apart, and the seed tubers planted in the side that faced the morning sun. The warmth helped them germinate and grow; at night, rocks that had been laid out to gather heat during the daylight hours were placed around the mounds. To ensure that the young plants absorbed the greatest nourishment, the mounds were meticulously weeded by the women. Plagues of caterpillars of a native sphinx moth, unknown in eastern Polynesia, descended on the new shoots and leaves, as if dropping from the sky. Before the coming of the Polynesians and their favoured crop, these moths laid their eggs on the native bindweed. Now the caterpillars transferred their voracious attentions to the leaves of the *kumara*. The Maori gardeners picked them off by hand or destroyed them with smoke from smouldering *kauri* gum. So threatening was this annual infestation that the Maori encouraged flocks of black-backed gulls to help them with their work.

Every stage in the *kumara* calendar was observed with special reverence. The *kumara* became a *tapu* plant, associated with peace. Each year, the new season of autumn was celebrated as the time to lift the *kumara* from the ground and prepare the store for the long months of winter. It was a time for rejoicing. The gardeners who had nurtured their crop through the southern summer now celebrated with special games and dances.

Unlike their distant cousins in Hawaii, the Maori gardeners did not create irrigated terraces for taro; instead they planted this root crop in damp, rich soil, often on the banks of the numerous wide streams and rivers that wound their way from the mountains across the flat coastal plains. To help warm the soil, an upper layer of sand and gravel was imported from the shore. Laid on the rooting taro beds, this attracted the sun's heat and helped growth. Gardeners in modern Auckland still turn up patches of soil coloured with beach sand, a legacy of their first industrious countrymen.

The gourd plant (*Lagenaria siceraria*) was brought by the first settlers and grew reasonably well in the warmer early years of occupation. It was cultivated mainly to make containers, but the immature fruit could be eaten like marrows in early summer when other vegetables were in short supply. The fruits left to mature were often painstakingly trained into useful shapes. When ripe, the gourds were dried and hardened in the sun or by fires, and then their spongy contents removed to create the vessel. Large gourds were sliced in half to make bowls and funnels; others had a small hole bored at the stalk to convert them into water containers. The Maori had come from islands where the science and craft of making pottery had long been forgotten. New Zealand had abundant sources of clay, but with an ample supply of gourds, there was perhaps no stimulus to re-invent the skill. Just as with fine pottery, the most perfectly shaped gourds were decorated with handsome Maori motifs and handed down as heirlooms.

It must have been a frustration to the first Polynesian settlers to discover that the paper-mulberry tree did not flourish in the new land. Only in the far north was the climate sufficiently benign. In its place, the Maori utilized the inner bark of the lacebark trees (*Hoteria* spp.), which were common throughout the country in drier areas and at forest edges. In damp places the Maori discovered another fibrous plant, which they called *harakeke* and which we know as flax (*Phormium* spp.). Several native species grew in New Zealand and the Maori devised ways of using the plant to make cordage and nets, mats and simple fabrics for clothing. The green leaves could be woven into baskets or plaited into a fabric for sails.

The long, fibrous leaves of the flax sprout annually and, if carefully cut, the plant will produce another fan of foliage. Scraped and dried, the leaves were knotted into strings and ropes. The immigrants had no experience of weaving; making *tapa* had been quite a different skill. In time, the Maori developed a technique similar to the weft and warp style of weaving, which could produce a fine, closely textured fabric. Chiefs and other influential people wore capes of this cloth, into which were often woven *kiwi* or *kaka* feathers. For others, a simpler shaggy cape composed of rows of tied and twisted flax fibres was worn over the shoulders; like a thatch, it kept out the cold and shed the rain.

In winter, or any times of need, the roots of the *ti* plant provided extra energy. Brought from eastern Polynesia, it was valued for its sugary content and grew well during the first few centuries. It needs eighteen months to reach maturity and would have perished in cold winters. In time it became scarce in New Zealand and the Maori came to rely on the native species (*Cordyline australis*), which they now call *ti* but which is known more widely as the New Zealand cabbage tree. Harvested in the summer, when the sugar content was highest, its roots were baked in the earth-oven.

The same technique was used to extract nutrition from the rhizomes of another native plant, the bracken-fern (*Pteridium esculentum*). Although not as nutritious as the imported root-crops such as taro, yam and *kumara*, the

The Maori of New Zealand discovered that this native tree (*Cordyline australis*)
has a high content of sugar. They called it the *'ti'* plant, the name also
given to a very different sugary cordyline tree in Tahiti. Today
it is more commonly known as the 'cabbage tree'.

fern-root became an acceptable substitute. It grew wild and really needed
no cultivation, but the Maori gardeners discovered that when planted in rich
soils, the fern grew to ten feet in height and developed rhizomes two feet long.
Some of the best ferns grew on soil that had been left fallow after several
years of growing *kumara*. The bracken would invade from the wild or would
be intentionally planted. Three years later, a decent crop could be lifted in
early summer when the starch content was highest. The rhizomes were
soaked in water before being roasted in the embers of the fire and pounded
with a wooden mallet on smooth water-worn stones. The mealy part was
swallowed and the fibrous remnants spat out. Eaten with fish or baked into
cakes with wild fruits, bracken could even be palatable. It was a valuable source
of energy in times of famine, which often led to rivalry between neighbouring
tribes. The processed rhizome sustained the Maori warrior. Just as *kumara*
symbolized peace, the fern-root became the plant of war.

Skeletons have been found that date from the first centuries of New Zealand's new era of human occupation. They show the wear and tear of life during those early years. Although well-built and muscular, like their Polynesian ancestors, the Maori of New Zealand did not live long lives. They often died in their twenties or thirties. A man of forty was considered to be very old, and to reach fifty was exceptional. Nearly all the skeletons had degeneration of the joints and the lower spine, suggesting hard manual labour and the carrying of heavy loads. Many showed signs of bone deficiency from malnutrition, and almost all had lost the majority of their teeth. It seems that, even in more recent centuries, most people lost their first molars by the age of twenty-five. The disintegration then moved to adjacent teeth until all were lost except a few at the front. The principal culprit was probably the fern-root. Perhaps chewed as dried sticks, the rhizome wore away teeth at a particular angle which anthropologists call the 'fern-root plane'. In time, whatever the cause, most Maori lost their teeth. Unable to eat the limited and often harsh diet, an early death was inevitable. Back on the tropical islands of Polynesia, life not only seemed less strenuous but the diet was kinder on the teeth. Raw bananas and coconut, cooked root-crops and fermented bread-fruit were all easy on the palate and the jaw. Even elderly people retained most of their teeth. The secret may have been in the taro root which, unbeknown to its cultivators, contained a rich content of fluoride. It was in the Austral Islands that a twentieth-century American dentist noted the perfect teeth of the islanders and patented the idea of fluoride toothpaste.

The people who came to New Zealand from tropical islands were already accomplished gardeners. It had been because of their understanding of the soil and the business of plant husbandry that their ancestors had settled the eastern Pacific. At first, the settlers may have relied on wild birds, fish and native plants until they could establish their domestic crops. It would soon have become apparent which imported plant species were going to survive the change in climate, and tolerant varieties would have been selectively developed.

Polynesians had always been physically and spiritually attached to the coast; the Maori of New Zealand were no exception. Their settlements were mostly at the mouths of streams and rivers or at coastal sites that made good harbours for their canoes. Although there were no coral reefs and lagoons, sea fishing remained an essential way of life. They developed nets and lines to catch the numerous new species of fish, and invented pots and traps that would lure the large crayfish and crabs. In New Zealand there was no shortage of different hardwoods, stones, shells and large bird-bones from which to fashion hooks and lures. In time, the making of these fishing accessories became a Maori art-form.

Sea-birds and sea-mammals were harvested by the new inhabitants. The middens of shells and bones contain evidence that a wide range of species were taken as food. Many oceanic birds came ashore to breed. A shearwater, known to New Zealanders as the mutton-bird (*Puffinus griseus*), nests in burrows during the New Zealand winter. When the fledglings are almost ready to leave, they make easy prey. On North Island, thousands of them were harvested annually at every major colony. Plucked, cleaned, cured and stored, they provided a larder for winter. Licences are still issued to Maoris who have a hereditary right to take the mutton-birds.

In autumn, vast flocks of godwits (*Limosa lapponica*) gathered on the harbours and shores of North Island, in preparation for their migration to warmer islands. Netted or taken in snares, they offered the Maori a windfall opportunity to top up their larders for the oncoming winter months. In spring and summer, all sea-bird colonies provideed a bonanza of eggs. Gulls were favourite; their large-yolked eggs were rich in protein. Shearwaters, prions, petrels, shags and cormorants probably all contributed to the Maori diet. Each year South Island became a focal point for many ocean birds. Being so far south in the Pacific, it was, and still is, an important breeding region for extreme southern species. Several penguins, notably the now rare yellow-eyed penguin (*Megadyptes antipodes*), the small endemic Blue penguin (*Eudyptula minor*) and the Fiordland crested penguin (*Eudyptes pachyrhynchus*), breed on South Island during New Zealand's winter or early spring. Clumsy on land, they were easily caught by hungry islanders.

On the headlands of South Island there were large colonies of the royal albatross (*Diomedea epomopora*). This is New Zealand's most handsome sea-bird and worthy of its name. Called *toroa* in Maori, these great birds glide above the southern oceans, hunting fish and crustaceans and preying on octopus and squid. Far out to sea, this nomad was seen by Polynesian voyagers who thought of it, like themselves, as a wanderer far from home. The bird survives the salty environment by excreting a saline solution through its tubular nostrils; *roimata toroa* means 'albatross tears', as the bird was thought to be weeping for its distant homeland. They are long-lived birds; the oldest on record had voyaged the Pacific Ocean for more than fifty-four years before it eventually expired on the shores of Aotearoa. Pairs mate for life and they return to their ancestral colony in September, each within an hour or two of each other. To see the famous colony on Taiaroa Head near Dunedin is a highlight of a spring visit to New Zealand. Rising on the updraught, these magnificent white birds epitomize the spirit of the southern seas.

The Yellow-eyed penguin (*Megadyptes antipodes*) – one of several southern species that provided the first New Zealanders with a source of oily meat.

Nowhere in Polynesia was the destruction of the native forest so extensive and so consequential as in New Zealand. This was achieved by fire. Flames had swept through the eastern forests of South Island long before human settlement, but it was the coming of people that began the wholesale clearance of great tracts of woodland. The burning was often to encourage the growth of bracken-fern, but in North Island it was part of a deliberate scheme to create more space for cultivation. From the coastline, the forest was steadily nibbled away as settlements moved inland. The area around Hawke's Bay, now famed for its vineyards, was one of the first to be transformed from dense forest to open ground. Many fires sped through the forest, out of control; far more was destroyed than was needed for horticulture.

As on other Pacific islands, the 'big burn' became an annual event; there seems to have been an innate desire to 'cleanse' the land with fire. In New Zealand it happened on a grand scale. It has been estimated that in the three centuries between 1200 and 1500, a few thousand Maori destroyed eight million acres of forest, reducing it to open grassland and scrub. The disappearance of the tree cover led to widespread erosion and to loss of soil fertility. Rather than attempt to rejuvenate the land by use of composted vegetation, the communities continued the ancient but relentless process of 'slash and burn'. Compared with their former oceanic islands, space in New Zealand was not at a premium. The Maori transformation of the landscape was, of course, not one of conscious destruction; nor were they in any way less responsible than we are today. As in Hawaii and Easter Island, the Polynesians living at this third corner of the Triangle began a process of extinction from which there would be no retreat. The difference between their respective impacts on the various island groups was simply a matter of scale.

New Zealand's forest had been full of birds, many of which fed on nectar. The disappearance of the trees and the spread of grassland devastated these species. Unlike many of the native birds of Australia which are seed-eaters and thrive on grass and other cereals, they could not adapt to the new landscapes. Those that survived the changes began to fall victim to the new four-legged predators suddenly inflicted on the land. The domestic dogs, introduced by the first settlers, had a great impact on flightless species and on ground-nesting birds which had never been harassed by such predators. Trained by their Maori owners to flush out game-birds, these dogs plagued the native wildlife.

The Polynesian rat, known to the Maori as *kiore*, also came with the first settlers, probably deliberately imported as a valued source of meat. Bred in captivity and then released into the wild, the species thrived in its new home. In the absence of any native ground predators, it too had the run of the place to itself. It was soon living everywhere and had adapted to its new omnivorous diet of seeds and fruits, birds' eggs and fledglings, and reptiles such as geckos and skinks. At night these small rodents would move to new feeding grounds, running in single file along well-trodden paths worn smooth by their tiny feet. The Maori invented ingenious traps which they set along these rat-runs. Their fur plucked or singed, the *kiore* were roasted and eaten by the basketful, or preserved in their own fat and stored in gourds for a cold, rainy day.

It does seem extraordinary that the first New Zealanders, from wherever they came, arrived without their traditional domestic supplies of meat. For generations, their ancestors had reared the jungle fowl until it had become as much a part of tropical island life as the coconut. The same applied to the pig. Throughout the rest of Polynesia, except for Easter Island, the domesticated pig was prized for its tasty flesh. It had successfully been introduced to Hawaii but not, it would seem, to New Zealand. No archaeological digs have yet turned up pig bones, nor are there any recognizable signs of the domestic chicken. It is conceivable that the animals failed to survive the long journey or were eaten en route by desperate voyagers. What is difficult to believe is that this would happen many times. The idea of a great fleet sailing together seems equally unlikely. Another explanation for possible arrival but extinction of these two valued domestic creatures is the natural store of meat that was waiting to be plundered. When the first New Zealanders encountered flocks of giant, meaty, wingless birds, they could be excused for neglecting their own imported stock. Maybe the poor, travel-weary pigs were roasted in celebration of the canoe's safe arrival and the chickens ignored in favour of the native fowl now to be known as *moa*.

From the day that man set foot on New Zealand soil, a close association began between the hunter and his prey. It was to last for centuries but was finally to result in the complete extinction of the *moa*. It was a pattern of human impact which can be traced back to the beginnings of the Polynesian people's settlement of Pacific islands. Colonization of Fiji and the other islands of the western Pacific left its mark on the birds and other wild creatures of those islands; megapodes soon became rare or extinct, as did many species of flightless rail. Giant clams rapidly disappeared from the reefs and turtles from the lagoons. Wherever and whenever people first settled remote oceanic islands, the balance of nature was changed forever.

In New Zealand, all eleven species of *moa* were probably extinct before AD 1500. Bone and fossil records also show that about a dozen other endemic birds were hunted to extinction. This list included an eagle, a harrier hawk, a crow and a pelican, as well as various swans, geese, ducks and rails. Other species almost went the same way. Pigeons were caught with nooses as they gorged on ripe fruits in the forest canopy; in the mountains, *kea* parrots were lured by tame

Above The *kea* (*Nestor notabilis*), the alpine forest parrot of New Zealand.
Fearless flocks scavenge human settlements and pester tourists for scraps.
The name *kea* given them by the first maori settlers describes their noisy call.
This is a juvenile.
Right The *kakapo*, literally 'parrot of the night' (*Strigops habroptilus*). This large
flightless bird was easy prey for hunters; its nocturnal habit helped save it from
extinction. Very vulnerable to introduced mammalian predators, this wonderful
creature is great cause for conservation concern.

decoys and then speared; sought after for their feathers as well as their meat, the *kakapo*, the large flightless 'night parrots', were hunted with dogs; even the sonorous *tui* was considered a game-bird and snared in traps cunningly baited with blossom. The Maori hunter, in his seemingly limitless land, assumed that its edible resources were also endless.

South Island is regarded as having been the centre of *moa* hunting; there was a greater variety of species than in the north. It was the climate in the south that shaped the lifestyle of its people. Very few of the introduced domestic crops would grow there, which made horticulture difficult. Their best option was to capitalize on the wild resources, as hunters and gatherers. Compared with the tribes that settled in the north, the Maori of South Island moved around the country in response to its seasons. They established coastal camps for fishing and for hunting fur seals, and inland they set up the now famous 'moa-hunter' sites.

The larger species, such as *Euryapteryx geranoides*, must have been formidable quarry. They moved in flocks but, when alarmed, could run much faster than a man. With one slash of their claws they could disembowel a hunter armed with spears and stones. The most effective method of hunting was for a party of men to ambush the birds and kill them at close quarters with their spears. Dogs were specially bred to be tenacious hunting companions, able to hang on to the *moa* with powerful jaws and neck muscles. Snares set on *moa* trails through the bush would catch unwary birds by the feet, making their capture less hazardous for the hunters. Although far fewer people lived in the south, it is reckoned that during the first few centuries of occupation, 100 000 *moa* fell victim to the accomplished Maori hunters. The charred remains found in thousands of earth-ovens around the island bear witness to the importance of this incredible bird that the Maori hunter called a chicken.

The intensive hunting of *moa* and other land-birds, together with the exploitation of seals and other marine life, began to threaten the survival of people in some parts of New Zealand. Their rats and dogs also hunted for food, while other wild creatures competed with the human inhabitants for the natural resources of the land and sea. The cultivated crops were pillaged by opportunist wildlife and infested by pests. The centuries of settlement and adaptation were changing to an era of competitive survival. Not only were the resources dwindling, but the Maori population was increasing. From the initial founding group of perhaps 100 immigrants, it would have taken four centuries to reach a total population of 5000. During the next four or five centuries until European contact, the figure increased perhaps twenty-fold to 100 000.

This expansion phase in New Zealand's pre-European times coincided with a marked deterioration of climate. Throughout the world, temperatures dropped a couple of degrees centigrade below those enjoyed in the Little Climatic Optimum. In England it was enough to regularly freeze the River Thames each winter and kill all the vines. The so-called 'Little Ice Age' was felt around the globe. In the Viking outpost of Greenland, the Norse people lost their lush pastures. In time, their crops failed and their herds of cattle perished. It was the end of their colony.

In the Pacific Ocean, the greatest effects were felt outside the tropics. In temperate New Zealand the glaciers on the west coast of South Island began to grow. Many of the inland areas became less hospitable and some tribes moved north. Year by year, as winters became noticeably more severe, houses were modified to give more protection. Small and thick-walled, they were equipped with a porch and tightly thatched with bundles of grasses and bark of trees. Much like those of windy Easter Island, they were entered on hands and knees through a low tunnel. Characteristically, Maori dwellings had an internal hearth and a single window to let out the smoke. With the onset of less temperate weather, warm houses and warm clothes became essential for survival.

The extinction of the *moa* and the disappearance of many colonies of sea-mammals forced the Maori to rely increasingly on their fishing and horticultural skills, just like their Polynesian cousins in the tropics. Though four times larger in area than all the other Polynesian islands put together, the land of New Zealand was not as naturally fertile as many of the small volcanic islands further north. Most of the ground soils consisted of hard compacted clays, with thin skeletal topsoils. This, combined with the cooler climate, put pressures on an expanding population

Food was often in short supply. The *kumara* crops were the first to fail. Even in the warmer north, the storage pits were difficult to fill. To protect their stocks, each settlement built a fortress around its principal garden areas, *kumara* stores and chiefly buildings. These *pa* were designed for easy defence against envious neighbours who had not been so successful with that season's crops. Throughout New Zealand's landscape, you can still see clear signs of these fortifications. Some were constructed as a system of terraces or as ditches and banks; others were sited near the sea or with their backs against rivers. An entire hilltop might be converted into a *pa* by building circular palisades of logs. Many of the small volcanoes that are a feature of today's capital city, Auckland, were once fortified in this way. There are more than 5500 *pa* recorded in North Island while perhaps only 100 have been identified in South Island.

Maori culture seems to have always been very tribal, although there is little evidence of warfare in the archaeological records of the early centuries of

In a Maori *pa*, a fortified village, each family had its own cluster of buildings – for sleeping, food storage and cooking. Curiously, this engraving clearly depicts pigs; presumably they had, by then, been introduced by Europeans. In New Zealand, pigs became known as 'Captain Cookers'.

settlement. Each tribe had staked its regional claim and there was space and resources for everyone. It was in more recent centuries that rivalry and conflicts became a regular feature of New Zealand life. To die like a man was the ambition of every Maori warrior. They became the most formidable fighters in Polynesia.

As in the other Pacific islands, the birth of a boy was an occasion for celebration. Taken by his parents to a stream, the infant would be named at an elaborate ritual conducted by a priest. The gods would be invoked to give strength and stamina to the new warrior. From an early age, most boys were professionally trained to fight; athletics helped promote a high level of mental and physical agility. As in the Marquesas and other eastern Polynesian islands, the art of body tattooing became highly developed in New Zealand. Called *moko*, the Polynesian word for 'lizard', this prestigious decoration was reserved for people of high status, which included warriors. Women were also tattooed, although normally only on the chin, lips and forehead. Men were adorned with circles and other curving shapes, including motifs based on the coiled leaves of *koru*, the native fern. Warriors were tattooed with a privileged blue dye made from the soot of a resinous timber or from burnt *kauri* gum. The decorations were painstakingly and painfully inflicted on their faces, thighs and buttocks.

With his tongue defiantly extended in a gesture of threat, and armed with his spear and *patu* club, the Maori warrior was a fearful opponent. The land of his tribe was sacred; it was *whenua*, the earth mother. Like the *vanua* of Fiji and the *fenua* of Samoa and Tahiti, it was the place of his ancestors and, as a warrior, he would willingly die in its defence.

CHAPTER ELEVEN

The PIERCED SKY

The advent of man had a profound impact on the nature of the Pacific. He was the first predator to set foot on many of the islands. The Polynesians came with clear concepts of how to manage the landscape in the interests of their survival. They brought alien plants and animals which they would selectively encourage. Native vegetation was replaced with plantations of imported crops that would not have reached these islands on their own. The indigenous birds were forced to compete with introduced domestic fowl and were harassed by Polynesian dogs and rats. Pigs uprooted young trees and foraged for fruits and nuts which might otherwise have matured to take their place in the forest canopy. Full-grown trees were felled for their timber and their places taken by imported species favoured by the newcomers. Though the Polynesian population was small, its influence on the natural communities of these islands was substantial. It was, though, a drop in the ocean compared to the 'fatal impact' of the European.

On 6 October 1769, Europeans were poised to descend on New Zealand, the largest islands of Polynesia. It had been almost three months since Captain Cook's vessel, HMS *Endeavour*, had bid farewell to Tahiti, more than 2500 miles away in the eastern Pacific. Now his task was to explore and map the southern land which the Dutch navigator, Abel Tasman, had sighted 120 years before and named in honour of his European homeland. There had been a skirmish with the natives in which four of them were killed. Tasman had sailed away without setting foot on this unknown southern land. For several generations, there had been no further contact between these two worlds that lay at completely opposite sides of the globe.

William Hodges, the official expedition artist on board *Resolution*, romantically portrayed this encounter with a waterspout off New Zealand in May 1773, during Captain Cook's second Pacific voyage.

We lived at Whitianga, and a vessel came there, and when our old men saw the ship they said it was an 'atua', a god, and the people on board were 'tapua', strange beings or goblins . . . their eyes are at the back of their heads; they pull on shore with their backs to the land to which they are going. We ran away from them into the forest and the warriors alone stayed in the presence of these goblins; but, as the goblins stayed some time and did not do any evil to our braves, we came back one by one, and gazed on them.

Horeta Te Taniwha was a small child when Cook's men rowed ashore at Whitianga harbour. When he was an old man, he described his memories of that historic first encounter. Recorded faithfully in John White's *The Ancient History of the Maori*, published in New Zealand more than a century later, this Maori view of Captain Cook and his crew reminds us that these 'savages' were perceptive and rational people.

There was one supreme man in that ship. We knew that he was lord of the whole by his perfect gentlemanly and noble demeanour. He seldom spoke, but some of the goblins spoke much. He was a very good man, and came to us children and patted our cheeks, and gently touched our heads. His language was a hissing sound, and the words he spoke were not understood by us in the least.

Captain Cook and his European 'goblins' had sailed to New Zealand in the wake of the Polynesians who had first discovered this southern land at least five centuries before. The first voyage had been by double-hulled canoe, made entirely of timber and other plant material, and crewed by experienced mariners whose main navigational aids were the sea and the sky. Cook's vessel was held together by iron and navigated with the help of instruments made of metal and glass. Both voyages had been powered by the wind and both had set off in the hope that, a long way to the south-west of Tahiti, there was an even larger land. In their own way, they were equally epic voyages of discovery.

Whilst Daniel Solander, Joseph Banks and the other naturalists recorded the native wildlife and natural resources of this new land, James Cook investigated the life of its human inhabitants. Wisely, he had brought Tupaia as guide and interpreter. This man, born on Raiatea, knew the legends about Kupe's 'island of birds' but, although well travelled in eastern Polynesia, he had never been there. After the to-and-fro voyages of settlement, it is probable that no further Polynesian sailing canoes came this far south. For twenty or so generations, the people of New Zealand lived in isolation from the other island groups of Polynesia. Tupaia was a foreigner but he was not a 'goblin'. He looked much like the Maori and spoke a language which they could under-

stand. Cook, Banks and probably all the crew discovered that the Tahitian and Maori languages shared many words. James Magra, the only American on board, who was clearly a widely travelled man, marvelled at their similarity.

> *It deserves to be remarked, that the people of New Zealand spoke the language of Otahitee but with very little difference, not so much as is found between many counties in England; a circumstance of the most extraordinary kind, and must necessarily lead us to conclude, that one of these places was originally peopled from the other, though they are near two thousand miles distance; and nothing but the ocean intervenes.*

Magra drew many other parallels between the Tahitian and Maori people and their cultures. He pointed out their similar physical features, the way they tattooed their bodies and tied their hair on top of their heads, but noted that the Maori were browner in complexion than Tahitians; he drew attention to the identical way they cooked food in earth-ovens and to the similar design of such artefacts as axes and fish-hooks. He observed that the Maori were more courageous in their warfare but that they did not use bows and arrows as he had

Above The Maori of South Island crossed the high passes of the
alps to reach the braided rivers of the west coast, source of greenstone
with which to make tools, weapons and ornaments.
Left English officer bartering with Maori for crayfish. The painter
of this watercolour sketch is thought to have been Joseph
Banks, the botanist on Cook's first voyage to New Zealand. Banks'
journal for 7th March 1770 refers to 'sea crawfish and lobsters'
being traded with the native people.

seen practised by the archers on Tahiti. He concluded that the warfaring Maori
would never have dispensed with such an advantageous weapon, and therefore
the Tahitian people must have migrated from New Zealand and invented the
skill on Tahiti. Theories surrounding the origins of the people and the dates of
settlement of all the island groups in Polynesia have intrigued experts ever since;
it is unlikely that we have heard the last.

For the Maori of New Zealand, Cook's arrival brought awareness of a wider
world. They could converse with Tupaia. From him they learned of Tahiti and
the distant lands that were remembered in their folklore as 'Hawaiki'. They
discovered that Tupaia and his people shared the same beliefs, the same gods and
the same reverence for their ancestors. They knew the same sea-birds and fish,
and they had the same names for many of the plants and animals essential to their
way of life. They had much in common.

Above The *haka* was often a prelude to physical conflict between tribes. The stylized posturing, grimaces and chanting of the warriors presented a fearful challenge to their opponents. Today the *haka* is enthusiastically performed when members of different tribes meet socially and for competitive sports. The more provocative the presentation, the more welcome the guests.

Top European traders introduced iron axes and muskets and dramatically changed the course of Maori warfare. In this war-dance, they brandish their new weapons in place of traditional *patu* clubs and *taiaha* batons.

By now, Tupaia could speak some English. He could converse with Captain Cook and his crew, with whom he exchanged ideas. They told him about England and the other countries beyond the horizon, foreign lands that the Polynesian mind had not been able to conceive. By sailing into the Maori world, the European explorers had breached its isolation. These 'goblins' who came to New Zealand with their strange ways and strange ideas had not only come from another world, they carried part of it with them. When they sailed away, they would leave part of it behind.

In the Maori language, the white-skinned 'goblins' were commonly referred to as *pakeha*, a term that might derive from their word for the indigenous white turnip. Other explanations are even less polite! In Tonga and Samoa, the equivalent term for white foreigners is *palagi* (pronounced 'palanggi'), the original meaning of which may have been 'sky-piercer'. The euphemism not only graphically describes how these aliens descended on their world, but also conveys the impact of their arrival. For the Polynesian, the universe was an ocean of islands embraced by the vast dome of the sky. Those who came from beyond the furthest horizon had pierced the boundary of their world. Nothing would ever be the same again.

The Maori had not seen iron before, nor any other kind of metal. Like their cousins throughout Polynesia, they were still essentially a Stone Age culture. Iron fired their imaginations and changed the tempo of their lives. Metal axes and adzes sliced through timber with a speed that stone could never match; iron picks and hoes cut the sod and turned the soil in a way that could never be achieved with the humble digging stick. Armed with metal spear and hatchet, the Maori warrior would be invincible; with the goblins' fiery weapons his tribe would rule the land.

Captain Cook visited New Zealand on each of his three Pacific voyages; his journals reveal that he developed a great affection for the land and its people. It was in New Zealand that he first recorded his growing concern about the changes that this new era of European encounter would inevitably bring to the people of the South Pacific. Venereal disease, measles, influenza and other contagious European ailments had a devastating effect on the Maori population. Trading their greenstone war clubs for muskets and powder, warfaring tribes embarked on a wholesale slaughter of each other. Within a few decades of Cook's last voyage, the Maori population had dramatically fallen. Offshore, foreign vessels were slaughtering seals and whales in a frenzy of exploitation.

Some alien imports and ideas brought great social and physical benefits. Potatoes from Europe grew well in New Zealand and, together with other introduced crops, helped feed the Maori population. Pigs and chickens, the traditional Polynesian livestock missing from the Maori way of life, were introduced by Cook. They helped compensate for the disappearance of the native *moa* and other birds wiped out by generations of exploitation and deforestation. When Cook sailed away from New Zealand, he also left goats, which bred so prolifically that they accelerated the transformation of the landscape to open country. With the introduction, first of horses and cattle from Australia in 1814, and then the plough, the process became almost irreversible. British sheep soon followed, together with British people and other European immigrants who were convinced that New Zealand should mirror their distant homelands. Just like the Polynesians before them, they sought to impose their own familiar landscapes on this wild southern land.

The new settlers also brought wild plant and animal species which they thought would benefit their adopted country. The most favoured imports were birds. Some, such as partridge and pheasant, Canada geese and mallards, were introduced as game birds; others were to adorn the new land with the grace of their plumage or the reassurance of their song. The early settlers from England yearned for the song of the skylark, their emblem of pastoral plenty. It was imported to New Zealand and flourished on the newly created grassland. For similar reasons, 'acclimatization societies' sponsored the introduction of other familiar northern European birds, such as the songthrush and blackbird, starling and chaffinch. They all excelled in the new habitats. Some did so well that they became pests.

Unlike most native New Zealand birds, the yellowhammer is a seed-eater. It wreaked havoc wherever European settlers tried to establish new pasture by sowing seed. This imported bird became such a problem, particularly in South Island, that a price was put on its head. The house sparrow was a similar story. Introduced into Britain at the time of the Roman invasion, it was brought to New Zealand to help control insects that were devastating the crops of the colonists. Instead of solving the problem, it devoured the crops it was supposed to protect. So widespread was its success in the latter half of the nineteenth century that the house sparrow became the object of the new nation's Small Birds Nuisance Act of 1882.

From Australia came kookaburras and cockatoos; from Asia came myna birds and exotic peafowl; from America came wild turkey and Californian quail. In all, thirty-four species of birds were introduced. To these were added Australian lizards and frogs, fourteen species of fresh-water fish from around the world, and thirty-three species of mammals, including zebras from the African plains and llamas from the High Andes. For tens of millions of years, New Zealand had evolved on its own, cut adrift from the rest of the world. By the beginning of the twentieth century, Kupe's fabled 'island of birds' had become a menagerie of strangers.

The reason for the re-stocking of New Zealand was simply because most of its native plants and animals would not adapt to the new landscapes created by European settlers. Most of the native species were essentially forest-dwellers; as the trees disappeared, so did they. The exotic species introduced by the zealous acclimatization societies flourished in the alien landscapes created by their benefactors. Only snakes and foxes were forbidden entry by act of Parliament, but many of the new wildlife residents were far more injurious to the ecosystem. Some became such a nuisance that predators such as stoats, ferrets, weasels and even hedgehogs were brought from Europe to control the European pests. From Australia came possums which, in the absence of natural controls on their numbers, bred unhindered in the wild. Today possums are public enemy number one as they devastate the *rata* (*Metrosideros*) and other native forest trees. Natural vegetation has been stripped by more than a thousand species of introduced insect, many of them voracious pests. Not only has New Zealand lost most of its native forest plants and animals, much of the country has been transformed into landscapes which the first Polynesian settlers would barely recognize.

Exotic plants and animals were introduced by European settlers to beautify their adopted country; lupins now dominate much of the South Island landscape.

In the wake of explorers came opportunist traders from Europe, America and Asia. They came to raid the forests of the Pacific islands for their native timbers. Sandalwood soon almost completely disappeared from Hawaii, Fiji and the Marquesas. In place of the forests, new crops were planted. In Hawaii today the pineapple is far more conspicuous than the pandanus. The fertile lowlands of Tahiti and her neighbouring islands sprout modern cash crops of coffee and vanilla in place of taro and yams; even the traditional copra trade in coconut has been overtaken by the times. On the higher slopes, orchards of orange trees have replaced the ancient groves of Tahitian chestnut. Even on sacred Raiatea, the invasive miconia shrub is rapidly increasing its stranglehold on the remnants of wild forest. On the islands of western Polynesia, from Tonga to Fiji, the native forest has been replaced by vast tracts of imported pines and endless acres of sugar-cane. None of these crops supports the native wildlife of the islands, nor do they preserve the traditions of the island people.

Like the native plants and animals of the islands of Polynesia, the native people had evolved their own very special way of life. Over generations of experiment and adaptation they had developed an understanding of their ocean environment which had enabled them to reach and settle almost every oceanic island in the Pacific. The further from the mainland they voyaged, the more dependent they became on the resources they took with them. The landscapes they created on each new island were landscapes for survival. As they sailed eastward across the Pacific, they did so with increasing confidence in their ability to prosper on its natural wealth. They were prudent in their plant and animal husbandry and conscious of the limits of nature's benevolence. With taboos they regulated the exploitation of the world around them. If their well-proven system began to fail them, they moved on to new horizons. The islands that they left behind were returned to the wild. The Polynesian experience on Easter Island holds a salutary economic and environmental lesson for us all. Until we know for sure what lies beyond the horizon, and that we have the ability to reach it, we must live within the confines of the world we know.

Polynesian voyaging involved an act of faith, but it was rationally and strategically planned. Very little was left to chance. Like voyagers in space, these explorers travelled with their self-contained life-support system. When they landed at their destination, they used their ancestral skills and wisdom to create a landscape which would provide for their needs. But like the native people of North America, to which in the distant past they are surely related, the Polynesian people saw themselves as belonging to the land and the sea, not owning them. Like the American Indians, they were not environmental saints, but they knew that their survival depended on the way they capitalized on the natural resources of their island world. They were adaptable and resourceful. The flowering of their culture was an expression of their success. In wood and stone, in music and dance, in ornate tapa-cloth and tattoos, each new colony of Polynesians celebrated their relationship with the land and its nature. To the Polynesian, *fenua*, the land, is everything. It is not a solely territorial concept, but a spiritual bond.

The Europeans who pierced those distant horizons came with very different ideas. For them the land and the sea were there to be exploited for short-term profit, not for long-term well-being. Today, one of the most appealing traits of the Polynesian people is their ability to enjoy each day for its own sake. It is a quality which the first European visitors to the South Seas found both alarming and alluring. What the outside world failed to respect was the Polynesians' commitment to their land and to their ancestral line. Like the Maori of New Zealand, all Polynesians have a strong sense of belonging. They are part of the sea and the sky, the land and its nature. They have a collective tradition of inheritance and of obligation. Such worthy concepts are central to the new wave of environmental concern that has gripped the conscience of us all. For Polynesians, these principles have always been a very natural part of life.

On Easter Island, the felling of the last trees heralded the dramatic decline of the culture; in New Zealand it was the destruction of the forest, not the extermination of the *moa*, which changed the basic nature of the country. It was a process started by the Maori and all but completed by the more recent European settlers. Perhaps because there was so much forest in New Zealand, both cultures took it for granted. Whatever the explanation, New Zealand has lost more of its forest, more rapidly, than any comparable part of the world.

The *kauri* is a giant among trees; some individuals are 2000 years old, perhaps more. They can reach 180 feet into the sky and measure fifty feet in girth. Their sheer size gives the *kauri* their great distinction. Its timber is tough and straight-grained but also silky-textured and the colour of honey. As it grows skyward, its trunk does not seem to taper, but climbs with even strength until it towers above the canopy of lesser trees. California's famed sequoia trees are older and often taller, but the surviving *kauri* of Waipoua Forest in New Zealand's Northland are truly majestic. It is not surprising that they are considered to have great *mana* and that they represent all that is powerful and benevolent about Tane, the god of nature. In the early nineteenth century, the reputation of this magnificent tree brought timber-traders from Sydney. For a time it became the new nation's principal export, the native Maori and immigrant Pakeha collaborating in its exploitation. By 1885, half the *kauri* forest had been plundered and by the end of the century, only a quarter remained. For today's New Zealanders, both Maori and Pakeha, the *kauri* is now a symbol of their country, as beloved as their ubiquitous silver fern.

In the centre of North Island is the region called Tongariro, an area of active volcanoes, ancient forest and barren desert. The Maori have always held it in great esteem. For many generations, the Ngati Tuwharetoa tribe buried their chiefs on the side of its principal mountain. For centuries, the region was feared and respected as *tapu*. Towards the end of the nineteenth century, at a time when much of New Zealand was being reshaped by axe and fire, the tribe's ancestral claim to the ownership of Tongariro came under threat in the Maori Land Court. To ensure that the *tapu* mountains would not fall into the hands of exploiters and others who would despoil the land, chief Te Heuheu Tukino gave the mountains to the nation, stipulating that they should be 'for the purposes of a National Park'. In 1894, an act of Parliament formally established Tongariro National Park. It was the first such park in New Zealand, and the first to be set aside in any of the islands of Polynesia.

Above European and American whalers came to New Zealand waters to slaughter fur seals and whales; now enterprising Maori have developed a new and profitable way of exploiting the marine mammals off their shores. At Kaikoura, whale-watching is big business, but relatively harmless to the whales.
Right On Tahiti, Polynesian people protest against France's nuclear presence on the atoll of Moruroa. Throughout French Polynesia, there is a growing awareness of the importance of solving the islands' many ecological problems. The ancient Polynesian concept of *rahui*, a form of taboo involving 'restraint', has taken on a new political meaning.

Today, ecologically and politically, Polynesian people are reasserting their concern for the land and its nature. In New Zealand in particular, Maori claims to the country's natural landscapes and resources have become a sensitive issue. They are highlighting differences of attitude to issues of landscape and wildlife conservation. In French Polynesia, there is a similar renaissance of pride in their culture and in the nature of their islands. In Hawaii, the resurgence of interest in the islands' native wildlife is matched only by concern about the demise of its native people and their distinctive cultural heritage. The most 'endangered species' in Polynesia may now be the Polynesian.

In October 1992, people from every corner of Polynesia were drawn together
for a Festival of Pacific Arts held on Rarotonga in the Cook Islands. It was an
event staged for themselves – not for the entertainment of the outside world.
For the Polynesian musicians and dancers, craftsmen and navigators, story-tellers
and historians, it was a very real celebration of their common heritage – and an
expression of the recent renaissance in their Pacific pride.

The great age of Polynesian voyaging came to an end almost 1000 years ago. A tenacious, seafaring people had abandoned the shores of south-east Asia and sailed into the Pacific. As their culture developed, they acquired new skills of survival, and new knowledge of the ocean world which became their home. The further they sailed eastward, away from the security of mainland life, the more they came to depend on their own resourcefulness as well as the resources of the islands they discovered and settled. The vibrant Polynesian culture that grew and flourished on the remote islands of the Pacific is testament to the invention and adaptability of its people. Its distinctiveness derives in part from the ancestral way of life brought by the first voyagers, but mainly from the singular nature of the oceanic world that they adopted as their new homeland.

Auckland is now the largest Polynesian city in the world. Not including the native Maori of New Zealand, its cosmopolitan population includes 60 000 immigrants from other Polynesian islands. There are now more Cook Islanders living in Auckland than live on their own home island, Rarotonga. At the northern apex of the Polynesian Triangle, Hawaii is the adopted land of 14 000 people from Samoa, 2500 miles away. A further 15 000 Polynesian islanders have moved to the American mainland and live in sprawling Los Angeles. Long-distance migration remains part of the Polynesian spirit; the nomad is still within them. Besieged by an alien tide that came from every horizon, they travel in search of other worlds. Paradoxically, the one they leave behind still seems, to us, like paradise.

GLOSSARY
of Polynesian Words

Many words and terms are very similar throughout Polynesia, Fiji and many of the islands of South East Asia. These linguistic affinities provide fascinating clues to the origins and migrations of the Polynesian people. Certain sounds have changed with distance and time, but there are remarkable similarities between the native languages of the far-flung islands of the Pacific. Today's Fijian language, though not strictly Polynesian, has many words in common with its oceanic neighbours and their voyaging ancestors. The words selected for this glossary are those used in the main text of the book, but others have been included in the definitions to serve as interesting comparisons.

An apostrophe ' indicates a glottal-stop as in *i'iwi*
In Samoan and Fijian **g** is pronounced '**ng**'
In Fijian **q** is pronounced '**ngg**' and **b** sounds like '**mb**'

The following abbreviations indicate the island group to which the text refers, but many terms have a more widespread use.
EI Easter Island   F Fiji   H Hawaii   M Marquesas   NZ New Zealand   S Samoa   SI Society Islands (Tahiti etc)   T Tonga

ahi'ahi afternoon (SI)
ahu/ahu moai temple/with statue (SI/EI)
aito ironwood tree (SI) also known as *toa*
aitu spirit
ama candle-nut tree (M)
ao day
ari'i chief (SI); elsewhere *ariki, aliki, ali'i*
arioi religious sect (SI)
ati hardwood tree (SI) (*Calophyllum*); also known as *tamanu* (SI), *temanu* (M), *kamani* (H), and related to *damanu* (F)
atua god
aute paper-mulberry tree (SI); also *koute* (M), *wauke* (H)
auti sugar-producing cordyline tree, also known as *ti* (SI), *ki* (H), *qai* (F)
auwai irrigation ditch (H)
ava'a gods' bed (SI)
avatea mid-day hours (SI)

balabala tree fern (F)
bokola cannibal victim (F)
bulu spirit world (F)
bune orange dove (F)

dalo taro plant (F), *talo* (S), *ta'o* (M), *kalo* (H)
damanu (see *ati*)

elepaio wren-like bird (H)

fenua land; also *vanua* (F) and *whenua* (NZ)

hare house (EI); *hale* (H) and *fale* (S)

hau beach hibiscus (EI); *vau* (F) and *purau* (SI)

ie'ie freycinetia vine (H, SI)

kaka red-breasted musk-parrot (F); forest parrot (NZ)
kakapo nocturnal flightless parrot (NZ)
kalo (see *dalo*)
kapa bark-cloth (H); *tapa* (SI); *masi* (F)
kapu taboo (H); *tapu* (SI); *tabu* (F) etc.
kauri primitive pine-like tree (NZ)
kava word derived from Tongan name for pepper-plant used to make intoxicating drink: also *ava* (S, SI); *awa* (H); *yaqona* (F); similar plant known as *kawakawa* in NZ
kea mountain parrot (NZ)
kiore/kio'e Polynesian rat
kiwi flightless ratite bird (NZ); cf. *ivi* curlew (SI etc)
koa Hawaiian acacia tree (H)
kula parrot-like collared lory (F)
kulawai red-throated lorikeet (F)
kuluvotu multi-coloured fruit dove (F)
kumara sweet potato (NZ, EI); *umara* (SI); *umala* (S); *uala* (H) and *kumala* (F) (interestingly, *kumar* on west coast of S. America)

lovo earth-oven (F) (see *umu*: also *hangi* NZ)

ma fermented bread-fruit (SI)

magimagi coconut fibre (F); *ma'oma'o* (S)

makahiki annual harvest festival (H)

mana supernatural power/prestige

manahune commoner (SI); cf. *menehune* legendary 'dwarfs' (H)

mao giant forest honeyeater (S)

mape Tahitian chestnut (SI); also *ifi* (S) and *ivi* (F)

marae sacred site (SI); *me'ae* (M); also *malae* etc.

mare asthma (EI); cough (SI)

masi bark-cloth (F); (see *tapa*)

mata'a obsidian spearhead (EI)

matatoa warrior leader (EI)

me'ae (see *marae*)

miro Pacific rosewood (*Thespesia*) (SI); *milo* (S, H); *mulomulo* (F)

moa chicken/fowl (S, SI, EI etc); extinct giant flightless birds (NZ)

moko lizard; also tattoo (NZ)

momoko commoner (EI)

naio tree used in house construction (H)

neinei Rarotongan sunflower tree (Cook Islands)

nene Hawaiian goose (H)

nono Indian mulberry (SI); *noni* (M, H), *nonu* (S), *kura* (F)

ohi'a endemic *Metrosideros* tree (H)

opou tattoo 'victim' (M)

ou'a assistant to tattoo artist (M)

pa fortified village (NZ)

patu war club (NZ)

pili grass used as thatch (H)

po night

pukao topknot of statue (EI)

pulotu underworld (S); also *burotu* (F)

purau beach hibiscus; also *vau* (F and T), *'au* (Cook Islands), *fau* (S and T), *hau* (H, M); *ra'au* (SI); *rakau* (EI, NZ)

ra'atira lesser chiefs (SI); also *rangatira* (NZ)

rakau tree (SI); wealth (EI); weapons (NZ)

sau spiritual power (F); see also *mana*

tabili hollowed log for pounding kava roots (F)

tabu (pronounced 'tambu' in Fiji) sacred/ prohibited; also *tapu* (SI), *kapu* (H)

tamanu hardwood tree (SI); see also *damanu*

tangata people (EI, NZ etc)

tanoa wooden bowl (F)

tapa bark-cloth (SI etc); see also *masi*

tatau tattoo (SI)

ta'ua patu tiki tattooist (M)

ti (see *auti*)

tiare gardenia flower (SI)

ti'i tiki figure (SI)

tohua community centre (M)

totara native podocarp tree (NZ)

tou shoreline tree used for timber and medicines (SI, M); also *kou* (H)

tupa land-crab (SI)

tutui candle-nut tree (SI)

umu earth-oven

uru bread-fruit tree (SI); also *ulu* (S, H), *uto* (F), *kuru* (Cook Islands)

va'a canoes (SI); also *vaka/waka* (Cook Islands, NZ etc)

vanua (see *fenua*)

vesi hardwood tree (F)

wauke paper-mulberry tree (H) (see also *aute*)

whenua land/earth mother (NZ)

wiliwili endemic Hawaiian tree

yaqona kava plant, also the intoxicating drink made from its roots (F) (see *kava*)

BIBLIOGRAPHY

GENERAL

Bellwood, P. *The Polynesians – Prehistory of an Island People*, Thames and Hudson, 1978 and 1987

Buck, P. *Vikings of the Sunrise*, Whitcombe and Tombs, 1954

Cameron, I. *Lost Paradise – The Exploration of the Pacific*, Century, 1987

Cook, J. (ed. Beaglehole, J.) *The Journals of Cpt. J. Cook on his Voyages of Discovery 1768–1780*, Hakluyt Society, 1955–68

Danielsson, B. *I James Cooks Kölvatten*, Bra Böcker, 1991

Irwin, G. *The Prehistoric Exploration and Colonisation of the Pacific*, Cambridge University Press, 1992

Jennings, J. (Editor) *The Prehistory of Polynesia*, (various authors) Harvard University Press, 1979

Kane, H. *Voyagers*, Whalesong, USA, 1991

Kirch, P. *The Evolution of Polynesian Chiefdoms*, Cambridge University Press, 1984

Mitchell, A. *A Fragile Paradise – Nature and Man in the Pacific*, Collins, 1989

Stanley, D. *South Pacific Handbook*, Moon Publications, 1989

Suggs, R. *The Island Civilisations of Polynesia*, The New American Library, 1960

TAHITI AND THE SOCIETY ISLANDS

Eyraud, A. *Tahiti Today – and All its Islands*, Les Editions j.a., Paris, 1990

Howarth, D. *Tahiti – A Paradise Lost*, Harvill Press, 1983

Oliver, D. *Ancient Tahitian Society* 3 vols., University of Hawaii Press, 1974

Stanley, D. *Tahiti – Polynesia Handbook*, Moon Publications, 1989

THE MARQUESAS

Handy, E. *The Native Culture in the Marquesas*, Bishop Museum Bulletin No. 9 Kraus Reprint 1971

Ottino, P. & M. *Hiva Oa – Glimpses of an Oceanic Memory*, Department of Archaeology, Tahiti 1991

Sinoto, Y. *The Marquesas*, In Jennings, J. (Ed.) 1979 (see above)

Thomas, N. *Marquesan Societies*, Clarendon Press, Oxford 1990

Thomson, R. *The Marquesas Islands*, Written in 1814 Institute for Polynesian Studies, Hawaii 1978

FIJI, SAMOA AND TONGA

Clunie, F. *Birds of the Fiji Bush*, Fiji Museum, Suva 1984

Green, R. *Lapita*, In Jennings (Ed.) 1979 (see above)

Lonely Planet *Guides to Tonga and Samoa*, 1990

Ravuvu, A. *The Fijian Way of Life*, University of the South Pacific 1983

Ryan, P. *Fiji's Natural Heritage*, Southwestern Publishing, Auckland 1988

Williams, T. *Fiji and the Fijians*, First Pub'd: 1858 Fiji Museum, Suva (Reprint) 1985

HAWAII

Abbott, I. *La'au Hawaii – Traditional Uses of Hawaiian Plants*, Bishop Museum Press 1992

Carlquist, S. *Hawaii – A Natural History*, Pacific Tropical Botanical Garden 1980

Kirch, P. *Feathered Gods and Fishhooks – an introduction to Hawaiian Archaeology and Prehistory*, University of Hawaii Press 1985

Berger, A. *Hawaiian Birdlife*, University of Hawaii Press 1972

Insight Guide *Hawaii*, A.P.A. Publications 1988

EASTER ISLAND

Bahn, P. & Flenley, J. *Easter Island, Earth Island*, Thames and Hudson 1992

Englert, S. *Island at the Centre of the World*, Scribner 1970

Heyerdahl, T. *Easter Island – The Mystery Solved*, Souvenir Press, London 1989

Lee, G. *Easter Island – an Uncommon Guide*, International Resources, California 1990

NEW ZEALAND

Anderson, A. *Prestigious Birds*, Cambridge University Press 1989

Davidson, J. *The Prehistory of New Zealand*, Longman Paul 1984

Insight Guide *New Zealand*, A.P.A. Publications 1992

Leach, H. *1000 Years of Gardening in New Zealand*, AH & AW Reed, Auckland 1984

Orbell, M. *The Natural World of the Maori*, David Bateman, Auckland 1985

Salmond, A. *Two Worlds – First Meetings between Maori and Europeans*, Viking 1991

INDEX